The Book of
Money

The Book of Money

Edited by Mike Palmer and Ryan Markish

Editorial Research: Greg Yenoli and Ned Harper
Graphic Design: Jennifer Costigan
Publisher: George Rayburn
Founding Publisher: Porter Stansberry and Bill Bonner

Editorial Interns: Adam Hopkins and Deb Streusand

Table of Contents

Foreword

What Really, Really Works on Wall Street

By Bill Bonner

Most people imagine that the market is like an ATM machine that just dispenses cash without debiting your account.

You just have to stand at the machine long enough... and you get rich. No brains required.

Yes, of course, the machine sometimes goes on the blink... but it is soon repaired. Best to stay in line even when it's not working well... so you'll be ready to collect your money when it starts up again.

This view is the one held by most people today. It is the view that informs the investment decisions of millions of people... and that undergirds most of the financial industry. It is a view reinforced by experience... the last two decades of market history provides no convincing counter-example. Stock prices (almost) always go up.

This, we believe, is a very dangerous view for you to take as an investor.

The economist John Maynard Keynes once commented, "practical men, who believe themselves to be quite exempt from any intellectual influences, are usually slaves to some defunct economist."

Keynes was, himself, the defunct economist to whom two generations of economist were enslaved. He viewed the economy as a vast machine that could be adjusted by turning a few knobs and pulling a few levers. Thus were his successors chained to their posts at central banks and councils of economic advisors, fiddling with the instruments of their respective economies... and generally making a mess of them.

Now, most economists understand that an economy is much more complex than Keynes imagined. Economies are unbounded systems. They cannot be successfully commanded and controlled, nor even predicted... but merely modeled, based on probabilities.

A stock market is the same sort of thing. It is an equally unbounded system. It is not a mechanistic, automatic, wealth-distributing machine. It is more like a living thing. Real investors know that this is so... they give pet names to the different "moods" of the market... anthropomorphically describing it as a "bull" or a "bear."

They know from experience that it can be many things. But it is definitely not a machine.

One of the best financial writers of the past 50 years is Richard Russell. He says that "whatever your weakness... the market will find it." He often describes a bear market as "vicious" or "cunning" and "out to take as many people down with him as possible." What machine would do that? Is this just hyperbolic writing... or does the market actually have a mind... a will... and even malicious desires?

The answer is yes. And no. And maybe.

There... I hope that's settled.

A market reflects and influences the economy that supports it. Not surprisingly, the qualities that make for success in the economy... or perhaps I should say, in real life... are generally those that serve investors well.

What works in an economy? Effort, discipline, patience, and humility.

Perhaps no one illustrates these qualities more than the greatest investor of our time—Warren Buffett. Buffett works extremely hard getting to know every detail of the businesses in which he invests. He does not invest on hunches. He does not guess about which technology is likely to succeed. He does not check out the buzz on Internet chat rooms. He applies a discipline and training that he has worked on for many years.

When he decides to invest in a company, he does so recognizing that it could take many, many years before his investment really "pays off." He's very patient. And he's smart enough to be humble. He does not invest in things he doesn't understand. He has never bought stock in Microsoft, for example, even though he plays bridge with Bill Gates. When stock prices generally do not make sense to him... he attempts to get clear of the market... as he did in the late 60s. And as he is doing again in 2004.

By contrast, what hurts you as an investor is what hurts you in the rest of life.

Vanity: such as when you think you are smarter than other investors. *Sloth*: such as when you can't be bothered to study an investment before buying it. *Pride*: when you won't admit that you've made a mistake... and don't cut your losses. *Greed*: when you think you can get a 20% return every year... without working... or when you think you'll make a killing on an Internet stock... even though you have no idea what it's all about. *Timidity*: waiting too long to make your move... needing the reinforcement of others before making an investment decision.

In short, this book is an attempt to help you make use of the investment strategies that work... while avoiding the things that hurt.

It is a collection of some of the best secrets, techniques, and strategies we've learned at Agora Publishing over the past 25 years.

We started Agora with a single newsletter in 1979, and operated out of a small office in Baltimore.

Today we publish more than 50 financial newsletters and have published dozens of books. We still have our main offices in Baltimore—although our operations now take up several large row-house mansions in the city's historic Mt. Vernon district. I live in France with my family today, and work in our London office. We also have operations in Ireland, Poland, Spain, Germany, and South Africa, just to name a few.

This book was created when one of our editors came to me and said he wanted to collect some of the best financial advice we'd published in our books and newsletters in the past few years, and put it in a single volume.

We also contacted several financial writers and experts outside of the Agora fold (such as Richard Russell and Michael Checkan), whose work we have admired for many years. They graciously allowed us to include several of their essays.

The result is one of the most useful financial books I have ever seen. I can say that because I had nothing to do with producing it.

This is a book of ideas and information—pure and simple. It represents 25 years of accumulating knowledge about how people really get wealthy—how ordinary men and women can accumulate riches without taking risks with their savings or winning the lottery.

This book will not help you get rich quick. Ordinary people do not get rich quick. Only people with extraordinary luck do that.

When you get right down to it, the whole idea of "get rich quick" is nonsense. It happens. But so rarely and so randomly that it is not a prudent way to approach the subject of wealth. If you try to get rich quickly… by taking one of the crazy offers you get in the mail, such as the self-liquidating loan… where you pay $250 to some fellow in the Caribbean for his help in arranging a $25,000 loan that you never have to pay off… you will never get rich. You will get poor.

The fastest way to get rich, as we explain in more detail throughout this book, is to take a long-term approach. It may take a few years, or even a decade or more. Depending on your circumstances, we believe that a fairly average family could add $100,000 to $300,000 to its net worth in several years. That's a spectacular growth of wealth. It's getting rich as quickly as possible. But it depends on not falling for one of the silly "get rich quick" promises you see so often promoted. And it depends on not relying on a large and popular financial institution to identify for you the best investment opportunities.

Another key observation, made over more than two decades of study, that you will see is a big part of **The Book of Money**, is that small things add up. This is the hub of the concept of compound interest, for example. But it has broader application. Small habits—and we credit Aristotle for this observation—have a remarkable effect on big outcomes.

You've heard the story about how "for want of a nail" a shoe was lost… and then a horse… and then a soldier… and then a whole battle. The same is true in the battle for wealth. Little things mean a lot.

Wealth, after all, is an accumulation of little things (represented by money) over time. These have a way of growing—to which a metaphor of compound interest barely does justice. For often, it is the combination of capital, skill, circumstance, and habit of operation that come together to create what would have to be seen as a form of souped-up or turbo-charged compounding. That is how you get the "lift"… or what we describe as reaching escape velocity.

Cutting your losses quickly, for example, will ensure that you never lose much on a single investment, no matter how far it drops. The same goes for putting your money into the right mix of assets. Using the right broker will ensure that you get a decent entry price on every stock you buy. These "little things" add up in a big, big way.

Finally, you'll notice that the financial advice in this book is "different."

There's a reason for this. There would simply be no advantage in our giving you the same advice, information, and point of view that you receive in the pages of the financial section of your local paper… or in the other financial media available… or in a thousand "free" websites.

Nor would there be any benefit to you in reading what you have already read, or following the same course of action that other services have already recommended. You are reading this precisely because you are not completely satisfied with the results of the actions you have taken to date.

This advice is different because it holds the promise of producing an outcome that is different. If you want to do as everyone else does, you will end up as everyone else does.

If you take the same approach to investing as the average man, you will produce an average amount of wealth for yourself. If you continue to think and act as you do now… you'll continue to get the same results.

The Book of Money offers you the opportunity to think differently, to act differently, and to end up with a much different result. And, we believe, a better one.

I hope you enjoy and benefit from these ideas as much as I have.

Bill Bonner

Bill Bonner

Founder, Agora Publishing Inc.

What You Can Expect From This Book

Dear Reader,

This book is clearly about money and investing.

But this is not a book filled with common-sense ideas you've already read somewhere else.

You see, at Agora, we offer ideas, information, and insights that are very different from those presented by the traditional publishing house.

Our health publications, for example, show readers how to use alternative medical treatments your doctor is never likely to tell you about. Our retirement and real estate publications show you how to live and own property in places most Americans would never dream of going—like Panama, Nicaragua, and Honduras.

In short, if our messages at Agora have something in common, it is that they all celebrate the virtue of thinking independently and taking responsibility for your own life.

That's the theme of this book too.

It's about money, yes. But more importantly, it's about how to take responsibility and think independently about wealth, money, and investing.

Why should you do this? What's wrong with following the advice everyone else is following in mainstream magazines and newspapers? Simple. When you do the same thing as everyone else, you're guaranteed to get the same mediocre results. It's why the majority of investors will never beat the stock market averages.

The Book of Money, however, offers you a different perspective.

This book is a collection of the best financial advice and ideas I've encountered during my nine years of working at Agora.

Some of these concepts, I assure you, will be completely foreign. But all are explained in simple terms… and each one is proven to work where it matters most—in the real world.

The people you will meet in these pages are among the smartest and most successful investors and analysts I've ever known. Porter Stansberry, for example, knows more about technology investing than anyone I've ever worked with. Dr. Steve Sjuggerud knows more about alternative investments than anyone I've ever met. In addition to writing newsletters and books, he's worked as a stockbroker, mutual fund vice president, and even ran his own hedge fund.

Michael Masterson knows more about how to run a profitable business than anyone I know. During the past 30 years, he's done it more than 3 dozen times... everything from art galleries and real estate developments... to publishing businesses and a martial arts school. Chris Weber is a true expert on currencies and precious metals. He started investing in gold coins at age 16 and has made millions since, without ever going to college, and without ever holding a "real job."

These are just a few of the people you'll meet in these pages.

The point is, there are some really smart people here, sharing their real world secrets on what has made them successful, and very often, rich.

I hope you enjoy this book—and learn as much as we did putting it together.

Michael Palmer

Editor, The Book of Money

Chapter 1

The Most Important Rules of Investing

3 Things Most Investors Don't Know About the Stock Market

By Porter Stansberry

Last Saturday I was doing a live radio interview broadcast from Monterey, California when the host asked me a very good question: "What are the three things that most people don't know about the stock market, that if they did know, would make them much better, more professional investors?"

It was such a good question that I thought I'd share my answer with you.

#1. I believe the number one thing most people don't understand about the stock market is that the value of common stocks is heavily dependent on the level of short-term interest rates. When investors can earn a very high rate of return on short-term, low-risk investments, money will not flow into the stock market, and the overall price level for stocks will fall.

Imagine the stock market as a bathtub and individual stocks as rubber duckies. When short-term interest rates are low or heading lower, water flows into the tub, lifting all the duckies. But when you turn the water off, it takes one heck of a ducky to rise above the scum line. And when the yield curve is inverted—when short-term bonds are paying out more than long-term bonds, it's like someone lifting the drain plug.

#2. The second thing most folks don't understand about stocks is the nominal price of a stock has absolutely nothing to do with its intrinsic value. (I'm sure that 95% of you guys understand this, but, believe it or not, the most frustrating thing I have to do when speaking to novice investors is to explain—usually in vain—that stock splits are neither bullish nor bearish. A related problem is trying to explain why a stock that trades at $10 can be more expensive than a stock that trades at $100).

Remember: To evaluate stocks you must realize that the board of directors of each company decides how many shares to have outstanding. If a company desires, they can reduce the number of shares outstanding, (which would cause the nominal price to rise) or they can increase the number of shares outstanding (which would cause the nominal share price to fall).

To get a rough idea if a stock is cheap or expensive, you must look to its technology, its income statement, and to its balance sheet relative to the total value of its shares outstanding. And be careful about book value: Some companies trading at book value are actually trading on inflated goodwill.

#3. The third thing most investors don't understand is this: The popular indexes are actually a very poor measure of the overall health of the market. The NASDAQ and the S&P 500 are "market cap weighted," which means prices of bigger stocks like Intel, GE, and Microsoft move the indexes much more than dozens of other companies combined. The Dow Jones Industrial Index is even more strangely skewed. It's price weighted, which means stocks with high nominal prices influenced the index proportionally more than other stocks.

If you really want to know whether the general trend is higher or lower overall, you have to look at either the advance/decline line or an index that "weighs" each stock equally, like the Value Line Index. You can find the Value Line Index on Yahoo! Finance (finance.yahoo.com) under this ticker: ^VLIC.

Originally published: January 3, 2001

Porter Stansberry is the Editor of Porter Stansberry's Investment Advisory, an investment newsletter that focuses on the best ways to profit from emerging technology trends. After the launch of his newsletter in 1999, Porter founded Stansberry & Associates Investment Research, a private firm that publishes 7 other investment newsletters and financial advisory services, which cover value investing, biotech, insider buying, day trading, alternatives to the stock market, and microcap stocks. For more information on these services, go to: www.stansberryresearch.com.

The Perfect Portfolio in Just 15 Minutes a Year

By Alexander Green

Imagine a place where time is yours to spend as you wish... Where you spend time only with people you want to be with... Working on the things you enjoy... Traveling the world... Spending time with your kids or grandkids... Or going fishing.

That's what the Perfect Portfolio can do for you. That's the idea behind what I call The Gone Fishin' Portfolio.

Get ready to watch your investment dollars compound. And enjoy the satisfaction and peace of mind that come from knowing you are using a system that has the highest statistical probability of long-term success.

That's not just my opinion, by the way. It's the opinion of the Nobel Prize Committee as well. I'm going to detail exactly what this simple investment system is all about, why it's so incredibly effective, how you can put it to work immediately, and why it only takes 15 minutes a year to use. <u>That's right, 15 minutes a year. And you'll be maximizing your investment returns with the least risk possible...</u>

Where It All Started...

In 1990, Dr. Harold Markowitz won the Nobel Prize in Economics for his groundbreaking discovery of the math behind the Gone Fishin' Portfolio. Although many of the concepts used by Dr. Markowitz are hard to understand, he won the award because he showed how investors can master uncertainty and, at the same time, generate excellent investment results.

You don't even need a computer to implement this strategy. All the adjustments you'll need to make to your portfolio can be done once a year—with a single 15-minute phone call. The rest of the time you're supposed to go fishing... or you can just spend your time however you choose. Because this strategy works.

Instead of struggling with trying to figure out when to get in and out of the market, do something simple: Spend 15 minutes a year on your Asset Allocation—a nominal amount of time when you consider the impact it can have on your portfolio... and your life.

What Asset Allocation Is

Asset Allocation is the process of developing the most effective—optimal—mix of investments. In this case, optimal means that there is not another combination of asset classes that is expected to generate a higher ratio of return to risk.

And what does it consist of? Quite simply, it's breaking down your portfolio into different baskets, or classes of investments, to maximize returns and minimize risk. As the cliché goes, *"Don't put all your eggs into one basket."*

So let's take the first steps in breaking down your portfolio into baskets, or asset classes. By the way, an asset class is a group of investments that have similar financial characteristics. For the purpose of today's letter, let's focus on the five principal types of long-term investments—stocks, bonds, cash, real estate, and precious metals.

How To Spread Your Eggs Around

Diversification is a strategy designed to reduce exposure to risk by combining a variety of investments, which are unlikely to move in the same direction. In other words, you don't want to put all your money in investments that will perform similarly.

One of the best ways to diversify your portfolio is by placing your money into mutual funds. Because mutual funds are generally invested in a diverse portfolio of investments, they provide the greatest degree of diversification. By owning several investments, you lessen the chance that you'll suffer if one or two of them drop in value. One mutual fund can hold dozens or even hundreds of different securities at the same time.

The Gone Fishin' Portfolio allows you to put this strategy to work through the lowest-cost group of mutual funds in the country, the Vanguard Group. Here's how you would asset allocate your "Nobel Prize" portfolio:

The Gone Fishin' Portfolio
Vanguard Total Stock Market Index (VTSMX) - 15%
Vanguard Small-Cap Index (NAESX) - 15%
Vanguard European Stock Index (VEURX) - 10%
Vanguard Pacific Stock Index (VPACX) - 10%
Vanguard Emerging Markets Index (VEIEX) - 10%
Vanguard Short-term Bond Index (VFSTX) - 10%
Vanguard High-Yield Corporates Fund (VWEHX) - 10%
Vanguard Inflation-Protected Securities Fund (VIPSX) - 10%
Vanguard REIT Index (VGSIX) - 5%
Vanguard Precious Metals Fund (VGPMX) - 5%

Notice that we have a 30% allocation to U.S. stocks. It is divided between small-cap and large-cap stocks. Likewise, the 30% allocation to international markets is evenly divided between Europe, the Pacific, and Emerging Markets.

You might wonder how including some of these riskier assets—like emerging markets, gold and small-cap stocks—actually makes your portfolio less volatile. By combining these riskier—but non-correlated—assets, you actually *increase* your portfolio's return while *reducing* its volatility.

It is also important to note that the **Gone Fishin' Portfolio** is not exclusive to the Vanguard Group. We selected Vanguard as our family of funds simply because they have the lowest expense ratios (in fact, for the moment, Vanguard has stopped admitting new investors to two of these funds). In an effort to maximize returns through Asset Allocation, reducing expenses with the Vanguard Group provides the best fund platform. But it can be used with any fund family.

If you'd like to imitate the above portfolio and don't know where to start, Schwab is a good company to contact: www.schwab.com. Simply use the same percentage breakout as noted above for your Asset Allocation. Then select, from the list of funds available to you, the ones that most closely mirror the Vanguard funds.

Who Should Consider the Gone Fishin' Portfolio?

For those of you who are conservative investors, who are retired or close to retirement, who need to exceed inflation while taking as little risk as possible—and who prefer casting purple worms to trading stocks—the Gone Fishin' Portfolio is designed with your serious money in mind.

Key Points To Remember

- **Asset Allocation is time tested**. It has worked and will continue to work because it takes the guessing out of investing.

- **Asset Allocation is a Nobel Prize-winning strategy**. No other strategy shares this seal of approval.

- Research demonstrates that **Asset Allocation accounts for approximately 90% of investment returns**, making it nearly 10 times as important as stock picking and market timing combined. There is no other investment strategy that can boast the same.

- The world's most successful and respected investors swear by it. As Paul Sturm of *Smart Money* puts it, Asset Allocation is *"a simple strategy that comes as close to guaranteeing long-term success as anything I've seen."*

-Its benefits are unparalleled: significantly reduced expenses, protection against inflation, maximized returns with minimal risk—the list goes on.

And the best part about it—it's simple. With the Gone Fishin' Portfolio, all you have to do is make one phone call—*15 minutes a year.*

Originally published: September 5, 2003 by The Oxford Club

After 16 years on Wall Street, Alex Green left institutional investing to become Investment Director for The Oxford Club, a private, international network of investors and entrepreneurs. In addition to writing on global investing for Wall Street Week's Louis Rukeyser, Alex has been a writer or contributor to several financial publications, includ-

ing Global Insights, The Daily Reckoning, The Financial Sentinel, World Market Perspective, and The Fleet Street Letter.

Mr. Green has been responsible for introducing a long line of highly profitable "safe money" investment strategies to the Oxford Club. He's also created a number of trading techniques that have recently earned Oxford Club members who followed them gains as high as 68% in a matter of weeks. He currently edits The Momentum Alert, The Oxford Short Alert, The Insider Alert, and The International Trader Alert. For more information on these services and The Oxford Club, visit: www.oxfordclub.com.

3 Traits of World Class Investors

By Porter Stansberry

Most people don't understand the important differences between EQUITY SELECTION, ASSET ALLOCATION and POSITION SIZING. I have earned a reputation for being a good stock researcher—a good stock picker. But I have told people for as long as I have been writing investment research that 90% of the money I actually make in the market is generated by how I buy stocks, not which stocks I buy. And today I'd like to explain this concept again—it's one of the most important differences between WORLD-CLASS investors and everyone else, professional or amateur.

World-class investors do three things that you probably don't:

They sell stocks.

They manage their asset allocation carefully against a benchmark.

They never break their position-sizing discipline.

Most amateur investors won't sell stocks. They simply won't cut their losses, no matter how many times they promise themselves that in the future they will. Call it human nature. People don't like to admit they're wrong. But if you're managing other people's money, you don't have the luxury of soothing your ego with the simple platitudes that your broker will feed you (at least not for very long).

The second thing that world-class investors do is to manage their asset allocation carefully.

Asset allocation is how much money you put into different asset classes. For example, what percentage of your assets is in stocks, bonds, cash, real estate, private equity, and commodities? Believe it or not, these choices are the most important parts of your investing.

I don't give you advice on asset allocation because it's going to be different for every single individual (based on risk-tolerance, age, trailing stops, etc.) But, there's a simple rule of thumb that I would recommend to you.

Take your age. Subtract it from 100. Under normal market conditions you should allocate this percentage of your assets into stocks. So, if you're 40 years old, under normal market conditions, you should put 60% of your investment assets in stocks.

Finally, the last difference between world-class investors and everyone else is that most people regularly break their own position sizing rules. They tend to get excited about one or two stocks and they invest too heavily into those few stocks. This almost always results in big losses.

You'll improve your actual investment results and sleep better at night if you institute a little discipline into your trading. Make sure that you follow your stop losses. Make sure that you adjust your asset allocation to account for market conditions—but don't get 100% invested in stocks or 100% out of stocks. And finally, don't go overboard for a stock, ever.

Originally published: September 28, 2001 by Stansberry & Associates Investment Research

For more information on Porter Stansberry go to: www.stansberryresearch.com.

Control the Price You Pay

By Dan Ferris

Warren Buffett is by far the world's most successful investor. Every $1,000 invested with him in 1965 has become $195 million today. That's a 195,000 percent rise in value over a period of 37 years. By contrast, the S&P 500 is up just 4,742% during the same period.

How did he do it? What did he do that was so different from what everyone else does?

What Warren Buffett did was simple. It's too simple, in fact. That's why most people overlook it. It's why most people don't make a fortune in stocks. And it's what you need to know if you're going to be successful in the stock market.

The one thing Warren Buffett does is that he controls the one and only thing any investor can control in any investment transaction: the price he pays. Warren Buffett looks at a company, decides what its stock is worth, and refuses to pay more than a fair price.

That's how he makes all of his investments. When he bought three million shares of media moguls Capital Cities in the mid-1980s, he did a few calculations and told them he'd pay exactly $172.50 per share. The deal was done.

He bought over $1 billion in Coca-Cola shares because they were trading for less than $11, which he considered a bargain.

Buffett likes to remind interviewers that he's been allocating capital since he was 11 years old, and hasn't changed much since that time.

Even today, as he told his shareholders at their last annual meeting, "We have no master plan... Charlie [his partner at Berkshire Hathaway] and I don't sit around and talk about the future of industries. We have no reports or staff. We just review what comes in and look for companies with a durable competitive advantage at an attractive price."

Asked why he bought shares in furniture rental chain Cort Business Services, Buffett remarked, "a fine though unglamorous business, an outstanding manager and a price that made sense."

Buffet walked into the Nebraska Furniture Mart on a summer's day in 1983.

He looked around the floor for Rose Blumkin, the crotchety founder. She was patrolling the aisles in a golf cart, scolding employees and smiling at customers. Buffett walked up to her and asked her if she wanted to sell the business. She said, "yes." He said, "How much?" She said "$60 million." He shook her hand, wrote up a one-page deal and wrote her a check. The whole thing took a couple of days from start to finish.

That's the way it is with Buffett. He decides what something is worth, and as long as the price is right, he's in. No matter what else Buffett likes about any business, he always must get it at a price that makes sense to him. That one rule is universal. Everything else is open to change.

Buffett is as clear in writing as he is in person: "The critical investment factor is determining the intrinsic value of a business and paying a fair or bargain price."

Did you catch that? If imitating the investment results of the greatest investor in history is what you want to do, you don't even need to pay a bargain price. A fair price will get you there. You don't need to buy an endless string of bargains to get rich.

That's very different than the way most people invest. They buy stocks without knowing what the business they're investing in is really worth.

They don't know what price they should pay, so they lose. They look at price charts and try to predict the stock's price one year away, or one month, or one week... sometimes even one hour! It's totally unnecessary... sitting there watching prices go up and down every day.

Buffett says he wouldn't care if the stock market closed for ten years. He doesn't watch the up and down movements of the market from day to day. And he never loses sleep as an investor.

As long as he's paid a fair or bargain price, and as long as the business he's invested in hasn't changed significantly, there's no need to worry about the future. Paying the right price is the one thing you can do as an investor that will give you unshakeable peace of mind.

Originally published: October 3, 2002 in Extreme Value

Dan Ferris is the editor of Extreme Value, a monthly newsletter that looks for the best undervalued long term investments, companies that are worth more (when you add up their cash, land and other assets) than the listed value in the stock market. Safe and cheap—that's the strategy behind this investment service. Dan models his service in the tradition of legendary value investors such as Benjamin Graham, the grandfather of value investing, and his famous pupil, Warren Buffett. For more info on Dan's service, visit www.stansberryresearch.com, and click on "Extreme Value."

Don't Get Taken by the Trader

How to get the best possible prices on stocks and options

By Dr. Steve Sjuggerud, PhD

I've learned a lot over the years about the *correct* way to place a trade. Early in my career, I had no idea just how important the details could be. But I learned quickly...

Having been a broker, an institutional trader, and a hedge fund manager (among other things), I've traded every type of financial instrument and placed every type of order. Today, we'll look at what types of orders you should use to trade smartly and how to avoid giving anything away to the trader, like I did trading options a long time ago...

The Trader Killed Me...

I knew I was going to make a mint that day... it didn't matter what price the trader gave me... or so I thought.

I was just starting out. And I felt strongly that this particular option was worth $4 and that it could well close at $6 by the end of the day, for a 50% profit in a day. So I put in a "MARKET" order to make sure I got in that morning, at any price.

The trader killed me—he filled my trade at $7 and then moved the market to $4. The option closed at $6. But instead of making a 50% profit, I took a loss. All because I didn't know what I was doing. I didn't know how to properly place orders.

I don't know about you, but losing money is a powerful teacher. Like touching a hot stove, you quickly learn you want to avoid that miserable experience if at all possible.

Knowing When To Fight The "Spread"

Before we get into "MARKET" orders and "LIMIT" orders, you've got to understand something called the "SPREAD." The best way to understand the spread is to look at how used cars are bought and sold.

Let's say you've got a 5-year-old car worth $12,500. You take it to a dealer to see if he'll take it off your hands. He says he'll give you $10,000 for it. But you say: "Hey that's not fair. You've got the exact same car on your lot for $15,000!"

My friend, the difference between $10,000 and $15,000 is the spread.

If you sold your car, you'd like to get $12,500, not just $10,000. And if you were looking to buy, you'd much prefer to pay closer to $12,500 than the $15,000 the dealer is asking. So when you're buying a car, in order to get the best deal, what you're looking to do is *eliminate the spread...*

In big stocks, like Microsoft, Intel, and basically any other company you've already heard of, the spread is not a concern. There are so many buyers and sellers, you're best off just putting in a MARKET ORDER, and you'll own the shares immediately at the market price. (In fact, the spread on Microsoft, a $25 stock, is only 1.5 pennies as I write.)

Unless you are some kind of lightning-fast day trader, *you should always use a MARKET order on major stocks.* For a simple rule of thumb, we'll define a major stock as one with a market cap (market value) of over $1 billion. That pretty much covers most stocks that you'd probably consider buying. And it covers nearly all of the stocks that are household names.

Now some may quibble with this $1 billion rule. Some people may try to save a little on the entry or the exit with another type of strategy. But for nearly all investors, a market order is fine. You'd hate to miss a huge great gain over a measly half of a percent.

How To Fight The Spread—And Avoid Getting Burned In Small Stocks

However, in small stocks (less than $1 billion in size) and in options, you're better off wheeling and dealing—fighting the spread. Options and small stocks can have a significant spread. Here it's more risky to put in market orders, especially at the open (as I shared with you above). The lesson I learned above was this: *Don't use market orders on thinly traded positions—especially not at the open!*

Let's look at a real stock. Let's take Qualcomm.

If you wanted to buy shares of Qualcomm right now, you'd find that there are two prices quoted—the **BID PRICE** ($33.09) and the **ASK PRICE** ($33.11)

The **ASK PRICE** (sometimes called the **OFFER PRICE**) is what you'd pay if you wanted to buy the shares right now, at any cost. Now take a look at that spread. It's two pennies. Is it really worth haggling to get the trader to lower the price for you to $33.10? I don't think so. It sure isn't the $5,000 spread the car dealer has.

To buy at the market price (to accept the trader's price of $33.11), you would simply place a **MARKET ORDER** with your broker, which instructs him/her to buy the shares for you at the current market price, whatever it may be.

When it comes time to sell, you receive the **BID PRICE** instead of the ASK PRICE. So you would receive a price of $33.09.

If you were buying, and you didn't want to pay the asking price of $33.11, but thought that $33.10 was a fairer price, you would enter a **LIMIT ORDER** to buy at $33.10. Since that price is below the current price, chances are your order won't be filled right away. But it might. Again, I wouldn't bother with this penny. But if I had put in a limit order on my options trade of $4 instead of a market order, I wouldn't have been hammered by the trader.

Orders default to what's called a "**DAY ORDER**," which means it's good for that day. Unless you specify "**GOOD 'TIL CANCELLED (GTC)**" or "**FILL OR KILL (FOK)**," a DAY ORDER is what you've entered. These are all self-explanatory. A day order lasts all day. A GTC order is open for days and weeks until you cancel it. And a FOK order is a one-shot deal. I never use GTC orders (as I've seen people forget about them). And I've only rarely used FOK orders. Market orders and limit orders (both of which are day orders) should cover things.

You can also enter a **STOP ORDER** to limit your downside, but I don't recommend these either. Imagine buying an option at $4 and then putting an order in that you want to sell at $3 if it falls there. That is a bad idea. That is like buying a house for $400,000 and telling everyone you're willing to sell it for $300,000. As a general rule, don't show your hand—use MENTAL stops (stops that you keep in your head)—not actual stop orders.

Well, that about covers the basics of placing an order. Summing up our rough guidelines:

* Use MARKET orders on stocks that are valued at over $1 billion
* Use LIMIT orders on options and stocks below $1 billion
* Don't bother with the rest of the types of orders

If you follow these three simple guidelines, you should avoid getting burned by a trader... either on the "spread" or by inadvertently tipping your hand.

Originally published: April 17, 2003 in Investment U

Dr. Steve Sjuggerud runs a free investment education course on-line called Investment University. Twice a week, he covers the most important investment concepts, rules, and strategies. He also explains what's currently happening in the investment markets, and which investments make the most sense right now. To sign up for Dr. Sjuggerud's free Investment U service, go to: www.investmentu.com.

How to Know What Other Investors are Doing

By Dr. Steve Sjuggerud, PhD

"When everyone thinks alike, everyone is likely to be wrong."
~Humphrey Neill in "The Art of Contrary Thinking," 1951

A s the Nasdaq soared from 2000 to 5000, everyone joined in. After all, nearly everybody in America was thinking alike—that making money in the stock market was easy.

But we all know the outcome. It turns out that many Americans were just following the crowd—right off a cliff.

If you looked at a list of the world's most successful investors—Warren Buffett, George Soros, John Templeton—you'd find that they all did remarkably different things to make money. But they all share one thing in common—they had the courage to do the opposite of what "the crowd" was doing, and did so with regularity.

Now over 90 years old, Sir John Templeton predicted a Nasdaq bust in January of 2000. Going against the crowd, he put about $2 million each on 84 different Nasdaq stocks, short-selling so he would profit as they fell in price. He took losses early if the stocks went against him, and he rode many to 100% profits—as many of the companies he bet against went out of business.

You too can make a lot more money in the markets by doing the opposite of what the crowd is doing.

In order to make these large profits, I like to size up "the crowd" from every angle. I like to know what professional investors are doing. I like to know what the investment writers are saying. I like to know what individual investors are doing. And finally, I like to know what the man in the street thinks. Let me show you what I watch to know when the time is right…

Professional Investors

I've been a "professional" investor, and I've run funds, so I know what motivates professional investors.

When the stock market is going straight up, if a professional manager has too much cash in his portfolio, he'll get left behind. So in order to keep up, he'll keep trimming his cash holdings to try to catch up. Inevitably, at market peaks, professional managers are caught loaded to the gills in stocks, with very little cash.

On the flip side, in pessimistic times, professional managers don't want to lose their investors' money. So they hold a lot of cash, reasoning that cash will stay above water, even if stocks fall.

What's amazing is that history shows us professional investors are great contrarian indicators, always holding the wrong amount of cash. If professional managers are scared and holding a lot of cash, history shows us it's a great time to buy stocks. And if professional managers are *not* scared and don't have any cash—run for the hills!

The Investment Company Institute (www.ici.org) publishes the cash holdings of mutual funds monthly. When mutual fund liquid assets are above 9.5% (when professional investors are scared and holding a lot of cash), stocks rise 18% a year. But when mutual funds hold little cash (less than 6% of their portfolio) stocks only rise 1% a year. My study uses data going back to 1970.

Investment Writers

Ah, the great prognosticators. My brethren. I hate to break it to you (if you didn't already know) but investment newsletter writers, as a group, are bad prognosticators. But don't hold it against them—they're no worse than professional investors or individual investors.

Barron's publishes the "Investors Intelligence" report (an oxymoron?) weekly—a report on percentage of bulls and bears among newsletter writers. If you take the percentage of bulls versus the percentage of newsletter writers that take a stand as bullish or bearish, you'll actually find an equal and opposite relationship between what they say and what actually happens in the markets. Uncanny. But true.

When newsletter writers are bullish, stocks generally lose money. And when they're bearish, stocks rise by about 20% a year. (Figures, from www.chartcraft.com, go back to 1970). A reading above 60% on the number of bulls versus the number having an opinion would be optimistic. We don't make money under those circumstances.

Individual Investors

The American Association of Individual Investors (www.aaii.com) publishes a weekly survey of individual investors. In short, when individual investors are bullish, nobody makes any money in stocks. This fact becomes even more amazing when you realize the survey has only been around since 1987—so it's only seen one down-turn. So even in bullish times, you don't make any money.

The Man in the Street

How do people feel out there? Are they optimistic or pessimistic about the future?

The University of Michigan has asked this question since the 1960s. And, like all the others above, there's an equal and opposite relationship between how people feel and stock returns. If people are pessimistic, stocks do very well. And if people are optimistic, returns on stocks are pretty bad.

The most popularly quoted figure is the University of Michigan's consumer senti-ment figure (www.athena.sca.isr.umich.edu). But I prefer a subcategory in the study—consumer *expectations*.

When expectations are high (a reading above 95) stocks only rise at 3% a year.

If it rises above 95, it's unanimous—everyone and everything is optimistic. Unfortunately, with history as our guide, WE'RE FEELING TOO GOOD ABOUT OURSELVES TO BE ABLE TO MAKE ANY MONEY IN THE MARKETS.

Originally published by Stansberry & Associates Investment Research

For more information on Dr. Sjuggerud's True Wealth advisory service, go to: www.stansberryresearch.com, or call (888)261-2693.

Margin of Safety—How to Make Sure You Don't Lose Money

By Dr. Steve Sjuggerud, PhD

It can be simple. Richard Russell reminded me of this in his latest newsletter, with a little story... a story that teaches us about the value of avoiding invest-ments that contain more risk than potential return.

Back in 1974, Russell notes, Texaco and Exxon were paying out 10% a year in dividends. Based on that alone, Russell figured that he'd be up 30% in three years time on the dividends, no matter what happened.

It was a bear market back then, a scary time to invest. The market lost half its value during 1973-1974. In 1974, Russell figured that even if the stock prices of Texaco and Exxon fell by 30% over the next three years, he'd still have broken even on his investment, because of the dividends.

After sizing up the risks and the rewards, Russell determined, "The margin of safety was so attractive that I bought both stocks."

In this example, the "margin of safety" principle is where you believe you've got ample dividend yields to cover your risk in the stock.

According to Russell, "*Today it's very difficult to find stocks or bonds that fit into this [category]...*"

But Russell does name a large handful of utility stocks where the big dividends over the next three years should provide you plenty of safety to cover your risk of loss. Readers of my newsletter know that I think a few real estate stocks (REITs), which pay dividends of 7% or better, also fit this "margin of safety" concept.

Buying At A Mega Discount

The term "margin of safety" was made famous by Ben Graham, the father of "value investing." Graham and Dodd's *Security Analysis*, written in 1934, is still the bible for budding analysts.

Instead of having income cover your risk of loss, Graham prefers to buy stocks ridiculously cheap—consider that his "margin of safety." Graham knows that his "margin of safety" concept is not without risk. In his book, *The Intelligent Investor*, he reminds us: "*Even with a margin [of safety] in the investor's favor, an individual security may work out badly.*" You've still got to spread your bets.

Dan Ferris, a good friend who also likes to buy super cheap, recently recounted the story of Mason Hawkins, one of the longest-running success stories in the investment world, who, like Graham, likes to buy ridiculously cheap. Hawkins' track record is compelling. Over the past two decades, he has made investors an astounding 44 times their money.

Dan says that Hawkins' technique is simple in principle: Hawkins tries to determine what he considers the "real" value of a stock, and then he refuses to buy unless it trades for at least 40% less than that value.

By doing this, Hawkins ultimately believes that two-thirds of his returns come from closing of the gap between the price and the "real" value, and only one-third of his returns come from the business growing.

In whatever context, the concept of margin of safety is good to keep in mind. As you consider your next investment, ask yourself:

- Will the income from this investment over the next three years cover my risk of loss in that period? If not...

- Am I buying at a minimum 40% discount to what I really believe is the value of this business?

Investing can get complicated. Asking these two questions before you invest is a great reality check. They may save you from taking on an investment with more risk than potential return.

Originally published: May 27, 2003 in Investment U

To sign up for Dr. Sjuggerud's free Investment U service, go to: www.investmentu.com.

Rich Man, Poor Man—The Power of Compounding

By Richard Russell

Making money entails a lot more than predicting which way the stock or bond markets are heading, or trying to figure which stock or fund will double over the next few years.

For the great majority of investors, making money requires a plan, self-discipline and desire. I say, "for the great majority of people," because if you're a Steven Spielberg or a Bill Gates, you don't have to know about the Dow or the markets or about yields or price/earnings ratios. You're a phenomenon in your own field, and you're going to make big money as a by-product of your talent and ability. But this kind of genius is rare.

For the rest of us, we must have a financial plan. In view of this, I offer below a few items that we must be aware of if we are serious about making money.

Rule 1. Compounding: One of the most important lessons for living in the modern world is that to survive you've got to have money. But to live (survive) *happily*, you must have love, health (mental and physical), freedom, intellectual stimulation—and money. When I taught my kids about money, the first thing I taught them was the use of the "money bible." What's the money bible? Simple, it's a volume of the *compounding interest tables.*

Compounding is the royal road to riches. Compounding is the safe road, the sure road, and fortunately, anybody can do it. To compound successfully you need the following: Perseverance, in order to keep you firmly on the savings path. You need intelligence in order to understand what you are doing and why. And you need knowledge of the mathematics tables in order to comprehend the amazing rewards that will come to you if you faithfully follow the compounding road. And, of course, you need time to allow the power of compounding to work for you. Remember, compounding only works through time.

But there are two catches in the compounding process. The first is obvious—compounding may involve sacrifice (you can't spend it and still save it). Second, compounding is boring—b-o-r-i-n-g. Or I should say it's boring until (after seven or eight years) the money starts to pour in. Then, believe me, compounding becomes very interesting. In fact, it becomes downright fascinating!

In order to emphasize the power of compounding, I am including this extraordinary study, courtesy of *Market Logic*, of Ft. Lauderdale, FL. In this study we assume that investor (A) opens an IRA at age 19. For seven consecutive periods he puts $2,000 in his IRA at an average growth rate of 10% (7% interest plus growth). After seven years this fellow makes NO MORE contributions—he's finished.

A second investor (B) makes no contributions until age 26 (this is the age when investor A was finished with his contributions). Then B continues faithfully to contribute $2,000 every year until he's 65 (at the same theoretical 10% rate).

Now study the incredible results. A, who made his contributions earlier, over just 7 years, ends up with MORE money than B, who made 40 contributions but at a *later time.* The difference in the two is that *A had seven more early years of compounding than B.* Those seven early years were worth more than all of B's 33 additional contributions.

This is a study that I suggest you show to your kids. It's a study I've lived by, and I can tell you, "It works." You can work your compounding with muni-bonds, a good money market fund, T-bills, or with five-year T-notes.

Rule 2. Don't Lose Money: If you want to be wealthy, you must not lose money, or I should say must not lose *big* money. Absurd rule, silly rule? Maybe, but <u>most people lose money</u> in disastrous investments, gambling, rotten business deals, through greed or poor timing. Yes, after almost five decades of investing and talking to investors, I can tell you that most people definitely *do* lose money—big time—in the stock market, in options and futures, in real estate, in bad loans, in mindless gambling, and in their own business.

Rule 3. Rich Man, Poor Man: In the investment world, the wealthy investor has one major advantage over the little guy, the stock market amateur, and the neophyte trader. The advantage the wealthy investor enjoys is that *he doesn't need the markets.* I can't begin to tell you what a difference that makes in both one's mental attitude and in the way one actually manages money.

The wealthy investor doesn't need the markets, because he already has all the income he needs. He has money coming in via bonds, T-bills, money market funds, stocks, and real estate. In other words, the wealthy investor *never feels pressured* to "make money" in the market.

The wealthy investor tends to be an expert on values. When bonds are cheap and bond yields are irresistibly high, he buys bonds. When stocks are on the bargain table and stock yields are attractive, he buys stocks. When real estate is a great value, he buys real estate. When great art or fine jewelry or gold is on the "give away" table, he buys art or diamonds or gold. In other words, the wealthy investor puts his money where the great values are.

If no outstanding values are available, the wealthy investor waits. He can afford to wait. He has money coming in daily, weekly, monthly. The wealthy investor knows what he is looking for, and he doesn't mind waiting months or even years for his next investment (they call it patience).

But what about the little guy? This fellow always feels pressured to "make money." And in return, he's always pressuring the market to "do something" for him. But sadly, the market isn't interested. When the little guy isn't buying stocks offering 1% or 2% yields, he's off to Las Vegas or Atlantic City trying to beat the house at roulette. Or he's spending 20 bucks a week on lottery tickets, or he's "investing" in some crackpot scheme that his neighbor told him about (in strictest confidence, of course).

And because the little guy is trying to force the market to do something for him, he's a guaranteed loser. The little guy doesn't understand values so he constantly overpays. He doesn't comprehend the power of compounding, and he doesn't understand money. He's never heard the adage, *"He who understands interest—earns it. He who doesn't understand interest—pays it."* The little guy is the typical American, and he's deeply in debt.

But here's the ironic part of it. If, from the beginning, the little guy had adopted a strict policy of never spending more than he made, if he had taken his extra savings and compounded it in intelligent, income-producing securities, then in due time he'd have money coming in daily, weekly, monthly, just like the rich man. The little guy would have become a financial winner, instead of a pathetic loser.

Rule 4. Values: The only time the average investor should stray outside the basic compounding system is when a given market offers outstanding value. I judge an investment to be a great value when it offers (a) safety; (b) an attractive return; and (c) a good chance of appreciating in price. At all other times, the compounding route is safer and probably a lot more profitable, at least in the long run.

Originally published in Richard Russell's Dow Theory Letters

Richard Russell began publishing Dow Theory Letters in 1958, and has been writing it ever since. Dow Theory Letters is the oldest advisory service continuously written by one person. It is also one of the best. For more information on Mr. Russell's Dow Theory Letters, go to: www.dowtheoryletters.com.

The Single Most Important Factor that Determines Your Investment Success

By Dr. Steve Sjuggerud, PhD

The most important lesson in investing is: *How* you divide up your assets among the three classes is infinitely more important than *which* stocks you choose...

It's the same with the food you eat. A diet of *all* meat would literally kill you. But a diet of all vegetables, while it may not kill you, will likely lead you to inferior overall performance. We all know this. And we know that some balance of these is optimal—hence the phrase "well-balanced" diet.

The same holds for investing. Investors with "all stock diets" have just been killed over the last few years. Bond investors (like broccoli eaters) haven't been killed—except by boredom—as bond yields have fluctuated between approximately five and six percent for a few years now. We know that some mix of stocks and bonds over the long run must be the "optimal" mix, to give us healthy gains and (at the same time) ward off portfolio heart attacks.

Asset Allocation Accounts for 90% of Portfolio Performance

Now-famous studies (by Gary Brinson in 1986 and 1991) show that over 90% of portfolio performance and variability can be explained by asset allocation—your mix of stocks, bonds, and cash. The other 10% is made up of factors including market timing and stock selection. This makes sense. If your asset allocation is 100% stocks, and the market falls 20%, chances are you'll be down pretty close to 20%, regardless of the stocks you choose. And if your allocation is 100% bonds, and bonds earn 6%, chances are your bond portfolio would have made you 6%.

Clearly, by far, the most important decision you make is how you divide up your pie of assets. If those studies about portfolio performance are even remotely correct (they do intuitively make sense), it basically means that spending your time picking stocks is a waste of time—because a rising tide raises all ships. (And, yes, unfortunately, an outgoing tide has the opposite effect.)

So we've established that for a long-term investor, the asset allocation decision is by far the most important investment decision. So what have you done about this? Have you spent time doing the critical thinking, considering *your* asset allocation—your mix of stocks, bonds, and cash? Are you happy with it? Are you certain that your allocation makes sense, and that it's right for you?

I recommend that you spend some time thinking about your current asset allocation, how you arrived at it, and if you think it is the optimal asset allocation for you, and why. If it's not optimal... exactly *why* is that the case? And what are you going to do to change it?

Originally published: June 3, 2002 in Investment U

To sign up for Dr. Sjuggerud's FREE Investment U service, go to: www.investmentu.com.

Stocks with Warts—A Lesson From the Oakland A's

By Dan Ferris

"What gets me really excited about a guy is when he has warts, and everyone knows he has warts, and the warts just don't matter," says Paul DePodesta, the assistant general manager of the Oakland Athletics major league baseball team.

DePodesta wasn't merely describing baseball. He was discussing the unique art of winning an unfair game... a sort of legalized cheating.

DePodesta continues, "We don't get the guys who are perfect. There has to be something wrong with them for them to get to us."

Paul DePodesta's fascination with "warts" began at Harvard. As an undergraduate there, DePodesta entered reams of data into a computer to find out which metrics in baseball were correlated with winning. In other words, which numbers mattered. Most baseball fans would be surprised by what he discovered.

There were only two numbers that really mattered: on-base percentage and slugging percentage. Both statistics give runners credit for earning walks, while the more popular batting average does not.

As you know, serious baseball fans revel in statistics. But, looking carefully at the numbers, Paul DePodesta found everything else—all the stuff fans pay and overpay for—is meaningless. What turns out to be truly valuable in the game of baseball, the thing that really wins games, is simply avoiding outs. Getting walked or slapping grounders past the infielders. That's how you win baseball games. No matter what anyone tells you, that's what the numbers say.

Does this sound familiar? What the Oakland Athletics baseball team calls avoiding outs, value investors refer to as "not losing money." That translates into one boring, slightly screwed up—but incredibly cheap—investment opportunity after another. Stocks with "warts."

Look at a few of the companies with warts that I've had in my portfolio recently: 1) A company that own lots of land that just sits there year after year: 2) a ladies clothing company no one's ever heard of, or is ever likely to hear about in magazines, radio or TV; 3) a company that grows trees that just announced the sale of all its timber land.

Here's what I look for: companies with cloudy near term outlooks; companies that buy assets in the jungles of Africa; companies that can't find anything better to do with cash than buy their own shares.

There's always something wrong with the stocks I buy, the same way the Oakland A's baseball players seem too slow or too old or too awkward to win.

But I'm not buying these "warts" for the novelty. I'm buying warts because it turns out they produce more wealth for investors than any other method of investing in common stocks.

In fact, it was proven by two professors from the University of Chicago—Eugene Fama and Ken French, who published their results in the *Journal of Finance*, the oldest and most prestigious journal in academic finance. In short, what these guys found was that the cheapest stocks (the ones with the most warts), were not only the safest investments, but also the best performers. (A great book on this subject is called *The New Finance* by Robert Haugen.)

In both investing and baseball, the bureaucrats and experts are just as willfully ignorant.

The 5 Keys to Finding Perfect Stocks
By Dan Ferris

The perfect investment doesn't exist.

But if you want the greatest possible degree of success as an investor, you must know what perfection is and in which direction it lies.

In fact, it's easy to identify the characteristics of a perfect investment. The perfect investment would adhere to five basic criteria:

1.) High rate of return: A compound rate of return that outperforms inflation, taxes and other investment alternatives. (Stocks have averaged 11% a year since WWII.)

2.) Complete safety: No concern that any part of the investment could ever be lost. (Government bonds have this, but you give up the compounding and the high return.)

3.) Always liquid: The ability to redeem the investment for cash at any time of night or day, every day of the year, without fear of penalty. (Stocks, bonds, and futures all have this; real estate, coins and antiques do not.)

4.) No income taxes: No income taxes due on the investment growth; the investor keeps all profits. (If you buy and hold, stocks can come closer to this than any other investment.)

5.) Total passivity: No special skill or knowledge would be required to make the investment. No active management would be required. You could just forget about the investment and enjoy life. (Most people don't understand futures. Some don't even understand bonds. But everyone knows what it means to own a piece of a company. Children buy stocks. Everyone understands the phrase, "buy and hold.")

Several low-budget teams made the playoffs in the 2002 baseball season, and no mega-budget teams were in the World Series. But Major League Baseball commissioner Bud Selig still insisted that the Oakland A's days were numbered, because they didn't have enough money for a new stadium.

The fact that the A's turned a profit last year and won their division must have escaped commissioner Selig... the same way investors who lose money consistently buying expensive hyper-growth stocks don't notice that the richest investors and most successful fund managers—Warren Buffett, Bill Nygren, Marty Whitman, Bill Ruane, Mario Gabelli—are all disciplined value investors.

Think about what's popular in baseball, what really drives the fans wild. Foot speed, base stealing, homerun hitting... all of which *Moneyball* (see below) author Michael Lewis reveals to be highly overvalued by the market for major league baseball players.

Likewise, rapid earnings growth, stock splits and hot new technologies all send most so-called investors into a buying frenzy. That's what's popular among investors, and it's all dramatically overpriced.

DePodesta's comment is equally true of stocks. I don't get the stocks that are perfect. Perfect stocks are priced for perfection, like eBay, the online auction house, which is currently priced as though it's a sure thing to repeat last year's record earnings performance—91 more years in a row.

I like to buy the cheapest of the cheap, warts and all, knowing that the low price I'm paying is more important than any problems the company has. The fact that most people see the warts and don't understand the importance of price gives you a decided edge over other investors.

*The full story on Paul DePodesta and the Oakland A's is detailed in a book called *Moneyball: The Art of Winning an Unfair Game*, by Michael Lewis. It's the riveting story of how the Oakland Athletics baseball team wins so many games, even though it has the second lowest payroll in all of major league baseball.

Originally published: October 2003 in Extreme Value

For more info on Dan Ferris' Extreme Value service, visit www.stansberryresearch.com, and click on "Extreme Value."

The Only 2 Things That Affect the Value of Your Money

By Dr. Steve Sjuggerud, PhD

In my PhD work on international currencies, I found that there are only two clear things that affect the value of a "rich country" currency. In other words, how much our U.S. dollars are worth to the rest of the world.

People will say other things matter—things like budget deficits and current account deficits. But they don't.

The two things that affect the value of your money are 1) "purchasing power" relative to other currencies, and 2) real interest rate differentials.

These things sound complicated, but they are really pretty simple. Let me explain.

The concept of "purchasing power parity" is simple.

Think of it this way… the price of a Big Mac should be roughly the same wherever you are. The ingredients are homogenous, cheap, and widely available. And so driving across the border from the U.S. to Canada, you shouldn't see a huge difference in Big Mac prices. But sometimes you do.

In fact, right now a Big Mac is US$0.37 cheaper for Americans in Canada than it is in the U.S. So if you're planning a trip to Niagara Falls, you can check out the falls from the U.S. side. But make sure you spend all your money on the Canadian side. You'll save a heck of a lot of money.

Should a McDonalds in Niagara Falls Canada sell a burger for US$0.37 less than a McDonalds in Niagara Falls New York? Does this discrepancy in prices in rich countries make sense? Not in the long run. In the long run, currencies revert back to equal values—to their purchasing power parities. Of course, that long run can be a very long time. But they always return.

The second thing that affects the value of your money is interest rate differentials. This one is easy to understand too.

Money flows to where it's treated best. All things being equal, if one country is paying 5% interest, and another is paying 1%, money will flow to the country paying 5% interest. Where would you rather have your money? Obviously in a place that pays you more interest for your savings. That flow will cause the value of the 5% currency to increase as people flock to it. It's simple supply and demand.

Originally published: January 2003 in True Wealth

For more information on Dr. Steve Sjuggerud's True Wealth advisory service, go to: www.stansberryresearch.com, or call (888)261-2693.

The Caribou Factor—What to Look Out for with Every Investment You Make

By Dan Ferris

In the 1970s, it was feared that construction on the Trans-Alaskan pipeline would disrupt the migratory patterns and feeding habits of the Porcupine Caribou Herd.

Speaking on behalf of their cloven-hoofed brothers, environmentalists held up construction of the pipeline for about eight years. The stretched timetable caused Atlantic Richfield, the pipeline's owner, to re-price the bonds it had issued to finance the project (i.e., to lose money).

Since then, costly complications that turn up halfway through a big project have been referred to in the investment community as "the caribou factor."

When you think about it, though, it's not just the big financial projects where such factors redound. Recognizing the caribou factor is a simple acknowledgment that you don't own a crystal ball, and that you know as much about the future as everyone else—nothing.

All of life is a kind of caribou avoidance and recovery game. From inflation, war and corporate downsizing to icy streets, drunk drivers, and empty parking lots late at night. There are caribou everywhere.

Investing, as ARCO learned in the 1970s, is no different than anything else in this life.

Consider all the variables most common stock investors watch. Revenues, profits, returns on equity, debt, and dividends. Not to mention share volume, intra-day highs and lows, and closing prices.

You control none of those things. To you, they're all potential caribou herds, waiting to migrate to your portfolio.

After you buy, your money is out of your hands. It's in the hands of the market and the company of which you've just bought a portion. It's in George Bush's hands, Saddam Hussein's hands. It's in the hands of Alan Greenspan and his inflation, Congress and its tax increases (or decreases), the Department of Justice and its anti-trust laws.

Your money leaves your control when you buy stocks and bonds.

Marty Whitman, chief of Third Avenue Funds, refers to you and me (and often himself) as OPMIs. That's Outside Passive Minority Investors. If that doesn't sound like a very powerful position, you're right, it's not.

In a bankruptcy, OPMIs, in their normal role as common shareholders, are last in line. They usually leave empty-handed. The best bankruptcy workout for common shareholders that I've seen happened a month or two ago. I can't remember the name of the company, but 130 of the old shareholders got 5% of the new company. The rest got zip. Their shares—and the money they bought them with—were real one minute, caribou feed the next.

So-called investment professionals can't help you much, either. It's common knowledge that over 90% of all mutual funds fail to beat the market, fail to avoid the caribou. They should call themselves financial safari guides. They seem to find caribou for a living.

Grim as it all sounds, I'd stop short of paraphrasing Lord Keynes: "In the long run, we're all caribou too." I wouldn't go that far. There is a powerful ray of hope for caribou-phobic investors.

You can call it your timing, when you buy, or even what you buy. No matter how you arrive at it, no matter what incantations you intone, what stars you plot, how much accounting you know, or how many numbers you run, if you're Warren Buffett or John Q. Public.

Investing boils down to one, simple assessment that you, the investor, and you alone must determine: the price you pay.

Given that the caribou factor takes over after you buy, it behooves you to spend more time on assessing the price you pay, and its relation to the assets in which you seek to purchase an interest, than on anything else.

That goes for any passive investment you make: stocks, bonds, futures, options, MITTs, TIPs, you name it. Your number one concern is what it's worth to you, how much you'll pay. All other factors move across your financial landscape, on bad days alternately devouring and befouling it, on good days ignoring you, not benefiting you one iota more.

If you want to obsess about something as an investor (and let's face it, we all want to obsess about something as investors), obsess about the price you pay.

Not only is the price you pay the only thing you control. The price you pay determines how much you'll make or lose on a given investment.

Buy a $10 stock trading at half of book value, and you could profit, even if the company shuts down. Buy the same stock at $40, and you're placing a long shot bet that caribou won't like the flavor of your money.

If you buy the S&P 500 at 20 times earnings, and it reverts to its historical mean of 16 times earnings... and then falls in half from there, well, don't be surprised. That kind of price (i.e., high) is a signed, sealed invitation to every caribou in the countryside. When stocks fall well below 16 times earnings, the food supply dries up, and caribou herds thin out.

In the stock market, tilting the odds in your favor—by controlling the price you pay—is the best you or anyone else can do. In fact, buying low price to book value stocks and selling them every two years produced a 22% average annual return between 1930 and 1980. Those aren't entirely caribou-free returns, but they're as good as it gets.

Buying value at extreme lows in price is one of the most reliable caribou repellents around. Maybe cheap stocks smell like Eskimos. High prices, on the other hand, smell like female caribou in heat.

Fortunately, you get to choose which scent you'll wear, what price you'll pay.

Originally published: March 6, 2003 in Extreme Value

For more info on Dan Ferris' Extreme Value service, visit www.stansberryresearch.com, and click on "Extreme Value."

The Curse of the Fool—
A Surprisingly Accurate Way to Judge
the Psychology of the Market

By Porter Stansberry

Anyone who has been around the market for a few years knows that investor psychology is at least as important as earnings-to-share prices. Yes, I know, in the long run earnings are all that matter. If you're a patient value investor, then the emotions of other investors hardly matter.

But as Keynes said, "in the long run we're all dead."

So, what if there was a way to get as accurate a read on the psychology of a stock as you can on its estimated earnings? What if there was a good way to objectively measure the group psychology that makes the market bi-polar? There is. I stumbled onto it. This indicator is a sure way to know when NOT to buy a stock because it's too hyped. As you'll see, the same indicator also serves as a good broad market forecast tool.

What's my indicator? Message boards. They appear to be excellent "contrarian" indicators. Measured carefully, as I'll show you, the most active message boards on the Internet seem to be a nearly perfect sign that the stock in question will soon fall. Also, I suspect that a lack of posts on message boards that should be popular (but aren't yet) is a very bullish sign.

Similarly, is there a way to know when any particular newsletter writer, stock analyst, or investing style has become too popular to be useful or profitable? I think there is... and monitoring message boards plays a role. Imagine this matrix: On one side are incredibly overpriced stocks, corporate insiders selling in a panic and lots of message board posts (hundreds per day). On the other side are no message board posts for weeks, relatively cheap equity and insiders that are buying. Which stocks should you buy? Which stocks should you avoid? Thus, it seems to me that low frequency of message board posts is a good indicator of value and high frequency a sign of a hyped stock. Yes, I know it's obvious. But it's startling to me how good of an indicator this could be.

The idea of using message boards as indicators crystallized when I found a post on the Motley Fool, which is a website that primarily provides message boards for its subscribers. The post showed the number of new posters to the Fool, the number of total posters at the Fool, and the favorite message boards on the website for the year 1997 – 2002. The result is an amazing—and very precise—picture of the great equity bubble. Here's the data showing new posters and total posters for each year spanning the bubble.

NEW AND TOTAL MESSAGE BOARD AUTHORS AT THE MOTLEY FOOL WEBSITE (SOURCE: MOTLEYFOOL.COM) NEW TOTAL

	New Authors	Total Authors
1997	9,000	9,096
1998	28,000	31,345
1999	70,000	81,308
2000	90,000	118,223
2001	46,000	73,404
2002	8,000	23,256

You can see the air coming out of the tire, after peaking in 2000.

If you're new to investing, this 'contrarian' logic might seem very confusing to you. But trust me, over time you'll realize that doing the opposite of what's popular is the only way to make a lot of money in stocks. When everyone wants to buy, you have to have the courage to sell. And when nobody wants to buy, that's when it's time to load up the truck. It's not easy to always judge accurately exactly how the crowd feels, which is why using the Motley Fool message boards as an indicator might be so valuable.

To judge the predictive power of measuring chat board activity, let's look at the most popular single stock message boards at the Motley Fool during the years of the bubble. I wonder what we'll find. Do you think there's a strong correlation between popular message boards and poorly performing stocks?

—— 1997 ——

In 1997, out of the 20 most popular message boards on the Motley Fool website, eight were about individual stocks. As you'll see, eight out of the top 20 boards being about individual stocks reveals a very bullish crowd at the Fool. Here are the eight stocks, the number of posts about them, and their return to investors in the following year (1998). Keep in mind the Nasdaq ended the year up 40% in 1998. (If message boards serve as a good contrarian indicator, you'll expect these stocks to do worse than the market the following year.)

Iomega; 1,499 (-41%)

Microsoft; 1,085 (+114%)
Intel; 1,006 (+68%)
Dell Computer; 1,001 (+248%)
Apple; 796 (+212%)
Philip Morris; 780 (+26%)
3Com Corporation; 724 (+28%)
Solv-Ex Corp., 563 (delisted, -100%)

I calculate the average return of the most popular message board stocks to be 69%, a substantial outperformance of the general market for these kinds of stocks. Thus, taken as a whole, the "Curse of the Fool" didn't work for us in 1997-1998. However, I think you should note that Iomega was by far the most popular board. Iomega's message board had 50% more posts than the #2 individual stock message board, which belonged to Microsoft. (Microsoft is also a far larger company with many times more shareholders). In fact, Iomega was stock synonymous with the Motley Fool in 1996. It rose sharply during 1996, peaked, and has sold off continuously ever since. The sharp losses experienced by Iomega in the years after its huge popularity at the Fool would seem to prove my hypothesis, that stocks that are very popular on message boards tend to be very bad investments. One more thing: In 1997, the message board "Communion of Bears" was the 10th most popular message board in 1997. It was the only message board bearish in tone to make the top 20.

—— 1998 ——

1998 was a relatively bearish year for the Fools, perhaps because they were starting to lick their Iomega wounds. Whatever the reason, only four individual stock message boards made the top 20 most active list, about half as many as the year before. Or, said in other words, the Fools were only half as bullish during 1998 as they had been in 1997. As in 1997, there was one clear leader. It wasn't Iomega, it was Dell Computer, which had 30% more posts than the next leading single stock message board. Meanwhile, in 1998 stock market bears got a lot more attention at the Fool: Communion of Bears was #3 on the list; "Living Below Your Means" made its first appearance on the list at #9, as did "Shorting Stocks" at #16. Was the appearance of three relatively bearish boards in the top 20 a sign of good things to come for stocks in 1999? I think so. Here's the data on the most popular message board stocks for 1998. The format, again, is the name of the company, the number of posts about it and its return to investors in the following year (1999). Keep in mind the Nasdaq ended the year up 85% in 1999. If our contrarian indicator is working, the most popular single stock message boards should belong to stocks that underperformed the market in the following year.

Dell; 17,227 (+39%)
Iomega; 13,432 (-53%)
Amazon.com; 11,182 (+43%)
Coke; 4,726 (-12%)

Not surprisingly, the most popular stocks at the Motley Fool in 1998 were all underperformers of the stock market the following year, 1999. Taken as a whole, the group would have only brought investors fairly meager average gains (4.25%) during a year when the market soared. And, while the most popular stock at Motley Fool in 1998 did make money in 1999, its return was less than half of the market's average, not a strong performance. It also seems that making the list at the Motley Fool is especially bad news for companies not typically associated with aggressive investors, like Coke. 1998 saw the end of the incredible run in Coke's stock and it was also the year Buffett, in effect, began to unload his stake in the company, using his holding company's stock to purchase a large cash holding company. Should we call it the curse of the Fool?

—— 1999 ——

In 1999 the Motley Fool was inflamed with the passions of the crowd, which were running white-hot as the market approached its peak. Whereas in 1998 when the bears were out in force at the Fool, in 1999 the bulls made an amazing charge on the message boards. Example: The most popular message board at the Motley Fool in 1999 was "Day Trading—The Devil's Den." I'm not making this up. Talk about a contrarian indicator! Because of the bullish sentiment, we'd expect to find a lot of single stock message boards in the top 20 most active at the Fool in 1999. That's exactly what we see. Out of the top 20 most active message boards, *nine* were for single stocks, a number that beats even the bullish sentiment of the crowd during 1997. Here's the data on the most popular single stock boards during 1999: name, number of posts, and return in the following year. Keep in mind, as a whole, stocks did poorly in 2000, with the Nasdaq falling 41% on the year.

Dell; 35,657 (-65%)
CMGI; 26,172 (-97%)
AOL Time Warner; 24,635 (-54%)
Excite@Home; 22,002 (-90%)*
Amazon.com; 21,665 (-79%)
Iomega Corporation; 16,865 (0%)
Microsoft; 15,914 (-65%)
Berkshire Hathaway; 12,693 (27%)
Apple; 12,684 (-86%)

*(Note: the loss on Excite@Home is approximate and was probably worse than I document here. Because the company eventually went bankrupt (just days after being sold from the Motley Fools portfolio) I couldn't find accurate historical prices of the shares).

A couple of things stand out in the data from 1999. (First, it's a curse to be the most popular stock message board two years in a row.) After holding its own in the top cursed position during 1999, not even Dell could survive a double witching, as its shares fell hard in 2000. On the other hand, Warren Buffett is apparently so savvy that he could escape the curse of the Fool. Stocks like Berkshire, which don't normally generate attention from individual investors, should do badly when they get so popular that they make this list. But Buffett was up 27% in 2000. Also of note, there were NO bearish group boards in the top 20 most popular. As a whole, if you'd invested in the most popular stocks at the Fool, during the next year you did even worse than the market. On average this portfolio fell 85% on average in 2000... or about twice as bad as the market! As a contrarian indicator, message boards seem hard to beat. But... will it hold up?

—— 2000 ——

If our indicator is solid, it should be prepared for choppy markets. The year 2000 would qualify. The year 2000 started super bullish and ended very bearish. Would the rapidly changing market sentiment put a damper on the Fool's contrarian predictive power? Is there a genuine Fool curse? Out of the top 20 message boards at the Fool in 2000, only six were single stock message boards, reflecting a decline in bullish sentiment. But the Fool was still plenty bullish. Day Trading was still the #5 most popular message board. Here's the data—stock, number of posts, and return for the following year (2001). Keep in mind, as you probably know, 2001 was, yet again, a bad year for stocks in general. The Nasdaq fell 31% on the year.

Advanced Micro Devices; 36,970 (-37%)
Microsoft; 28,576 (+8%)
Celera; 27,925 (-46%)
Iomega; 27,206 (-59%)
Berkshire Hathaway; 24,007 (+12%)
Rambus; 22,198 (-83%)

So, despite the choppy results (to match the choppy sentiment shift in 2000), the results of our Fool indicator in 2001 were on target. On average, the popular stocks at the Fool lost 34% on the year, performing even worse than the market as a whole. And where we see the best indicator is again at the top of the list. The most popular single stock message board serves as a predictor of doom. Advanced Micro Devices lost heavily in 2001 and hasn't yet recovered. If you'd shorted the stock at the end of the 2000, because of its status as the most popular single stock board, you'd now be up 73%. That is, since its day in the sun at the Fool, the stock has fallen 73%. Talk about a curse! I'd call our indicator strong and reliable.

—— 2001 ——

There were still bulls at the Fool. Of the top 20 most popular message boards at the Fool, four were about single stocks. This is the smallest number of single stock message boards in the top 20 since 1998, the same year that we began to see bearish group boards making the top 20 list. And, as in 1997, bearish content has again crept into the top 20 list. The second most popular board in 2001 was "Living Beneath Your Means" and "Consumer Credit / Credit Cards" suddenly appeared in the #6 position. It's clear that the average individual investor is hurting, judging by the content of the Fool's boards. But they're still buying some stocks, and chatting about them too. Here's the list: company name, number of posts, and return in the following year (2002).

Advanced Micro Devices; 45,624 (-59%)
Microsoft; 33,718 (-22%)
Rambus; 30,255 (-16%)
Apple; 26,671 (-34%)

Conclusion: The Curse of the Fool

It looks unanimous to me. The more excited people become about stocks, the more they want to talk about them and the less cautious they become about the price they pay for the equity. In the stock market, great expectations are rarely met. And that might be the most important lesson you can ever learn about investing.

The lesson? Be careful with stocks where there's a lot of message board activity. Where you see it, it probably means you're investing alongside a lot of really excited investors who don't know what they're doing. Imagine you're in a herd of sheep, but instead of sheep, lemmings surround you. And they're all heading for a cliff. Be careful out there; avoid the curse of the Fool.

Originally published: January 16, 2003 by Stansberry & Associates Investment Research

For more information on Porter Stansberry go to: www.stansberryresearch.com.

The Only Two Things That Drive The Markets

By Dr. Steve Sjuggerud, PhD

There's such a glut of information these days: monthly investment magazines covering the markets, daily investment newspapers doing the same, and minute-by-minute coverage on CNBC. They're all trying to tell you what's driving the stock market, and they all *love* to tell you where the market is heading. And much of the time, they're wrong! It's enough to drive you crazy!

I'm going to make your life a lot easier. There are only two things that drive the markets. And you don't need to check on CNBC, newspapers, or magazines to follow them. Just two things drive the markets; I call them The Two "E's."

The Two E's... And How They Drive The Markets

The first "E" you can probably guess. The second "E" you probably wouldn't guess right away, but it's equally important, and much less talked about. Since that's the case, we'll spend a little more time on the second "E" today.

The first "E" is earnings. Everyone talks about this "E," and it is extremely important. The big question here is: What is the stock price in relation to the company's earnings? That tells you, in general, whether a stock is cheap or expensive. This is what we need to know, and the information is easy to find.

In my research, I've found that, throughout history, you don't make money in the stock market when the price-to-earnings ratio of the 500 biggest companies in America is above 17. Today, that number is *gulp* about 40.

What you need to realize here is that, unless stocks fall by over 50%—or unless earnings more than double—you don't even need to check this number. You *know* that stocks are expensive in relation to their earnings, and will be for a while. Just remember, history tells us we don't make money in stocks when the price-to-earnings ratio of the market is above 17. I won't say more here because so much is said and written on the topic of earnings in the mainstream financial press already.

The second thing—our second "E"—that drives the markets is *emotions*.

Emotions are a huge part of investing. Do you think it was earnings that drove the Nasdaq from 1,500 to 5,000, and then back to 1,500, all in four years time? Did earnings get 200%+ better? And then 70% worse? No. Was the Crash of '29, where stocks ultimately fell by 89%, due to earnings? No. Emotions played a big part in both of those examples.

10 Stages of the Stock Market

Human beings, with both rational and emotional urges, are the market players. And the thing is, those emotional urges can (and do) often overtake the rational side.

Instead of explaining this at great length, it's better if you just read my *10 Stages of the Stock Market* below and figure out where we are right now. This model is a tool for measuring the "emotional state" of the market today.

What are your friends and neighbors saying about the stock market? Ask them. Then figure out which quote below best sums up all their emotions. By doing this, you'll know exactly where we are in the stock market. Of course, you'll want to be a buyer somewhere around the end of the bear market and the beginning of the bull market.

Please read these *10 Stages*, and think about where you think we are now. When you do this, you'll *know* where we are in this market.

1) ***Bull Market, Late Stage***: "Darn it, other people not as smart as me are getting rich, and I'm just sitting here. I've got to get in on that!" (Late 1990s?)

2) ***Bull Market, Peak***: "Man, I am SMART. I've made a ton of money in stocks. And it couldn't have been any easier. Practically everything I buy goes up!" (Early 2000?)

3) ***Bear Market, Beginnings***: "It's just a correction. Buying the dips has worked like a charm in the past, and it'll work again!" (Late 2000?)

4) ***Bear Market, Early Stage***: "They say to buy and hold, so that's what I'll do, just keep on holding... it'll come back!" (2001?)

5) ***Bear Market, Middle Stage***: "The correction *has* to be almost over by now. I'd sure hate to sell out right at the bottom, only to have the market roar back." (Early 2002?)

6) ***Bear Market, Late Stage***: "Well, it's too late to sell now. So I'll just keep holding. Boy, I used to open my portfolio statement the second it came in the mail just to see my net worth going up, up, up! Now I dread opening my mailbox." (Late 2002?)

7) **Bear Market, Peak**: "Okay, I give up. It's time to start cleaning house and sell these stocks. Boy I really shouldn't have put so much money into these things." (Early 2003?)

8) **Bull Market, Beginnings**: Nobody *ever* makes money investing. I'll never put any money in the stock market ever again. (When???)

9) **Bull Market, Early Stage**: "Wow, prices have been going up lately. I hadn't even noticed—I'd given up. Those foolish buyers, they'll sure get what's coming to them! I'm going to get out now, while things are up!" (When ???)

10) **Bull Market, Middle Stage**: "Hey, things are looking up. Maybe there is something going on here... Nah, once burned, twice shy! I'm skeptical—I'll keep watching this sucker's rally!" (When???)

By reading these objectively, I'd say we're at about 5 right now, which means we're in the middle stage of the bear market. (The problem is, you never know how long one stage will last.) I hear everything from 4 to 6 regularly these days. What do you think? (Incidentally, the absolute *best* time to buy is between stages 7 and 8.)

Originally published: June 20, 2002 in Investment U

To sign up for Dr. Sjuggerud's free Investment U service, go to: www.investmentu.com.

The Only 3 Indicators You Need To Follow the Markets

By Dr. Steve Sjuggerud, PhD

Are you watching the CRB? The T-bond? The Russell? If you're not, then you may be missing the big picture—what's *really* going on. Most investors follow only the Dow, the Nasdaq, and maybe the S&P 500. But just following those two or three indexes could lead you to POOR investment decisions without you ever realizing it.

That's because—with just those three pieces of information—you won't have the right information to make informed decisions. Today I'll tell you about three simple—and quick—things you can do to make sure you have the right information every day. And I'll also tell you why the Dow really isn't a good stock market barometer...

What's Wrong with the Dow

The Dow Jones Industrial Average, the stock market index everyone talks about, is actually not a very good barometer of the stock market. If you're just watching the Dow, you're missing the overall picture. It's not bad. But it has a few problems.

1) **It only has 30 stocks.** If you really wanted an accurate representation of the market, you'd want as many as 500 stocks (the S&P 500 Index) or even 5,000 stocks (the Wilshire 5,000 Index, which now actually has 5,800+ stocks).

Of course, they have to be the right stocks. The Nasdaq Composite is made up of around 8,000 Nasdaq stocks. But since the Nasdaq is so small, it only represents about 19% of the total size of all stocks. So it is not necessarily a good indicator either.

2) **The Dow is a price-weighted index.** The 30 stocks in the Dow are not treated according to size, as you might expect. The higher the price of a stock, the more weighting it gets in the index. Here's what that means. Let's pretend that the index was 29 stocks at $1 a share and one stock at $100 a share. If each stock fell by $1, that should be a catastrophe. Any other index would crash over 90%. But the Dow would fall from $129 to $99, not really representing the crash. That's why a "price-weighted" index can contain misleading information.

In my mind a good index has a lot of stocks, is size-weighted not price-weighted, and is widely quoted and available. By that standard, the S&P 500 is a good stock market index.

The Important "Other" Indexes to Watch

There are three vitally important indexes—the CRB, the T-bonds, and the Russell—that you should follow regularly to get a gauge on what's going on. Keeping tabs on these three indexes doesn't take a lot of time, yet most investors would be much better off if they did. Let's examine each in greater detail.

• Of these, T-bonds are probably the most important, as it is the primary benchmark of the cost of money in the entire world. When people say "T-Bonds" they're actually referring to the 10-year U.S. Government Treasury bonds. Don't pay attention when they say "T-bonds rose 13/32s today..." Just listen for what happened, e.g. "the yield fell to 4.13%." As a general rule, stocks do well when interest rates come down, and they struggle in the face of rising rates. You can follow the T-bond yield at Yahoo! Finance. Go to: www.finance.yahoo.com. On the left side of the page you'll see the 10-year bond yield.

• The CRB Index is an excellent gauge of what's happening in commodity prices, as it's an index of a basket of 17 commodities. It includes metals, oil and gas, livestock and agricultural commodities. The index often moves in the opposite direction of bonds. Interestingly, the CRB index is up about 20% in the last year, signaling higher inflation and lower bond prices (higher interest rates) ahead. It's easy to track the CRB index on-line. Just go to: www.barchart.com. On the right side of the page, under "Market Information," you'll see a link for the CRB index.

• The Russell is the benchmark index of small stocks. It's actually the Russell 2000 Index. It's important to follow nowadays because we're coming out of a recession and the worst stock market crash since 1974. After that crash, small stocks absolutely trounced large stocks, beating them nine years in a row.

You can find the Russell 2000 Index on Yahoo! Finance too. Go to: www.finance.yahoo.com/m1?u. As a rule, you should also keep your eye on the S&P 500, and what Greenspan does when he tinkers with rates. After that, if you know what T-bonds, commodities, and small stocks are doing, you'll have a pretty complete picture of what's going on out there in nearly the whole investing world.

Originally published: January 14, 2003 in Investment U

To sign up for Dr. Sjuggerud's free Investment U service, go to: www.investmentu.com.

The "Technical Analysis" Debate
By Dr. Steve Sjuggerud, PhD

The topic of technical analysis is a touchy one. But before we dive into this heated debate, we should probably first come up with some sort of definition of technical analysis. How about this: Stock market technical analysis is, at its core, looking at *price action alone* to determine some course of action.

That said, there are essentially two heated sides of the debate, both with convincing arguments:

On the "technical analysis is a sham" side, the argument (from guys called "fundamental analysts") goes something like this: "The value of a company is purely determined by the fundamentals of that company's business, not by some silly squiggles on a chart. Therefore, the only worthwhile analysis is analyzing the company's business."

On the "technical analysis is the holy grail" side, the argument goes something like this: "Anyone who only looks at earnings and ignores emotions in the market is an idiot. The market is made up of live human beings, who always bid things up beyond any reasonable value, and sell things below any reasonable value. Sticking your head in the sand and ignoring market action is ridiculous."

Both make some sense when you read them, no? As a rule, these two camps are firmly divided—you either believe technical analysis is useful or you don't. Generally, there is no in-between. So by picking one side in this debate, I'm bound to outrage the other side. But where I stand on technical analysis actually makes neither side happy.

You see, I'm in the "in between" camp—I believe that both *earnings* and *emotions* matter. And therefore I like to mix and match the two. Here's what I mean..

Finding a Good Value, Without "Catching a Falling Knife"

I like to buy good values—cheap stocks. You find those through fundamental analysis. And I don't like to try to "catch a falling knife" in those stocks—I like to wait until the share price at least starts to recover to give me a margin of safety. I prefer to buy in an uptrend rather than in a downtrend.

The *Investor's Business Daily* newspaper is the most popular example of this. It ranks stocks based on both fundamental indicators (like earnings) and technical indicators, like what's called "relative strength." (Relative strength is just what it suggests: how well a stock is performing relative to the market or its industry. In the case of *Investor's Business Daily*, this is based heavily on the latest three months action. So if a stock has high relative strength, it's likely beginning an uptrend.)

William O'Neil, the founder of *Investor's Business Daily*, wrote a million-selling book called *How to Make Money in Stocks*, detailing his investment approach. His book established the most widely known use of both fundamental and technical analysis in an investment system. (I checked for you and found that it's available on Amazon for five bucks used—worth that price just for its list of "Common Investor Mistakes" alone.)

Earlier, you'll recall, we defined technical analysis as "looking at *price action alone* to determine some course of action." As an example, we pointed to O'Neil's *Investor's Business Daily* and its look at relative strength. Relative strength is based on the idea that O'Neil backs up with research—that the leading stocks are leaders for good reason, and are worth checking out.

Another basic concept used in technical analysis is the concept of "*support and resistance.*" For example, one might say gold has "support" around $250 an ounce, because every time it's sunk to that level in recent years, investors have come in to buy it, to "support" it. On the flip side, over the past 18 months, Microsoft has shown "resistance" to rising once it gets above $70. That seems to be a point where investors sell.

As your favorite stocks crashed in the last two years, the fundamental analysts over at Merrill and Goldman said, "The stock is cheap! Time to buy more!" Meanwhile, technical analysts wouldn't touch it. Because, based on their perspective, the stock had fallen below its support level. Once that happens (it's called a "breakdown below support"), technical analysts generally won't touch the stock until it starts an uptrend again. That concept alone could have saved all of us a lot of money over the last two years.

The Importance of the "Moving Average"

For one other example of useful technical analysis, consider the "moving average" of a stock price. While stocks fluctuate wildly over days and weeks, looking at the movement of the average over a period of time can smooth out the fluctuations and let you grasp the underlying trend. More importantly, moving averages can be a great way to significantly decrease your risk and slightly improve your returns.

Jeremy Siegel, author of *Stocks for the Long Run* and a noted Finance Professor at the Wharton School (University of Pennsylvania), broke with the tradition of academics and actually tested a simple technical analysis rule—the 200-day moving average—himself. During his test, when a stock's price moved above it's 200-day average, Siegel bought. And if a stock dipped below it's 200-day average, he sold.

What Siegel found is that since 1886, using the 200-day moving average as your indicator, you would have earned 2% points better than someone using a "buy and hold" strategy (11% instead of 9%, I believe), and you would have done so with significantly less risk. You were only in the market about 2/3 of the time. And my own research corroborates Siegel's. I've found that you simply don't make money in stocks when they are below their 200-day moving average.

One final thing here... I've found the more basic the technical indicator, the more valuable it can actually be. Relative strength is basic, but you can see its usefulness in spotting stocks starting to move. A moving average is basic, but it has a 100+ year track record of success.

However, once you start getting into the hundreds of bizarre and complicated technical indicators out there, chances are you're asking for trouble. The number of technical analysis indicators is mind-boggling. And quite frankly, I do believe that most of them are useless. (Some may work, sometimes, but be careful.) The same goes for fundamental indicators by the way. After crunching tons of numbers (both fundamental and technical,) I've actually found that simple ideas are best.

Bottom line: I like to combine both sets of indicators, both fundamental and technical. I want to buy a stock that is cheap (based on the fundamentals). But I don't want to try to catch a falling knife. So I use technical analysis to tell me when it's time to buy.

Originally published: May 30, 2002 in Investment U

To sign up for Dr. Sjuggerud's free Investment U service, go to: www.investmentu.com.

The Truth About Selling Stocks Short

By Dr. Steve Sjuggerud, PhD

Selling short is how you make money from falling stocks—in theory anyway. In practice, selling short is one of the most difficult skills to master in the markets.

Let's take a quick look at the mechanics of selling short, and then we'll get into how to make it work for you, and decide if it's even appropriate for you.

Short Selling is Simple

Short selling is so simple to understand, even a 12 year-old like Brandon Wallace can do it. Sixth-grader Brandon Wallace of Las Vegas, won the CBS MarketWatch trading challenge, beating over 40,000 other competitors by short selling instead of buying. Young Brandon said, "In fifth grade, I didn't understand it that much. But now I'm getting better."

Short selling is simply a regular trade in a stock, done in reverse order. Let's consider an example of a regular stock trade first. Then we'll look at a short.

When you buy a stock, here's what happens:

1) Buy 1,000 shares of XYZ company for $10
2) Sell 1,000 shares of XYZ company for $15
3) Collect your $5 per share profit.

When it comes to short selling, you simply reverse the order of #1 and #2:

1) Sell 1,000 shares of XYZ company for $15
2) Buy 1,000 shares of XYZ company for $10
3) Collect your $5 per share profit.

That's it. #1 and #2 were simply reversed. That's all you *need* to understand.

When you "short" a stock, you arrange to borrow shares from other investors. Almost any stockbroker (even online brokers) can do this. Why would you want to borrow stock? Because if you borrow shares of IBM at $99 and the price of IBM falls in half, then when you return the stock to the lender, you only have to return half of what you've borrowed.

You keep the rest as profit.

There's one major advantage to short selling: You don't have to have any money upfront to short a stock. Your broker will insist that you meet certain margin requirements, but if you want to borrow 100 shares of IBM, you don't have to pay for the shares right away—you're borrowing the shares, not buying them.

How The Pros Do It

I admire the professional short sellers—guys like David Tice of the Prudent Bear Fund, which is up over 100% since the market peak in March of 2000. Short sellers may be the most hated analysts on Wall Street. But they also are often the best.

They don't live the Wall Street life as depicted in movies—these guys spend their days poring over the minute details of accounting statements and government filings, looking for something that doesn't quite add up. And quite often, they'll uncover something, and sell short (at say, $20), only to see the price rise (to say $40 which would wipe them out) before whatever they discovered finally comes out in the open and the stock crashes. It's a tough life.

While that sounds rough, financial history is littered with exciting tales of bold short sellers, such as the short manipulation on the Erie Railroad by Jay Gould and Jim Fisk in 1868. Or Jesse Livermore, *King of the Bears*, making a killing in 1907 shorting Union Pacific railroad the day before the San Francisco earthquake. Or

Bernard Baruch's Amalgamated Copper short, also at the turn of the century. Or how about this: the President of Chase shorting his own company before the crash of 1929, closing his position in December of 1929 for a $4 million profit. Or George Soros, who made a billion dollars in a day shorting the British pound in the late 20th century.

The Prospects For Short Selling Are Much Different Today Than In 2000

At the peak of the bull market in 2000, the concept of shorting for profit was *"thought of by the smart circles of Wall Street to be extinct or the province of fools,"* says short selling expert Kathryn Staley. But short sellers sure look smart now—while most investors saw their net worth cut in half, short sellers saw theirs increase by 50%. Which investor looks foolish now?

Kathryn Staley wrote the book *The Art of Short Selling*. In it, she breaks down the three types of stocks to look for if you're going to sell short:

1. Companies where management lies to investors or obscures events that will affect earnings. (Did someone say Enron? Or WorldCom?)

2. Companies that have tremendously inflated stock valuations.

3. Companies that will be affected in a significant way by changing external events. She's talking about events that could make their business obsolete.

Importantly, Staley says, *"No mechanical method can capture this universe. And that is what makes short selling lucrative: It takes too much work for most people to fool with it."* She's right. It's tough. You can't simply type your criteria into a computer and have it spit out winners.

Stocks Are Still Expensive; Opportunities Abound For Short Sellers

So why would an individual investor even bother with selling short? There is a very good reason you'd want to sell short—to lower the risk in your portfolio… especially when stocks are very expensive.

While I don't envision a market crash any time soon, at the very least I don't expect to see the extraordinary gains we saw in the 1990s. And at worst, yes, stocks could still lose half their value from here. Taking a few short positions in your portfolio—which would rise in value as the market fell—would balance out your stock holdings, and thereby lower the risk in your portfolio. Shorting is not for everyone. And it's not for all markets. But it does make sense when stocks are highly overpriced.

No doubt, short selling is difficult. But for the right investor, at the right time, it has a place.

Originally published: December 5, 2002 in True Wealth

For more information on Dr. Sjuggerud's True Wealth advisory service, go to: www.stansberryresearch.com, or call (888) 261-2693.

Fiat Money and Deflation—What You Really Need to Know

By Dr. Steve Sjuggerud, PhD

"You can't have deflation in a fiat money society."
~ Albert Friedberg

Economist Gary Shilling wrote a fascinating book called *Deflation*. His book sparked the inflation/deflation debate that rages today—a debate that I find to be tired, and would like to put an end to in your mind right now, along with how to profit from the current environment.

I read Shilling's book in 1998 I believe, just after the Asian crisis. In essence, Shilling showed how interest rates and inflation had been falling for nearly 20 years, and how that trend was set to continue indefinitely. So far, Shilling has been right on track. The trends have continued as he suggested, and people extrapolate that those trends can continue indefinitely.

They can't.

What sealed the deal for me was reading a comment by Albert Friedberg around the same time. At the time, Al Friedberg had compiled the most amazing track record I'd ever seen. I believe the annualized return on his flagship fund was something like 40%+ a year over the dozen years it had been in existence.

Friedberg flatly stated, "You can't have deflation in a fiat money society."

He's right. And that statement is really the end of the story.

I'll explain this statement. But it really needs no explanation. It is complete in

54

itself. You see, when the government controls the money and printing of money, and that government wants to do everything it can to prevent deflation, the effect will be a concerted effort by the government—a massive inflation—to offset the deflationary trend by printing money.

"Fiat" money, if you haven't heard the term before, is "government decreed" money. Fiat money is a "promise to pay" by the issuer that has no intrinsic value. The U.S. dollar, for example, is fiat money. It is government-decreed money. It has no intrinsic value. It is a piece of paper that has a value simply because we believe it is worth something. That describes most money in the world today. The opposite extreme of fiat money would be the use of gold or silver coins where the value of the metal content of the coin is the value of that coin.

These days Friedberg is still pounding the table against deflation. He writes in his newsletter, "The steady fall of the U.S. dollar juxtaposed against rapid monetary growth [and] massive fiscal expansion… make nonsense of the fears of deflation."

Friedberg then points out that 15 out of 17 commodities are higher than a year ago—the highest reading in almost 20 years. He concludes his inflation talk by saying "In our view, an important acceleration of inflation is a certainty."

To bring us up to date, Martin Barnes of BCA Research, another of the few guys worth listening to out there, came to basically the same conclusion in *Barron's* over the weekend: "Not many people have noticed, but China's inflation rate has turned positive… By the middle of next year, deflation fears will be shifting to worries about inflation and concerns about the Fed raising rates."

We won't experience a prolonged bout of deflation. We can't. We've got a government committed to preventing deflation at all costs. And if that means accidentally overshooting and creating a massive inflation, that's what we'll see.

Friedberg's second sentence in his January newsletter is, "In fact, we firmly believe that we are in for the most sustained period of rising prices since the early 1970s."

Let's take a look at the annual returns of various asset classes over 1968 to 1979, the last period of rising prices:

19.4% Gold
18.9% Stamps
15.7% Rare books
13.7% Silver
12.7% Coins (U.S. non-gold)

12.5%	Old masters' paintings
11.8%	Diamonds
11.3%	Farmland
9.6%	Single-family homes
6.5%	Inflation (CPI)
6.4%	Foreign currencies
5.8%	High-grade corporate bonds
3.1%	Stocks

It's interesting to note that stocks and bonds are at the bottom of that list, actually losing money versus inflation. And gold is at the top of the list.

Who's right in this debate? I don't know. Nobody knows. But smart guys like Friedberg and Barnes make a good case. If they're right, it's time for a serious adjustment in thinking, away from stocks and bonds, and toward hard assets, like gold. How much of your portfolio is in hard assets? You'd better have some, if not a lot.

Originally published: June 3, 2003 in True Wealth

Why You Should Care About Dividends

By Dr. Steve Sjuggerud, PhD

Cash dividends don't lie. When a company pays you a *dividend*, that's cash in your pocket—from the company that you own, to you. One thing I like about dividends is that when a company pays you *hard cash*, there's very little room for fudging the numbers. If your stock has to pay you dividends in cash, the company must actually have that cash in order to pay you.

Dividends are crucially important. To understand why, let me ask you: What does it mean to be an *investor*? And just exactly what are we entitled to when we *invest*?

If we put our money in the bank and earn 2% interest on that money, what are we *entitled* to as an investor? That's easy—the interest on our money. And what's our risk? Well if we have less than $100,000 in that deposit, our risk is nothing.

If we loan $900 to a family friend, and we get it in writing that he'll pay us back

$1,000 in one year's time, what are we *entitled* to in a year? Our $1,000. That's a contract—and that arrangement is no different than another class of investment—a bond. What's our risk? Our risk is that he doesn't pay. But it is a binding contract, and we are entitled to our $100 in interest, which means we're getting paid about 5% a year for taking our risk.

If we invest $10,000 into Microsoft stock, what's at risk? *A lot*, as the stock is trading at an extraordinarily high number times sales. And what exactly are we entitled to when we invest in Microsoft? Are you ready for this? The answer is absolutely, positively, unequivocally nothing.

You see, the only things you're *entitled* to as a stock investor are *dividends*.

Before you make an investment in anything, you ought to say "what's in it for me?" And you ought to demand something concrete in addition to your speculative investment. Let's say you demand a dividend payment of 5% a year, to ensure that you will participate in the success of the business. Hey that's more than fair. You deserve it. In fact, that's not far from what investors demanded for 100 years, from 1870-1970.

But then the stock market crashed in the early 1970s. The blue chips cut their dividends. And the Wall Street brokerage firms, struggling to find a way to pitch companies to their customers that no longer paid healthy dividends, started focusing on earnings. After all, dividends were paid out of earnings they reasoned, so if you looked at earnings, you were looking at the source of dividends.

And so from the late 1970s to late 1990s, earnings were the rage, even though earnings are a step removed from *dividends*—the only thing that investors are truly *entitled* to.

By the late 1990s, when stocks started looking expensive on an earnings basis, Wall Street brokerage firms (again struggling to find a way to pitch expensive stocks to their customers) came up with two new ways to look at stocks like "pro forma" earnings (I don't speak Latin, but judging from the last few years, I can infer that "pro forma" must mean "completely made up to make a pipe dream look legitimate"). Of course, pro forma earnings are even further removed from what the investor is truly entitled to—which are corporate dividends.

Lately, we've heard the argument that companies are better off reinvesting their money than paying it to shareholders as dividends. Interestingly (to me at least), a study in the *Financial Analysts Journal* found that companies actually did a *miserable* job of reinvesting dividends. They found that you are better off *making sure you get paid*—accepting dividends instead of applauding stock buybacks.

The bottom line is, I don't want a pipe dream—I want to know what I'm entitled to when I invest in something. And quite frankly stocks like Microsoft are not making a compelling case for me to give them my money.

Making sure you get paid is quite often the difference between *investing* and *speculating*.

Speculating in real estate, for example, is buying a chunk of raw land on the hope that there'll be a greater fool out there who'll pay more than you did.

Investing in real estate is earning 7-9% in rent after expenses, and any capital gains are icing on the cake.

When considering your next investment, consider exactly what you're *entitled* to. No matter how good the story, if what's in it for you is not clear, what are you doing? My advice—regardless of the story is to make sure you know what's in it for you up front. One simple way to tilt the scales in your favor is to *make sure you get paid*.

Originally published: September 10, 2002 in Investment U

To sign up for Dr. Sjuggerud's free Investment U service, go to: www.investmentu.com.

The 50 Timeless Rules of Investing

By Dr. Steve Sjuggerud, PhD

The 50 Rules:

1. An attempt at making a quick buck usually leads to losing much of that buck.
2. If stocks in general don't seem cheap, stand aside.
3. "Buy and hold" doesn't *always* work.
4. Never throw good money after bad (don't buy more of a loser).
5. Cut your losers, and let your winners ride.
6. If the investment sounds too good to be true, it is.
7. Don't fight "the tape" (the trend).
8. Don't fight the Fed (interest rates).
9. Most stocks that fall under $5 rarely see $10 again.
10. The best hot tip: There is no such thing as a hot tip.
11. Don't fall in love with your stock; it won't fall in love with you.
12. Don't have more than 3% at risk in any one position.
13. The trend is your friend until the end.

14. Trading options often leads to a quick trip to the poorhouse.
15. Bear-market rallies are often violent; giving the illusion the bull is back.
16. Low-priced stocks don't double any faster than high-priced ones.
17. Valuations don't matter in the short run.
18. When a stock hits a new high, it's not time to sell. Something is going right.
19. Have a rose garden portfolio (don't trim your roses while your weeds fester).
20. It takes courage to be a pig (don't settle for taking 10% profits).
21. Not selling a stock for a gain, simply because you're afraid of the taxes, is a bad idea.
22. Avoid limited upside, unlimited downside investments.
23. When all you're left with is hope, get out.
24. Don't keep losing money just to "prove you are right." Nobody cares.
25. Forecasts are useless.
26. Have patience and stick with your discipline.
27. When it's time to act, don't hesitate.
28. Expert investors care about risk, novice investors shop for returns.
29. Don't lose money.
30. You can learn more from your bad moves than your good.
31. A rising tide raises all ships, and vice versa, so assess the tide, not the ships.
32. Stocks fall more than you think and rise higher than you can possibly imagine.
33. Very few people have had great success short selling, even in bear markets.
34. You can't know everything about everything.
35. Since you can't know everything, seek out specialists who know their areas.
36. If a company's sales are shrinking, the business isn't growing anymore.
37. Real estate cycles are not the same as stock market cycles.
38. Investing in what's popular never ends up making you any money.
39. Know your investment edge, and don't stray too far from it.
40. Bear markets begin in good times. Bull markets begin in bad times.
41. Buy value—stocks that are priced less than their underlying assets are worth.
42. Neglected sectors often turn out to offer good values.
43. There's usually only one reason corporate insiders buy stock.
44. Don't miss a good one by being too concerned with the exact price you pay.
45. Avoid popular stocks, fad industries and new ventures.
46. Buy shares in businesses you understand.
47. Try to buy a stock when it has few friends.
48. Be patient: Don't be rattled by fluctuations.
49. Mutual funds under-perform the averages over the long run. Buy index funds instead.
50. If you don't understand the investment, don't invest.

Whew. That's a lot of rules. Reasonably intuitive, yet millions of investors break these rules every day. I'd like to leave you with one more rule, which I often see with investors who have been burned in the market...

51. The people who suffer the worst losses are those who overreach.

Originally published: October 3, 2002 in Investment U

Dr. Steve Sjuggerud runs a free on-line investment education course called Investment University. Twice a week, he covers the most important investment concepts, rules, and strategies. He also explains what's currently happening in the investment markets, and which investments make the most sense right now. To sign up for Dr. Sjuggerud's free Investment U service, go to: www.investmentu.com.

Chapter 2

How to Evaluate Investments

Defining a "Good Investment"

By Dr. Steve Sjuggerud, PhD

What makes a "good" investment? How do you know if one particular investment opportunity is better than another? What are the important factors to consider when deciding whether an investment is "good" or "bad?" Specifically, what do you need to know?

Let's cut to the core: The lower the RISK and the higher the expected RETURN, the better the investment.

Of course, that sounds simple… until you try to define both the RISK and the expected RETURN, and then you try to compare whatever you come up with to other investment options. It's difficult because we just can't compare the RISK and RETURN very easily across different assets. Or can we?

How to Make a Valid Comparison of Investments

The truth is we *can* make an apples-to-apples comparison by simply coming up with a ratio of REWARD versus RISK. To get this ratio, we merely need to look at the performance of various indexes over a consistent period of time. And we need to adjust their returns for risk-free interest. (If we didn't adjust for risk-free interest, Treasury Bills would have the highest score, with a return of about 6% and a risk—or VOLATILITY—of only 2% a year.)

So to compensate, I've adjusted the return of each index down by 6%—that's the figure in the ADJ. RETURN column below. As you will see, by compensating for risk-free interest, the score for T-Bills immediately falls to the bottom of the list.

Investment	Score	Return	Adj. Return	Volatility
Dow Stocks	.87	19.5	13.5	15.4
Corporate Bonds	.59	11.2	5.2	8.9
Treasury Bonds	.57	9.9	3.9	6.9
Real Estate Stocks	.50	13.7	7.7	15.4
Russell 2000	.41	14.1	8.1	20.0
International Stocks	.39	15.0	9.0	23.0
Treasury Bills	.11	6.2	1.9	

Now that you've had a chance to see how the various investment categories stack up, I'll try to explain—as clearly and simply as possible—how the comparisons were made.

What the "Scoreboard" Means

To begin, the "SCORE" is the ratio between the ADJ. RETURN and VOLATILITY columns in the table. But in reality, it's also the REWARD versus RISK ratio I mentioned earlier. And it allows us to compare apples to apples.

What's interesting when you check out the scoreboard is that international stocks, which had the second-highest return, end up second from the bottom of the list because their risk (VOLATILITY) is so high. In fact, they're the riskiest investment on the "board."

It's also interesting that corporate bonds—relatively boring to most investors—come in second, even without having one of the highest rates of return… all because the risk is so relatively low.

People seem to be attracted to risk. They buy international stocks. And they buy tech stocks—the riskiest of all (and about three times as risky as stocks in general). I don't know if people haven't seen a table like this before, or if they just don't want "good-but-boring" investments such as decent corporate bonds, for example.

But when you take the time to compare the risk-reward ratios of different investments—in much the same way you would compare features of new luxury cars before purchasing—you give yourself a much clearer understanding of what to expect for your money.

As we proved here, it's easy to find out just how much return you can expect, and just how many sleepless nights you'll have along the way.

One more important thing to note: We only used 18 years worth of data in this chart, and that's probably not enough. If you just invested based on this table, you'd buy big U.S. stocks right now and shun small stocks, which could be a dangerous move. The table and the comparisons are only as good as the data used.

What Reward-to-Risk Ratio is Right For You?

The key message here is that when you evaluate any investment, you've got to consider both expected RETURN and RISK. Most people, dreaming about big potential returns, forget about the second variable—RISK. Don't include yourself in that list.

Before making an investment, ask yourself: "How much risk am I really taking, and what is my upside?" Personally, I like to have a three-to-one reward-to-risk ratio. If I can't potentially make three times whatever I have at risk in a stock, it's not worth it.

Let me explain this concept a little further. I use a trailing stop on all stocks I invest in, and that trailing stop is generally 25%. That means if I buy a stock at $100, I'll sell it at $75 to limit my risk. If I'm willing to risk 25%, then that means I'd better be looking for a return of 75% or more, or it's not worth buying.

Think about this: If you're not using trailing stops to protect yourself, you're actually risking 100% every time you invest. So you'd better be expecting a 300% return. Those odds aren't good—I can probably count the number of "real" stocks up 300% in the last year on one hand.

If you know your RISK—in my case 25%—and your potential return is favorable to you in relation to the risk you're willing to take—again, in my case, I'm looking for 75%+ return—then you've got a "good investment."

Originally published: February 7, 2002 in Investment U

To sign up for Dr. Sjuggerud's free Investment service, go to: www.investmentu.com.

What Any Business is Really Worth

By Dan Ferris

Before you can decide if something is cheap and safe enough to buy, you need to know as much as possible about what that something is.

An **ASSET** is something an individual or corporation owns that puts money in its pockets. A **LIABILITY** is anything an individual or corporation does, owns, agrees to, or encounters that takes money out of its pockets.

Your accountant wouldn't like these definitions. They don't conform to the Generally Accepted Accounting Principles, or GAAP, which you've heard much about if you've read a financial newspaper in the past two years.

Most accountants will tell you that an asset is anything of economic value that can be turned into cash. I don't like that definition. It doesn't speak to me as an investor. It doesn't tell me what a company's assets can do for me. I need an investor's definition, not an accountant's definition.

I'm interested in assets that work for me. And I'm interested in finding out all the liabilities that might work against me.

I promise you that if you use complex, standard accounting definitions to understand key financial terms, it'll be more difficult to figure out what's really going on with the companies you've invested in. But if you consistently refer to the kinds of alternative definitions I'm offering you here, you'll build wealth safely. You'll also find it easier to pass up those opportunities that might at first seem attractive, but turn out to be not-so-attractive.

Here's a good illustration of how our definitions of assets and liabilities can be useful to you.

Sears carries about $5 billion in inventory on its books. It's reported right there on the balance sheet, under current assets. In the accounting profession, current assets are assets that will be turned into cash within 12 months. Individual items (gas barbecues, shoes, dinnerware, furniture, etc.) do indeed turn into cash within 12 months and are appropriately accounted for as current assets.

But think about it… Sears *constantly carries* about $5 billion in inventory, every day of the week, month after month, year after year. Although accounting rules say it's a current asset, Sears' inventory really behaves more like a permanent $5 billion capital expenditure, a fixed asset. Fixed assets are depreciated. The risks to Sears' massive inventory have an effect similar to depreciation. Sears' inventory can go out of style, get stolen, or marked down at the end of a season. Inventory items can and do occasionally get lost. While the accounting rules say Sears' inventory is a current asset, it behaves more like a fixed asset. It isn't necessarily the ready source of cash it ought to be.

If we apply our new definitions to the Sears example, we see that Sears' inventory at times behaves like a liability, something that takes money out of the company's—and the shareholders'—pockets.

Let's say Sears has $1 million worth of designer sweaters. It's a really mild winter, so they only sell $100,000 worth. They should have $900,000 worth left.

But the season ends, and suddenly the remaining sweaters aren't worth $900,000 anymore. They're marked down at the end of the season. Those that are sold produce only $400,000 in revenue. The difference—$500,000—comes out of the shareholders' pockets. When shareholder's equity is calculated at the end of the year, the $500,000 won't be there.

This hypothetical example is greatly simplified, but it still works. Not all assets are created equal. Not all assets always conform to our definition of something that puts money in your pocket. Obviously, all companies are going to have some assets that have the potential to behave like liabilities and take money out of the company and shareholders' pockets. But some companies' assets are overwhelmingly of the variety that puts money into shareholders' pockets.

Am I saying I'd never buy Sears' stock? Not at all. If the price is right, I'm always game.

Originally published in Extreme Value

For more info on Dan Ferris' Extreme Value service, visit www.stansberryresearch.com, and click on "Extreme Value".

Graham's Number: Current Assets—Total Liabilities

By Dan Ferris

B enjamin Graham, the acknowledged father of the modern business of analyzing stocks and bonds, first discovered Graham's number. Graham was Warren Buffett's mentor. He taught Buffett at Columbia University. Graham referred to the number as "net current asset value." In places like the Value Line Investment Survey, it's referred to as net working capital.

I highly recommend spending some time repeatedly looking at balance sheets on Yahoo Finance.

One day, I looked at over 300 and found a bunch of companies with positive Graham's Number. Most of those that traded at a discount were businesses in trouble—but not all. There were some diamonds hiding in that rough.

Just subtract Total Liabilities from Current Assets. If the number is positive, it could be the sign of a conservatively financed company, like Microsoft. If the stock's market cap (the number you get by multiplying the total number of shares outstanding by the stock's share price) is less than Graham's Number, it could be a sign that you're about to make some money.

For most companies, Graham's Number is negative. For example, on its Sept. 30, 2002 balance sheet, IBM Corp. had $37.3 billion of current assets and $61.9 billion of total liabilities.

When Graham's Number is positive, it can be a very good thing. It means the company has plenty of liquid assets on hand, free and clear of all liabilities. If you owe $40,000 on your home and have $50,000 in the bank, then you have $10,000 that nobody has a claim on. Microsoft, for example, had about $50 billion in current assets and $16 billion in total liabilities on its Sept. 30, 2002 balance sheet. That means it has $34 billion in liquid assets free and clear, totally unspoken for by any obligations. That huge source of liquidity recently started making its way to shareholders, when Microsoft announced that they'd start paying a dividend.

Farmer Brothers (FARM), on the other hand, has $288 million in cash and securities that crotchety founder Roy Farmer refuses to part with. National Presto Industries (NPK), as of early February 2003, had $199 million worth of Graham's Number, and had a market capitalization of about $188 million, a 7% discount to Graham's Number. It's a similar situation to Farmer Brothers. In both cases, the company is majority owned by the founding family, and they're running it for themselves, not their shareholders. Neither company is likely to ever become a particularly good investment. If they both get a lot cheaper, maybe...

Originally published in Extreme Value

For more info on Dan Ferris' Extreme Value service, visit www.stansberryresearch.com, and click on "Extreme Value".

2 Tools for Your Investor Tool Box

By Porter Stansberry

Your first order of business as an investor is: Don't lose money. You should never be in a position to receive a Zerotrade statement in the mail. While I've made a career of finding speculative opportunities, the majority of your equity investments should be in stocks that represent outstanding value on an operating basis. To find stocks like that, you need good tools to evaluate value and ensure a margin of safety for your investment. These two simple tests should help.

Tool #1: Instead of using P/E ratios to measure the value of stocks, I want to talk about "earnings yield" instead. What is earnings yield? It's the P/E ratio measured in the opposite way. For example, if a stock is trading at 15 times earnings, it has an earnings yield of 1/15, or 6.6%.

Looking closely at earnings yield is the first step toward measuring value. It allows you to make a quick and simple comparison between stocks and bonds, which will prevent you from ever paying too much for a stock.

Let me explain how to do it. Ten-year corporate bonds yield 6.37%, according to Moody's. You could earn this return through investing in any number of no-load corporate bond funds. That's what's good about bonds: You know how much you'll make. Earnings will fluctuate with stocks, but you can nevertheless approximate the same kind of yield from equity. You figure a company's earnings yield by simply inverting its P/E ratio. I've done so for you below.

P/E:	Earnings yield:
50	2.0%
45	2.2%
40	2.5%
35	2.8%
30	3.3%
25	4.0%
20	5.0%
15	6.6%
10	10.0%
8	12.5%
6	16.6%
5	20.0%
4	25.0%

As I write this, the S&P 500 is trading for around 22 times this year's estimated earnings. Thus, as an equity owner, you will have an earnings yield of about 4.5% in blue chip stocks. Bonds represent better value. Bonds are paying out over 6%, with little risk. Stocks are only earning 4.5%, with lots of risk. It's not surprising to see stocks decline, given the clear advantage in bonds.

Of course, what's true of the market as a whole doesn't apply to every stock in the market in equal measure. For example, let's look at a company I've recommended before. I studied its business carefully. You can see this trend easily with a simple analysis of the firm's results: Revenue doubled in 2002, after rising 28%, on average, each year for past five years. I won't keep you in suspense. The company is Exelon (**NYSE: EXC**), and it's growing because of its superior technology (nuclear power) and its financial conservatism. As the rest of the power sector implodes, this firm is quietly—and profitably—picking up the pieces. The company's earnings yield—when I recommended it—exceeded 10% a year. And it paid a dividend of nearly 4% too. This was a growth stock that offered far more yield than a bond, and almost as much annual income.

Tool #2: Exelon passed the earnings yield test. It was paying 50% more than bonds of similar quality. But how do you know it's a safe stock to buy?

I measure safety by figuring out if the company I'm looking at can afford to buy itself. Are the balance sheet assets and cash flow of the company strong enough to accept new debt equal to the current market cap?

The market value of Exelon is around $15 billion (after discounting the cash on its balance sheet). Assuming the same interest rate we've been measuring against (AAA bonds) of 6.37%, management would have to borrow around $15 billion to buy back all of the stock. Interest on this debt comes to $955 million per year.

In 2001, Exelon made $3.6 billion in profits and spent $2 billion on capital expenditures. It also paid $500 million in dividends. Or, in other words, it had around $1 billion in cash flow, enough to carry the debt without canceling the dividend. And 2002 earnings are stronger than last year. Yes, this company could afford to buy itself.

When a company has a strong enough balance sheet and a strong enough business to buy back all of its stock—at least on paper—you have a large margin of safety. Essentially this gives you the same risk as a bondholder, which makes your greater earnings yield that much more attractive. You're only taking the risks of debt holder, while you will get the return of an owner.

Originally published by Stansberry & Associates Investment Research

For more information on Porter Stansberry go to: www.stansberryresearch.com.

Size Up Any Stock Quickly and Easily

By Dr. Steve Sjuggerud, PhD

The old way to size up a stock doesn't seem to be very valuable any more, so it's time to take a different look at things. Let me show you what I mean.

The Price-to-Earnings Ratio—the old standby measure of value—has become much less… well, "valuable" in sizing up investments. With companies like Enron out there pulling every accounting trick in the book to fudge its earnings, the "E" in the "P/E" equation is now highly questionable.

Just as a quick refresher, let's recap how we calculate the P/E ratio.

If Microsoft's Earnings-Per-Share is .816, and the stock is selling for 26, its P/E is the Price-Per-Share divided by the Earnings-Per-Share, or 31.86.

More Than Just Shady Accounting

But it's not just Enron—even the revered institutions are "messing" with their earnings numbers. The folks at Standard & Poor's for example, who publish the S&P 500 Index, (the general gauge of the overall stock market) have even gotten into the act of "messing" with earnings.

A few weeks ago, S&P told us that the P/E for the S&P 500 index was 40. But, in one week, that figure changed to 28. S&P said they "changed the way they calculate earnings." Hmmm… how about that?

Research outfit IBES says the S&P 500 market P/E is 24. And Bloomberg says it's 25. However, Bloomberg also lists the S&P P/E at a whopping 61 (counting write-offs and charges). So what's the "true" answer? That's still a mystery.

But here's why the discrepancy is important to you as an investor: Many of the traditional ways of analyzing the stock market are simply no longer relevant. They've fallen victim to "creative accounting" and "changes in procedure."

Whatever the real number is for the S&P 500, there is no doubt that by any measure, stocks are expensive. The historical average P/E is in the mid-teens. And the fudging of earnings numbers, Enron aside, is getting ridiculous.

So let me offer up a simple solution for us. Let's look at SALES instead of EARNINGS.

Introducing… the Price-to-Sales Ratio

The Price-to-Sales (P/S) ratio simply compares the price of a stock to the company's sales for that year. Here's why it may be a better guide to determining the "true" value of a company: It's much harder to fudge the top line (sales) than the bottom line (earnings). (Although companies like Global Crossing and Priceline.com found inventive ways to fudge the top line as well.)

And perhaps even more important, since most analysts and investors don't look as closely at the top line, chances are good it's a "cleaner" number for us to consider.

For example, in 2002 Wal-Mart's stock market value was about $280 billion, while sales were about $200 billion. So Wal-Mart was trading at a P/S ratio of 1.4. But what does this mean?

Well, stocks on average have historically traded for just under one times sales (0.9). So, at 1.4, Wal-Mart is expensive by historical standards but it's still cheaper than most stocks today. And, in fact, you may be willing to pay that premium for Wal-Mart because it is a successful company, especially given some of the real dogs out there today.

How the Price-to-Sales Ratio Measures Up

Crunching the numbers, the P/S ratio turns out to be a very valuable indicator. Not surprisingly, if you buy stocks when they are "cheap"—based on this ratio—you do much better than if you buy when stocks are expensive.

Specifically, if you buy the S&P 500 index when the P/S ratio is below 0.9, history tells us that five years later, you'd be up an average of 81%. This works out to an annualized return of 12.6%. However, if you buy when the P/S ratio is above 0.9, five years later, your average annualized return would be 4.7%. (A "buy and hold" strategy for the S&P 500 over last 50 years would have produced about 8.6%.)

Looked at another way, your returns would have been *almost 50% better* than "buy and hold" if you'd only bought "on the cheap." And your returns would have been almost 50% worse if you'd bought when things were expensive.

What P/S Ratio Tells Us Today

By this measure, stocks today are expensive. A conservative estimate of the up-to-the-minute Price-to-Sales ratio would be 1.3—or about 40% higher than the 0.9 historical average. Stocks aren't cheap.

The easy rule of thumb to remember as a rough "fair value" of a business is "one-times sales." (A Price-to-Sales ratio of one.) Again, this is just a rough gauge for whether or not you're paying too little or too much to invest. This ratio is easy to find; it's now listed on the Yahoo! Finance web page for each stock.

When you start applying this "one-times sales" rule of thumb, you'll find that many companies that have fallen a lot lately are still far from bargains.

I'm not saying you should "avoid all stocks that trade above one-times sales." What I am saying is, the Price-to-Sales Ratio is easy to understand. It's easy to find. And it's an easy gauge—one that you don't have to be an accounting expert to use—to know if a particular company is cheap or expensive.

Originally published: February 28, 2002 in Investment U

To sign up for Dr. Sjuggerud's free Investment Education service, go to: www.investmentu.com.

How Employee Stock Options Affect Your Investments

By Dr. Steve Sjuggerud, PhD

Former Global Crossing CEO Gary Winnick sold over a half a billion dollars worth of stock before Global Crossing went bankrupt. Shareholders are bust. And Winnick is a zillionaire. Is this right?

This is the question that's all over the papers as of this writing—both the *Wall Street Journal* and the *Financial Times* are focusing on CEO compensation, and on what's right.

While both sides of the fence yell about what's right and how it should be accounted for, the real question for most investors is, "How does all this affect me?" The answer is simple, and it's all you need to know.

Right now, giving employees stock options is a way to pay them without having that expense show up on company financial statements. That's not square, and it needs to be fixed. That's it.

As you can imagine, giving stock options in lieu of having a salary expense can make a business look a lot more profitable than it really is. And that can be a *dangerous* proposition for investors, especially in today's environment.

Because the reality is employee stock options have *value*. Let's take this matter to its logical extreme.

Imagine, for example, that a company not only paid its employees in stock options, but also paid its suppliers that way. Then the company's bottom line would look a LOT better. Heck, if it could pay the rent with stock options, then you'd have a company with no expenses, according to the accountants. That doesn't make any sense.

The simple reality is that by *not* reporting a *legitimate* business expense such as employee stock options, many corporations are, in fact, misleading investors. The danger, of course, lies in the fact that investors truly have no way of knowing what the books really look like... and therefore have no way of knowing just how overvalued a company may be.

What the Lobbyists Would Have You Believe

As you can see, there is a strong incentive for companies to keep options off the books. The lobbying is coming from all directions—politicians, CEOs, venture capitalists, etc. They say stupid things like, "No dollars changed hands." But the truth is, accountants have handled this issue for decades—it's called accrual accounting.

These "lobbyists" also ask, "How can you figure the value of these options?" But this is easy too, as those options have a MARKET VALUE. Regardless of how strong this lobby is, they've got to face this fact: Granting stock instead of salary is still payment—it's still a business expense, and needs to be treated as such.

Coca-Cola recently decided to voluntarily do this. GE joined in too. The reason is obvious—it's the fairest way to report what's happening at the company.

This Issue is Not About Executive Compensation

Let me be clear about this—I have no problem with CEOs making a lot of money. Consider an entrepreneur like Bill Gates. He took big risks. He dropped out of an Ivy League school to start his own company. Now that's gutsy. He took an enormous risk and literally invented Microsoft out of thin air. From scratch to $250 billion. Not too shabby. Good for him.

But I do have a problem—two of them, actually—with Microsoft and compensation. The first issue is what's called "options overhang." This is simply the ratio of options grants as a percentage of shares outstanding. At Microsoft, this number is around 28%. This number means that Microsoft has been extremely generous in passing out options. And that means shareholders will get seriously hurt (seriously diluted is the specific way to phrase it) as employees cash in. (As a comparison, Wal-Mart is at about 2%.) It will come back to haunt shareholders. No doubt.

The second issue is that the options creation, which is literally printing money, continues at Microsoft. Microsoft's option "run rate" is extraordinarily high as Microsoft is "printing" shares, in a way, at a rate of 4% a year. Again, this practice seriously cuts into the potential for shareholders to make a nickel. It's like inflation, only worse.

Microsoft is currently trading at nine times sales. That means if Microsoft were to pay out every penny of sales to shareholders over the next nine years (assuming sales were flat), shareholders would just break even. Of course, that's not going to happen.

Microsoft may be a great company, but it's an overvalued one that's printing money through options grants. And that makes it a horrible investment right now.

Summing up, stock options are a business expense and should be treated as such by appearing on the income statement. That's all you need to know. I think we'll see that in time. But when you hear some slick talker saying otherwise, just remember what you learned in this article.

Originally published: August 1, 2002 in Investment U

To sign up for Dr. Sjuggerud's FREE Investment Education service called Investment U, go to: www.investmentu.com.

4 Basic Rules for Biotech Companies

By Dave Lashmet

As a biotech investor, I look for the most profitable stocks in the entire market. However, during my search, I come across hundreds of compa - nies every year that have lots of promise, but little realistic chance of making money for investors.

Here are my four basic rules for investing in biotech. You'd be well served to apply this checklist to any biotech investment before you get involved:

#1. Don't listen to the hype about a new technology.

#2. Only the economic payoff matters.

#3. Look at the basic science, especially trial results in people.

#4. Look at the competition.

That's what marks a winning drug company from all the losers out there.

Let me give you an example.

Motley Fool's biotech guy was recently hyping a company called Nabi Biopharmaceuticals (Nasdaq: NABI), which has a vaccine for Staph infections in large Phase III trials, with final results due later next year.

The Fool says Nabi is woefully undervalued because it has a drug in Phase III tri- als and has generated $125 million in revenue over the past nine months. The Fool thinks Nabi is some sort of value play with a market cap of $600 million. They arbi- trarily attribute a market cap of $400 million to simply having a drug in Phase III trials.

But I disagree.

Instead, I apply my rules for Biotech, and Nabi just doesn't cut it. I see several major problems for investors:

First, don't listen to hype.

The stock is currently trading at its 52-week high with no new developments other than a recent stock offering. This suggests that the price is inflated due to the hype surrounding the offering.

Second, only the economic payoff matters.

Point one: StaphVax had a potential manufacturing issue. StaphVax is what's called a "polysaccharide conjugate" vaccine. In other words, it's built from the sugars on the outside of the Staph bacteria. That's what teaches your immune defenses how to identify this bug, in case you're ever infected.

The problem is that making a sugar-based vaccine is a lot harder than making a protein vaccine. Wyeth (NYSE: WYE) had this trouble with "Prevnar," its blockbuster vaccine to prevent ear infections.

Prevnar is a great vaccine for kids. And as soon as Prevnar hit the market, every school district in the country tried to buy some. But manufacturing difficulties stalled sales for two years. Prevnar is only now living up to its potential.

I'm not sure Nabi will have the same problems as Wyeth. Maybe things will go fine. But Nabi just changed partners to make its vaccine. It's going to take all of next year to prove that this new manufacturing process works. For now, this represents a major risk to investors.

Here's point two: Staph isn't a common illness. It's only common in people cut open, or people with weak immune systems. That's when staph infections are most deadly. So it's a tiny fraction of Americans who need this vaccine. It's not like flu, or strep throat, for example. It's not a childhood vaccine.

Third, look at the basic science. Especially trial results in people.

Nabi can't turn its current trial results into U.S. sales. The U.S. Food and Drug Administration (FDA) set the bar for approval of Nabi's Staph vaccine at 50% effectiveness. But in its first Phase III trial, "StaphVAX" was only 57% effective. That's very close to the bottom limit for winning FDA approval.

More importantly, the 95% confidence interval on the first trial showed that StaphVax's effectiveness was anywhere between 10% and 81%. So it's a coin toss whether or not it really works. And if StaphVax does fail the larger trial, Nabi's investors will take the hit.

Here are the major questions about Nabi:

*** Will this vaccine work?

*** Will it sell?

*** Can Nabi make it on a large scale?

*** And will StaphVax out-compete (fourth rule) new antibiotics that can do the same thing?

No one knows the answers. As I figure it, there's a better than even chance this vaccine will NEVER pay off for investors.

The way I see it, NABI at $600 million isn't a bargain. Wherever you turn, it's a potential disaster. Watch out for this minefield.

Originally published: December 31, 2003 in Diligence

For more information on Diligence, go to www.stansberryresearch.com, and click on "Diligence."

How to Evaluate a Biotech Company

By Porter Stansberry

When you invest in biotech companies, you want to know 1) That the technology is sound, and likely to work and 2) that you are getting the stock at a fair price.

Let's put the science aside and look today at the financial side of a biotech investment.

To do this, we'll use a company I recommended recently: Esperion Pharmaceuticals, which developed a breakthrough drug to treat clogging of the arteries.

Esperion, as a stock, is very expensive. And the more you pay, the more risk you take.

Evaluation Measure #1: Typically, I like to pay no more than a 100% premium to invested capital when I buy an unproven technical property. It's often hard to say what a new widget or drug is worth, but you can estimate a base value by looking at replacement cost.

Esperion has invested $116 million since 1998 in the development of its lead drugs. And currently the value of its technology is around $700 million.

Looking only at this company's capital and valuing its intellectual property only for what it cost to develop, I'd say a fair price for this company is $232 million—call it $200 million to deal in round numbers. And, because the company completed a large Phase II trial that demonstrated excellent efficacy, paying a 100% premium to its replacement value is probably warranted. So, I could see valuing the company at $400 million. At $23 where the stock is today, the company is valued at nearly $800 million—fully twice as much as I'd like to pay.

Evaluation Measure #2: My other rule of thumb in biotech is never to pay more than 100% premium to the last equity offering. Esperion raised $64 million at $16 per share in August, prior to the publication of its Phase II results. So, looking at the valuation this way, I'd pay up to $32 per share. And that means Esperion is well within my buy range. Truth is, I'm sure Esperion could sell it's leading drug ETC-216 today to any of half a dozen major pharmaceutical companies for $500 million, plus a 50% cut of future gross profits. *It's the only drug ever proven to reduce atherosclerosis—a $25 billion per year medical problem.* Statins, drugs that have a clearly inferior mechanism of action, sell billions each year, at 80% gross margins.

There's also another important consideration. By the end of the first quarter of next year (2004), Esperion will almost surely have a partnership with the very richest and best big pharma company—Pfizer. When Pfizer bought Pharmacia last year, one of the things it got was the remnant of Upjohn's preclinical portfolio, which included the right of first refusal on the marketing of Apo-AIM, a.k.a. ETC-216.

Thus, Pfizer can either agree to pay Esperion a licensing fee and, most likely, bear the cost of ETC-216's clinical trials, or Pfizer risks losing its chance to earn 50% of the drug's net profits in North America.

I think a partnership with Pfizer—and a big payday for Esperion—is a very good bet. Pfizer's decision has to be made 90 days from the time Esperion files its proposal, which is expected to happen in December.

EDITOR'S NOTE—Weeks after Porter recommended Esperion to his readers, it received a buyout offer of $1.3 billion from Pfizer, one of the largest pharmaceutical companies in the world. Esperion's stock gained 53% in a day, giving Porter's readers a great profit after owning the stock for just two weeks.

Originally published: December 2003 in Porter Stansberry's Investment Advisory

The Perfect Business

By Richard Russell

I once asked a friend, a prominent New York corporate lawyer, "Dave, in all your years of experience, what was the single best business you've ever come across?" Without hesitation, Dave answered, "I have a client whose sole business is manufacturing a chemical that is critical in making synthetic rubber. This chemical is used in very small quantities in rubber manufacturing, but it is absolutely essential and can be used in only super-refined form.

"My client is the only one who manufactures this chemical. He therefore owns a virtual monopoly since this chemical is extremely difficult to manufacture and not enough of it is used to warrant another company competing with him. Furthermore, since the rubber companies need only small quantities of this chemical, they don't particularly care what they pay for it—as long as it meets their very demanding specifications. My client is a millionaire many times over, and his business is the best I've ever come across." I was fascinated by the lawyer's story, and I never forgot it.

When I was a young man, just out of college, my father gave me a few words of advice. Dad had loads of experience; he had been in the paper manufacturing business; he had been an assistant to Mr. Sam Bloomingdale (of Bloomingdale's Department store); he had been in construction (he was a civil engineer); and he was also an expert in real estate management.

Here's what my dad told me: "Richard, stay out of the retail business. The hours are too long, and you're dealing with every darn variable under the sun. Stay out of real estate; when hard times arrive real estate comes to a dead stop, and then it collapses. Furthermore, real estate is illiquid. When the collapse comes, you can't unload. Get into manufacturing; make something people can use. And make something that you can sell to the world. But Richard, my boy, if you're really serious about making money, get into the money business. It's clean, you can use your brains, you can get rid of your inventory and your mistakes in 30 seconds, and your product, money, never goes out of fashion."

So much for my father's wisdom (which was obviously tainted by the Great Depression). But Dad was a very wise man. For my own part, I've been in a number of businesses—from textile designing, advertising, and book publishing to owning a nightclub and the investment advisory business.

It's said that every business needs (1) a dreamer, (2) a businessman, and (3) an

S.O.B. Well, I don't know about number 3, but most successful businesses do have a number 3 or all too often they seem to have a combined number 2 and number 3.

Bill Gates is known as "America's richest man." Bully for Billy. But do you know what Gates' biggest coup was? When Gates was dealing with IBM, Big Blue needed an operating system for their computer. Gates didn't have one, but he knew where to find one. A little outfit in Seattle had one. Gates bought the system for a mere $50,000 and presented it to IBM. That was the beginning of Microsoft's rise to power.

Lesson: It's not enough to have the product. You have to understand your market. Gates didn't have the product, but he knew the market—and he knew where to acquire the product.

Apple had by far the best product in the Mac. But Apple made a monumental mistake. They refused to license ALL PC manufacturers to use the Mac operating system. If they had, Apple today could be Microsoft, and Gates would still be trying to come out with something useful (the fact is Microsoft has been a follower and a great marketer, not an innovator). "Find a need and fill it," runs the old adage. Maybe today they should change that to, "Dream up a need and fill it." That's what has happened in the world of computers. And it will happen again and again.

All right, let's return to that wonderful world of perfection. I spent a lot of time and thought in working up the criteria for what I've termed the IDEAL BUSINESS. Now obviously, the ideal business doesn't exist and probably never will. But if you're about to start a business or join someone else's business or if you want to buy a business, the following list may help you. The more of these criteria that you can apply to your new business or new job, the better off you'll be.

(1) The ideal business <u>sells the world</u>, rather than a single neighborhood, city, or state. It has an unlimited global market (this is more important today than it has ever been before, since world markets have now opened up to an extent unparalleled in my lifetime). By the way, how many times have you seen a retail store that has been doing well for years—then another bigger and better retail store moves nearby, and it's kaput for the first store?

(2) The ideal business offers a product that enjoys an <u>"inelastic" demand</u>. Inelastic refers to a product that people need or desire—almost regardless of price.

(3) The ideal business sells a product that <u>cannot be easily substituted or copied</u>. This means that the product is an original, or at least it's something that can be copyrighted or patented.

(4) The ideal business has <u>minimal labor</u> requirements (the fewer personnel, the better). Today's example of this is the much-talked about "virtual corporation." The virtual corporation may consist of an office with three executives, where all manufacturing and services are farmed out to other companies.

(5) The ideal business enjoys <u>low overhead</u>. It does not need an expensive location; it does not need large amounts of electricity, advertising, legal advice, high-priced employees, large inventory, etc.

(6) The ideal business does <u>not require big cash outlays</u> or major investments in equipment. In other words, it does not tie up your capital (incidentally, one of the major reasons for new-business failure is under-capitalization).

(7) The ideal business enjoys <u>cash</u> billings. In other words, it does not tie up your capital with lengthy or complex credit terms.

(8) The ideal business is relatively <u>free of all kinds of government and industry regulations</u> and strictures (and if you own a business, you most definitely know what I mean with this one).

(9) The ideal business is <u>portable or easily moveable</u>. This means that you can take your business (and yourself) anywhere you want—Nevada, Florida, Texas, Washington, S. Dakota (none have state income taxes) or hey, maybe even Monte Carlo, Switzerland, or the south of France.

(10) The ideal business <u>satisfies your intellectual</u> (and often emotional) needs. There's nothing like being fascinated with what you're doing. When that happens, you're not working… you're having fun.

(11) The ideal business leaves you with <u>free time.</u> In other words, it doesn't require your labor and attention 16 hours a day (my wife is a lawyer who leaves the house at 6:30 AM and comes home at 6:30 PM… she's well aware of this criterion).

(12) Super-important: The ideal business is one in which your <u>income is not limited by your personal output</u> (lawyers and doctors have this problem). No, in the ideal business you can sell 10,000 customers as easily as you sell one (publishing is an example).

That's it. If you use this list it may help you cut through a lot of nonsense and hypocrisy and wishes and dreams regarding what you are looking for in life and in your work. None of us owns or works at the ideal business. But it's helpful knowing what we're looking for and dealing with. As a buddy of mine once put it, "I can't lay an egg and I can't cook, but I know what a great omelet looks like and tastes like."

For more information on Mr. Russell's Dow Theory Letters, go to:
www.dowtheoryletters.com.

How to Determine the Value of a Small Business

A Conversation with Michael Masterson, by Charlie Byrne

CB: Let's start with the basic question: Is there an easy way to figure out a fair price to pay for an existing business?

MM: Yes—but only if you have all the right information. What you're talking about is a "business valuation"—and there's a whole accounting industry built around doing this for big businesses.

CB: When they're looking to buy out an existing business?

MM: Yes—but also when they're selling, so they can get some help in setting a price. You'll also see this when a firm is raising capital or when there are lawsuits or divorces among the partners… things like that.

CB: Should you always have a professional valuation done before buying a business?

MM: I'm sure most of the so-called "experts" would say so, but I disagree. If you're going to buy a business, you should already know enough about it to figure out what it's worth. If you were going to buy something you don't understand, you would certainly need outside help. But then you're buying a pig in a poke—not a good way to invest, in my opinion.

Use experts for a second or third opinion, but trust your experience most of all.

CB: I did some research, and apparently there are lots of different ways to value a business: looking at assets, earnings, revenues, and combinations of those things…

MM: Yes, it can get complicated… but it doesn't have to be. Every business lends itself to a certain type of evaluation. The businesses I specialize in—publishing companies that market their products directly to customers—are best valued by either earnings or the value of their mailing lists, to give you one example. Other businesses, such as restaurants, may be better valued on a gross-sales basis.

CB: Let's say we're talking about buying a small, local service-based business. Do you start by considering paying the asking price?

MM: Are you kidding? The most important rule is to give that no credence at all. Sellers have emotional investments. They want to get paid back for all their time, their worries, etc. But that has nothing to do with what the business is going to do for you... so just ignore it.

For most businesses, most of the time, the No. 1 thing to consider is earnings. You need to figure out what the earnings of the business are and make an offer that's based on them. Earnings, by the way, is the same thing as profits—what you end up with after the business has paid all its expenses, including your salary.

CB: So how do you make an offer that is, as you say, based on earnings?

MM: The price you offer should be a multiple of earnings. You might, for example, be willing to pay three times earnings or five times earnings or even 15 times earnings, depending on a number of factors.

CB: Such as?

MM: Such as the way the business is managed, the industry outlook, profitability trends, and so on. Looking at all these factors gives you different ways to ask one critical question.

CB: Which is?

MM: How stable and predictable are the earnings of the business?

CB: And why is that important?

MM: Let's say I have a grocery store that you want to buy—and, last year, it made $50,000 in profits. You'd want to know how reliable that $50,000 figure is going to be in the future. If you knew that you could count on it year after year, you might be willing to pay five, six, even 10 times that amount ($250,000 to $500,000) for the business. But if you suspected that the $50,000 was a one-time thing—that the following year the business might make $25,000 and the year after that only $10,000—you certainly wouldn't be willing to bid anywhere near

$250,000. In that case, you might offer just $100,000.

CB: That makes perfect sense. So, how do you predict the stability of a business's earnings?

MM: The first thing you do is consider not just one year's worth of earnings but several. Most of the deals I've done have been based on the three most recent years. Three is a good number to start with. But you'll want to throw out any extraordinary years. For example, if you're buying a travel agency and one of the numbers you're dealing with is for a year when the Olympics were being held nearby, you'd eliminate that year. Consistent numbers are always better than numbers that are all over the place.

CB: How else can you determine the reliability of the profits?

MM: You look at the profitability of the industry as a whole. Is it trending up or down? Another thing is the locale. How is this particular business likely to do in this corner of the world? Another consideration is the sales and marketing apparatus of the business. Is it stable and self-running… or does it depend on something or someone that won't be there after the business is sold?

CB: You need to be sure that the business's human resources are not lost.

MM: I hate that phrase, but the concept is correct. It is the same for top management. You have to take into account the importance of the owner to the success of the business. Suppose you want to buy "Crazy Eddie's Stereo Sales." Everyone in town buys there because Eddie is on television and he's a fun, whacky character; there are free hot dogs and balloons at the showroom on Saturdays and he has great deals. But if you buy that business and Eddie retires, you may find that the magic is gone… and so are the profits. On the other hand, if you're buying Mayfield Appliances, which has been around for 100 years and has a reputation as the best store in the state, that's a different story. Because people feel good about Mayfield Appliances, not just one figurehead—and the goodwill (the reputation) stays with the firm when you take over.

CB: It sounds like you're saying that if you own a small business, you should actually make yourself less important as time goes on if you want to be able to sell it easily.

MM: Absolutely. And a lot of people don't do that. Ego can be a killer in business—but that's a separate discussion. Now, you might try to buy Crazy Eddie's and give Eddie a contract to stay on as a consultant. But you can run into a lot of problems doing that. Eddie is used to being the owner and the boss, and he might not like taking orders from you. It's also a bad idea to buy a business where the present owner has unique skills that you won't be able to reproduce.

CB: Such as Philippe Petit's Tightrope-Walking Academy.

MM: Right. Or Clancy and Evans' Fine Jewelry Repair. Do the customers insist on doing business only with Clancy and Evans? Do they think that Clancy and Evans have some special magic? If the answer is "yes," your answer should be "no."

CB: Let me see if I have this right. You begin by looking at the profitability of the business. You determine how reliable the earnings are by taking at least a three-year average and then accounting for anything that might affect those profits in the future. Once you've determined how much you can expect to make from the business, year after year, you can come up with a reasonable purchase price by calculating a multiple of that number.

MM: Exactly. The more reliable the profits and the less they will depend on key individuals in the future, the higher the multiple you can assign to it.

CB: Any other considerations?

MM: Yes. You must add or subtract any numbers that don't represent an arm's-length business transaction.

CB: Like?

MM: Let's say the owner had his wife and kids on the payroll but you are pretty sure they didn't actually do anything. Their salaries could be added to the profits.

CB: Making the value of the business higher.

MM: Exactly. On the other hand, the owner might be underpaying himself. Maybe he's a marketing genius or his own top salesman and yet he isn't paying himself an "arm's-length" salary for doing that job. In such a case, you'd need to figure out what it would cost you to pay someone to do it and subtract that amount from the projected profitability.

CB: Because that's what you will have to do.

MM: You're catching on.

CB: Anything else?

MM: If there is any real estate or some other major physical asset involved, deal with that as a separate transaction. In fact, you often don't want to actually buy the entire old business; you want to buy just the parts of it that are going to make you money in the future. You don't want to get stuck with old baggage that could involve lawsuits, hidden liability—those kinds of things.

And don't forget the final factor—the effect your involvement will have on the business. You could foul things up. Or you might make the business much better. You won't know exactly what is going to happen until you actually do it. But you should be prepared for either possibility.

Originally published: February 2, 2004 in Early to Rise

Michael Masterson has owned and run many businesses, starting with P&M Painting (at age 17), and including at least a dozen publishing houses, a discount jewelry outlet, a dozen direct marketing enterprises, two public relations practices, a career counseling service, at least a half dozen real estate development ventures, a fine art dealership, and a rare coin brokerage, just to name a few. He's been a partner in two businesses that grew beyond $100 million, two more that exceeded $50 million, plus at least a dozen that surpassed the $10 million mark.

These days, Mr. Masterson offers practical advice for growing wealth through his popular daily e-column, Early to Rise. He continues to act as advisor and consultant to dozens of start-up and established businesses—helping them to grow from struggling enterprises into multi-million dollar successes.

To sign up for Michael Masterson's free wealth-building advice, visit: www.earlytorise.com.

"SAI"—The Dirty Secret of Mutual Funds

By Dan Ferris

SAI doesn't really stand for Something Always Ignored, although that's what investor behavior suggests.

The SAI, or Statement of Additional Information, is a document all mutual funds publish. Most mutual funds don't send SAIs to investors unless they're requested.

To get a copy, all you have to do is call your mutual fund and explain that you'd like a copy of the Statement of Additional Information.

With the Vanguard Group's sterling reputation in the mutual fund industry, you'd think they provide the model for the treatment of SAIs. After all, Vanguard was the only mutual fund mentioned by Eliot Spitzer, Treasury officials, and others when asked to name a company that wasn't allowing late trading or market timing. Vanguard's spokesman said "the demand [for SAIs] doesn't warrant the resources necessary to maintain online availability." That's odd, since Vanguard is at least an order of magnitude larger than Longleaf, which seems to possess the "resources to maintain online availability" of its SAI.

The SAI can contain all kinds of information that would interest most mutual fund investors greatly.

For instance, what if you found out that a fund's directors didn't own any shares of the fund you were thinking of buying? Corey Colehour and J. Kenneth Dalton oversee 88 different funds at Rydex. And they don't have one thin dime in any of them. J. Michael Hagen and William Popejoy at Pimco oversee 70 different funds. Again, not a dime invested. David P. Gardner and Eleanor B. Schwartz at Waddell & Reed oversee 40 and 68 funds, respectively, with zero personal investment in any of them. (Data courtesy of Karen Damato at wsj.com.)

A spokesman for Van Wagoner actually said that the firm's directors "have greater objectivity by not being personally financially involved in the funds they oversee."

I hope you'll join me as I say to hell with objectivity.

I want a fund manager who is passionately dedicated to making me as much money as possible. Human nature being what it is, that's only going to happen if he gets rich at the same rate I do. Longleaf's 60-page SAI shows that all of its directors and trustees have over $100,000 invested in the funds.

All of the Independent Trustees of the Fund (they're like directors) have to get clearance before buying securities, to prevent conflicts of interest. They're required to invest in Longleaf Funds at least as much as they make in fees each year, which is $50,000.

All Trustees of the Funds, all directors, officers, and employees, as well as relatives, affiliated retirement plans, and foundations, own 2.2% of the Longleaf Partners Fund.

They also own 1.8% of its International Fund and 6.2% of the Small Cap Fund. That translates into $350.9 million as of December 31, 2003. At last May's shareholders meeting, Mason Hawkins made it clear that he and his managers have "virtually their entire net worths in Longleaf funds." Sounds like Warren Buffett, who says he has 99% of his net worth in Berkshire Hathaway.

The Longleaf Partners Code of Ethics requires all employees to limit their equity investments to Longleaf funds. All Longleaf employees are required to report their securities transactions quarterly. Longleaf's #1 governing principle is, "We will treat your investment as if it were our own."

Before you buy a mutual fund, call and ask for the fund's SAI form. You're likely to find information that will help you decide whether or not to buy.

Originally published: February 2004 in Extreme Value

For more information on Dan Ferris' Extreme Value service, visit www.stansberryresearch.com and click on "Extreme Value."

Chapter 3

When to Buy and Sell

Don't Lose Money: The Most Important Law of Lasting Wealth

By Dr. Steve Sjuggerud, PhD

Let's face it—most people don't know when to sell a falling stock. They become frozen inactivity, saying "Should I just keep holding and hoping, or should I cut my losses now?" This state of indecision is usually permanent, and often continues until you hear the all too familiar phrase, "Well, it's too late to sell now."

One of my good friends lost it all following the "it's too late to sell now" principle. He bought a ton of shares of a cable stock based on his friend's recommendation that it would take over the world. The shares soon tumbled in half, and his friend, who knows about the cable business, told him to buy more, so he did. The shares tumbled in half again, and he bought even more. He finally stopped buying when the shares hit a dollar per share. Now the shares trade for pennies—he would have to pay more in commissions than those shares are worth. He was uncertain about everything, and pretty soon it was all over.

After you've read this section, if you follow the advice here, your constant state of indecision will be gone. You'll never lose another night's sleep worrying about which way your investments will go tomorrow. Because, unlike most investors, you'll have a plan—knowing when to get out, and when to stay in, for the biggest possible profits.

Buying stocks is easy. There are thousands of theories out there for why and when to buy. But buying is only the first half of the equation when it comes to making money.

Nobody ever talks about the hard part—knowing when to sell.

We've all made expensive mistakes—either missing the full upside by selling too soon or taking a huge loss by holding a falling stock too long. But it's time to make big losses a thing of the past.

In order to invest successfully, you need to put as much thought into planning your exit strategy as you put into the research that motivates you to buy an investment in the first place. When you have a plan, you know in advance exactly when you're going to buy and sell. The strategy I'll show you will allow you to ride your winners all the way up, while minimizing the damage your losers can do. So please read closely here, and think about each point.

How do you evaluate businesses?

In business and in stocks, you've got to have a plan and an exit strategy. Before I get into the specific strategy, consider the following business example.

Let's say you're in the tee-shirt business.

You've made a ton of money on your tee-shirt business in the States, and you're now in the Bahamas looking for new opportunities. You size up the market, and you figure you can make money in two places: in golf shirts, geared at businessmen, and in muscle-tees, geared toward vacationing beach-goers. These are two products clearly aimed at two different markets.

You invest $100,000 in each of these businesses. At the end of the first year, your golf shirts are already showing a profit of $20,000. But the muscle-tees haven't caught on yet, and you've got a loss of $20,000. There are numerous reasons why this is possible, so you make some changes in your designs and marketing and continue for another year.

In the second year the same thing happens—you make another $20,000 on your golf shirts, and you lose another $20,000 on your muscle-tees. After two years, the golf shirts business is clearly a succeeding business, and the muscle shirts business is clearly failing.

Now let's say you're ready to invest another $100,000 in one of these businesses. Which one business do you put your money into?

The answer should be obvious. You, as a business owner, put more money toward your successful businesses. But as you'll see, this is the opposite of what 99% of individual investors in America do.

How do you evaluate stocks?

Let me start by asking you a question—what does "owning shares of stock" actually mean? This isn't a trick question. As you know, it means you're a partial owner of the company, just like you're the owner of the tee-shirt company in this example.

Owning your own business isn't fundamentally different from owning a share of a business through stock. However, 99% of investors treat them exactly the opposite.

Let's say the shares of your two tee-shirt companies trade on the stock exchange.

They both start trading at $10 a share. At the end of the first year, the profitable golf-shirt company is trading for $12 a share, and the unprofitable muscle-shirt company is trading for $8 a share. At the end of the second year, the golf shirt company is trading at $14, while the muscle shirt company is trading at $6 a share.

Which shares would you rather own?

Even though you know you should buy the winning concept based on the business example, most investors don't do so in their stock investments. They keep throwing good money after bad investments, hoping for a turnaround. They buy the "cheap" stock—the loser.

The Trailing Stop Strategy

In stocks (and in business), you must have and use an exit strategy—one that makes you methodically cut your losers and let your winners ride. If you follow this rule, you have the best chance of outperforming the markets. If you don't, your retirement is in trouble.

The exit strategy I advocate is simple. I ride my stocks as high as I can, but if they head for a crash, I have my exit strategy in place to protect me from damage.

Though I have many levels of defense and many reasons to sell a stock, if my reasons don't appear before the crash, the Trailing Stop Strategy is my last ditch measure to save my hard-earned dollars. And it works.

The main element of the Trailing Stop Strategy is a 25% rule. **I will sell any and all positions at 25% off their highs**. For example, if I buy a stock at $50, and it rises to $100, I sell it if it closes below $75—no matter what.

Don't Let Your Losers Become Big Losers

So with my Trailing Stop Strategy, when would I have gotten out of the failing muscle-shirt business? The shares started at $10 and fell immediately. Instead of waiting around until they fell to $6 as the business faltered, using my 25% Trailing Stop, I would have sold at $7.50.

And think of it this way—if the shares fall to $8, you're only asking for a 25% gain to get back to where they started. But if the shares fell to $5, you're asking for a dog of a stock to rise 100%. This only happens once in a blue moon—not good odds! (See the chart on this page to see how these numbers play out.)

What's so magical about the 25% number? Nothing in particular—it's the discipline that matters. Many professional traders actually use much tighter stops—the *Investor's Business Daily* newspaper, for example, recommends an 8% stop. Ultimately, the point is that you

You'll Never Recover

Percent fall in share price	Percent gain required to get you back to even
10%	11%
20%	25%
25%	33%
50%	100%
75%	300%
90%	900%

never want to be in the position where a stock has fallen by 50% or more. By using this Trailing Stop Strategy, chances are you'll never be in that position again.

Use Daily Closing Prices

I use end-of-day prices for all my calculations, not intra-day prices.

You should too. This makes things easier. If a stock has gone to $100, put at least a mental stop at $75. If, subsequently, the stock closes at or below that $75 level, sell your shares the next day.

I have to admit, it took me three years to truly follow my own advice on this one. I would always come up with some excuse to keep holding dud stocks. Nearly every time with those losers, if I'd practiced what I preached, I'd have been better off.

Now I always cut my losses. And once you get into the habit, and commit to doing it, it's easy.

One thing in life is certain: The future is uncertain. Nobody—not even the most astute analyst or investment advisor—can know enough about a particular company, industry or the nuances of the market to anticipate with 100% certainty the future price of a stock.

But common sense dictates two fundamentals: 1) taking small losses is much better than taking big losses and 2) letting your profits run is much better than cutting them off prematurely.

By following this simple plan accordingly, I strongly believe your investment results will start to improve immediately and dramatically.

Originally published: January 2002 in True Wealth

For more information on Dr. Sjuggerud's True Wealth advisory service, go to: www.stansberryresearch.com, or call (888) 261-2693.

Frequently Asked Questions About Trailing Stops

By Dr. Steve Sjuggerud, PhD

QUESTION: What's the rule for getting back into something that you were stopped out of?

ANSWER: Ah yes. The six-month "cooling off" period. That's the answer you're looking for. You are not allowed to consider going back into a stock you've stopped out of until a 6-month "cooling off" period has passed. "What's so magical about six months?" you may ask. The answer is "absolutely nothing." There is no scientific basis for it (just as there is no scientific basis for the 25% trailing stop rule). But it's not portfolio science we're concerned with—it is emotions. The whole purpose of a trailing stop is to get you out of a losing position, a stock that you like. Six months should hopefully give you enough time to let your emotions about the stock cool, and let you see it rationally again. Maybe it won't look so great the second time around.

The other rule is to make sure the stock has begun an up-trend. The simplest rule here is if the stock is above its 200-day (or 40-week) moving average. Those two rules should keep you from getting into trouble with stocks you're passionate about. The last rule, which trumps the above rules, is if the stock hits a new high, then you are allowed to consider buying it again. This is based on the rough idea that if a stock hits a new high after you stopped out of it, whatever caused the stock to fall by 25% in the first place is now water under the bridge. Whether you want to buy it at a new high or not is a different question. But you are ALLOWED to consider buying it again at a new high.

QUESTION: Steve, I have stop orders in with my broker, and…

ANSWER: Wait! Stop right there! I don't recommend having a stop with your broker, particularly with smaller stocks. Investors have been punished in the past for doing this. I know of a large group of investors who all must have had stops with their brokers at the same price. The trader promptly drove the price down by about 10%, took out all the stops, and then increased the price by 10%. All in the matter of a less than an hour. In particular, stocks that are smaller than $500 million deserve special attention. You should never have stops in the market in stocks this size—the trader *will* take you out. Chances are, you'll never have a problem with really big stocks. So you can use a stop order there if you prefer. But I think that even up to $1 billion market cap, it's still smarter not to show your hand…

QUESTION: Steve, I was wondering how I should handle stops in stocks with large dividends and "income" investments…

ANSWER: The stops are based on the total return. So you need to include any type of income. Fortunately, Yahoo! stock charts are shown adjusted for splits and dividends. Yahoo! Finance has a column called "Adjusted Close" in its historical quotes section, that provides the closing price adjusted for all splits and income as well. (An important note, Yahoo! does not do an Adjusted Close for open-end mutual funds, clearly defined by a five-letter symbol ending in "X.") You can easily import prices from Yahoo! into your financial program or Excel. Around the office, we automate it by using a program called XLQ (free to try, $45.00 as of 9/27/04 to buy at www.qmatix.com), but that may be a bit much for your needs. (While you're at that website, send an email to Leo and tell him you're really looking forward to the trailing stops program he's working on—that'll be our best solution when it's done.) You'd think that understanding and keeping track of this trailing stop stuff would be easier than it is. But as you can see, once you get into it, it is a little tougher than it first appears. But it's still not hard.

Originally published: August 12, 2003 in True Wealth

For more information on Dr. Sjuggerud's True Wealth advisory service, go to: www.stansberryresearch.com, or call (888) 261-2693.

The 1-2-3 Stock Market Model: How to Know Exactly When to Buy, Sell, and Hold Stocks

By Dr. Steve Sjuggerud, PhD

If you can understand traffic signals, you can invest using this simple model. It will tell you, in three easy steps, whether to buy, sell, or hold stocks. Let me explain.

Some time ago, I sat down and thought about what the most important factors are that affect the stock market. While an infinite number of factors are affecting the markets at any given time, there are three things that always affect the market. I built a simple "traffic light" model based on whether these three things are working for you or against you.

The model tells you this... If all three of these things are in your favor, I say we're under a "green light." Time to buy. Under green light conditions (which have occurred 26% of the time since 1927), stocks have risen 19.5% a year.

If two out of the three factors are in your favor, it's a yellow light. This has occurred 50% of the time, and stocks have returned 10.7% a year under yellow light conditions.

And if two out of the three factors are AGAINST you, it's a red light. Time to sell. Stocks have lost 9.7% a year under red light conditions.

If you had been armed with this knowledge, you would have known that we've been under red light conditions for the years 2000, 2001, and 2002. The stock market collapse would have come as no surprise to you.

When I created the 1-2-3 Stock Market model, I wanted to design something that was easy to understand, reflected the most important factors affecting stock prices, and consistently made money in all market conditions.

Since the model has proven itself over history and has been very well-received by both novice and sophisticated readers, I think I've achieved my goals. Let me share it with you...

So what are these three factors? It's best to phrase them in the form of questions. The following are the three most important questions to answer about the stock market:

#1) Is the stock market expensive?

#2) Are the Feds in the way?

#3) Is the market acting badly?

The answers to these questions cover nearly all the bases that affect the markets. So let's look at each question closely.

Question #1) Is the market too expensive?

How do we define expensive? Well, the clearest, time-tested measure of whether stocks are cheap or expensive, is the Price-to-Earnings (P/E) ratio.

If you're not already comfortable with what the P/E ratio tells you, the best analogy I can think of is a house. If the PRICE of a house you're considering is $100,000, and you're confident you can EARN $10,000 a year in rent after expenses, that house is "selling" at a "PRICE-to-EARNINGS ratio of 10. (10 x $10,000=$100,000)

If you could earn $10,000 a year on a $50,000 house, that would probably be a good deal (either that or something is seriously wrong with the house). This is because the house would be paid for in five years, and all the earnings after that would be gravy. A house with a $50,000 price that earns $10,000 a year in rent is at a "price-to-earnings" ratio of five. Clearly, paying five times earnings is better than paying 10. In other words, the lower the P/E ratio, the better.

However, paying a million dollars for this house, which would mean you're paying over 100 times earnings, would most likely not be a good deal. So it's interesting to note that the entire Nasdaq index was trading at a P/E of over 100 for a long time.

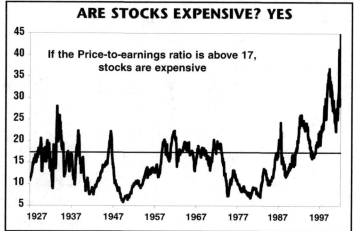

The same logic applies to the stock market.

From 1927 until mid 2002, if you'd bought stocks when the P/E was above 17.0 (when stocks were expensive), you would have made only 0.3% a year. The P/E was above 17.0 about 36% of the time.

However, if you'd bought when the P/E was below 17.0, which occurred 64% of the time, you would have made 12.4% a year in stocks. Buy and hold would have made you 8.03%.

Question #2) Are the Feds in the way?

Interest rates are probably the major factor affecting stock prices. Think about this for a moment. If the bank starts paying 12% interest, what would people do? Chances are, they'd move money out of the stock market and into the bank. Why take the risk of stocks when you can get the same returns with much less risk? So it only makes sense that as interest rates rise, people sell stocks.

But there's more to it than that.

Let's take the flip side. As interest rates fall, people take their money out of the bank, and bonds, and whatever else, to seek higher returns. Those funds usually end up in the stock market. Additionally, as interest rates fall, companies can take on projects with lower profit margins that wouldn't have been profitable under higher interest rates.

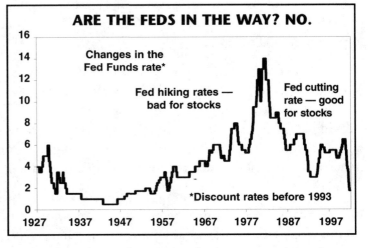

This is the natural push and pull of markets.

The interest rate movements that have had the most dramatic effects on the market have been changes in the interest rates set by the Federal Reserve—in particular, the Fed Funds rate. When the Fed is raising interest rates—look out!

Seventy-one percent of the time, the Feds are not in our way—they're not in the midst of raising rates. And when they stay out of the way, we earn 10.9% a year in stocks, versus the buy and hold return of 7.9%.

However, for the 29% of the time the Feds are in the way, it pays to be cautious. Stocks returned only 1.0% a year with the Feds in the way.

How do we define the 29% of the time the Feds are in the way? It's simple. It's the six-month period following a hike in the Fed Funds rate. The Feds are out of the way either 1) after the six-month period has ended, or 2) if the Fed cuts rates before the six-month period has ended.

Question #3) Is the market going up?

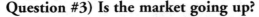

The market knows more than anyone can predict. No market model is complete without some indicator of market action.

Sixty-seven percent of the time, the market is strengthening, based on our simple market action indicator. If you are in

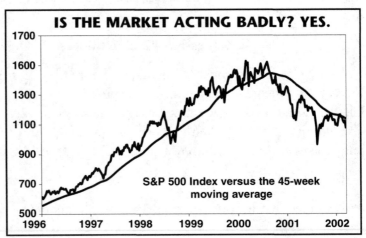

the market when this indicator says the market is strong, stocks have returned 12.6% a year.

The market is weakening 33% of the time, based on this indicator. If you are in the market when the indicator says the market is weak, stocks have lost 1.6% a year.

The market momentum indicator is simple. It's the 45-week average of stock prices. If the market is above its 45-week average, stock prices are strong. If the market is below its 45-week average, stock prices are weak.

Though I follow hundreds of indicators, all of them can basically fit into these three simple categories. If you just know the answers to the three questions above, and you use them, you will know whether you should buy, sell, or hold.

The 1-2-3 Stock Market Model Summed Up

Remember these three questions:

1. Is the market too expensive?

2. Are the Feds in the way?

3. Is the market acting badly?

Right now, stocks are expensive and the market action over the last 45 weeks has been weak. With 2 or more indicators negative, stocks return −9.7% a year. Red light. (Important note: These numbers are current as of mid 2002. Please see the current issue of True Wealth for the updated status of the 1-2-3-Stock Market Model.)

There you have it.

Red light, sell
When the answer to two or more questions above is "YES," stocks return −9.7%

Yellow light, buy and hold
When the answer to one of the three questions above is "YES," stocks return 10.7%

Green light, strong buy
When the answer to all three questions above is "NO," stocks return 19.5%

Originally published in True Wealth

For more information, go to: www.stansberryresearch.com and click on "True Wealth."

How to Sell Your $30 Stocks for $50 a Share

By Brian Hunt

Just two miles from my date's house in Iowa, a cow ruined my Friday night.

I popped over a hill and there it was, an Angus heifer standing on the right side of the road. I swerved to the left side of the road, but the spooked cow ran straight into my car, smashing the grill and hood.

Luckily, the cow was fine, and my insurance policy saved my car.

Just like driving, it's good to have insurance in the stock market.

A popular insurance policy is the stop loss. That's the price you'll sell your stock to cut losses. Stops are "insurance" that you won't hold a $50 stock all the way down to $2.

Many investors use stop losses, but almost nobody has heard of another insurance strategy I'm going to tell you about today: Using put options.

If you're unfamiliar with put options, they're easy to understand.

A put option is a contract that gives you the right, but not the obligation, to sell a stock at a certain price by a certain time.

You can also think of put options as you would insurance... you pay your insurance premium each year so you can sleep easy at night, knowing you're protected if disaster strikes.

If you're worried about disaster striking a stock you own, you can pair your stock position with a put option, which is called a "married put."

A married put is generally used with volatile stocks, like biotechnology or Internet high-flyers. The married put lets you hold a stock with big payoff potential—without having to worry about a sudden drop in price.

One high-flyer is Genentech (NYSE: DNA). Genentech is a big, profitable drug company that many investors own. But drug companies are vulnerable to inflated valuations, lawsuits, and failed drug trials. These events can send a drug stock down 10%, even 20% in a single day.

This is where a married put can come in handy. If you're one of the fortunate investors who bought Genentech in early 2003, you're sitting on gains of over

200%—gains you don't want to lose.

With Genentech currently selling for about $55, you could buy "insurance" in the form of an August 2004 Genentech put with a strike price of $50 a share (they're currently selling for around $1.00—or $100 for each 100 share contract).

Your put gives you the right to sell your Genentech shares for no less than $50 a share for the life of the contract. A market crash could knock Genentech down to $40—a failed drug trial could send the company down even more.

But no matter what happens, if the stock price is $30, or even $10 a share, you can sell for $50.

If Genentech continues its big run and rises to $70 a share, you give up the premium and continue profiting from capital gains, just as you give up the premium to your insurer if you're not in a car wreck.

Married puts aren't useful all the time—most investors will be well served by being disciplined with stop losses... and I'm just using Genentech as an example.

But in a situation like I just described, a married put strategy will provide you with the same kind of hedge as good car insurance.

Originally published: June 28, 2004 by Stansberry & Associates Investment Research

Brian Hunt runs a stock trading service called Microcap Moonshots, which focuses on the smallest and most potentially possible stocks in the entire market. For more information on Microcap Moonshots, go to www.stansberryresearch.com or call toll-free, 1-888-261-2693.

The Perfect Indicator—How to Spot a Recession Before It Starts

By Dr. Steve Sjuggerud, PhD

It's remarkable—an indicator you can't ignore. It has made only six predictions since 1970. And all six predictions were exactly right. The predictions were for recession. There were six predictions, and there have been six recessions since 1970. That's a perfect record for 33 years.

This indicator has a perfect record of predicting bad times. And it can be used to forecast good times as well. Best of all, it's simple to track, and I highly recommend adding it to your arsenal of investment tools. Knowing how to use this indicator to forecast a coming recession—or the lack of one—can keep you from rearranging your portfolio in anticipation of a market shift that never comes.

The Last Two Predictions

The last time this indicator said a recession was just around the corner occurred July 2000 to January 2001. According to the National Bureau of Economic Research (www.nber.org), the officials who date recessions, the last recession lasted from March 2001 to November 2001. So the prediction was perfect, signaling well in advance the oncoming economic downturn.

The previous prediction occurred June 1989 to December 1989. That recession lasted from July 1990 to March 1991, according to the NBER. The indicator was a little early that time, but still very accurate.

The other four recessions came in 1970, 1974, 1980, and 1982. All of these recessions were preceded a few months in advance by a prediction from this indicator.

What The Indicator Is and How to Use It

This indicator is really simple: When short-term interest rates rise above long-term interest rates, a recession will occur.

This is a rare occurrence. The last three times it's happened have been late 2000, late 1989, and mid-1981.

There is a good reason it's a rare occurrence: In a world with little inflation, long-term interest rates _should_ be higher than short-term interest rates.

It comes down to risk. If I lend you a dollar that you're going to pay back tomorrow, I don't worry about my risk, and don't demand much in interest. But if you're going to pay me back in 30 years, then my risk is higher, and it makes sense for me to ask for more in interest.

Why do short-term rates ever rise above long-term rates? It's generally because Alan Greenspan (the Federal Reserve Chairman) is trying to slow down the economy. His main tool to slow down the economy is short-term interest rates. If he raises them significantly—to levels above long-term interest rates—then he's bringing out all the stops. And it results in a recession a few quarters down the road. Judging by history since 1970, it happens every time.

Originally published: August 8, 2003 in Investment U

To sign up for Dr. Sjuggerud's free Investment U service, go to: www.investmentu.com.

8 Ways to Immediately Make More Money in Stocks

By Dr. Steve Sjuggerud, PhD

1. Pay No More in Commissions Than You Have To

Ameritrade.com charges eight bucks a stock trade. If you're trading your own ideas, but calling your orders into someone like Schwab, you're probably paying around 50 bucks per trade. If you place 10 orders a month, that's 120 orders a year, or $6,000 in commissions at Schwab, versus less than $1,000 a year at Ameritrade. Nothing against Schwab (I've got money with them myself), but why should you give away $5,000? For frequent traders, Ameritrade is a good mix of budget and quality. For a good all-around discount service, Schwab has been good to me. And for full service, Merrill and Morgan Stanley do a nice job. For more specific ratings of brokerage firms, both discount and full service, check out **www.gomez.com**.

2. Pay Attention to the Spread When Appropriate

Let's say you've got a 5-year old car worth $12,500. You take it to a dealer to see if he'll take it off your hands. He says he'll give you $10,000 for it. But you say "hey that's not fair, you've got the exact same car on your lot for $15,000!" My friend, that's the spread. If you sold your car you'd like to get $12,500, not just $10,000. And if you were looking to buy, you'd much prefer to pay closer to $12,500 than the $15,000 the dealer is asking. What you're looking to do, is ELIMINATE THE SPREAD.

In big stocks, like Microsoft, Intel, and basically any other company you've already heard of, the spread is not a concern. There are so many buyers and sellers, you're best off just putting in a MARKET ORDER, and you'll own the shares immediately at the market price. (In fact, the spread on Microsoft, a $50 stock, is only 3 pennies as I write.)

But in small stocks and options, you're better off wheeling and dealing—fighting the spread. Options and small stocks (say under $500M in size) can have a significant spread. With these it's more risky to put in market orders, especially at the open. I personally learned this lesson the hard way with an option when I was starting out—I paid $7 at the open for a $4 option. The option went up 50% to $6, and I still lost money. Lesson learned: Never use market orders on thinly traded positions, especially at the open!

3. Identify "Hidden Costs" of Mutual Funds

Bill Gross is the biggest bond fund manager in the world, and for good reason—he's earned double-digit returns for investors for 30 years. His flagship Pimco Total Return fund now has over $50 billion in assets. Wow. It's amazing that so many people have bought this. Consider this: Bonds only pay about 4.5% in yield right now, and this fund has a 4.5% UP FRONT CHARGE. By paying this hefty fee, you may just break even your first year. Even worse, annual fees clock in at around 1% a year. Meanwhile, Bill also manages a little-known fund called the Fremont Bond Fund, which does the same thing as the Pimco fund. Only it has no upfront charge and annual fees of only a half a percent a year. Amazingly, this fund has less than a billion in assets.

Why the big difference? My guess is, I'm sorry to say, investor ignorance. Brokers and financial planners sell the Pimco fund with the upfront fee because they pocket almost the entire 4.5% fee. If they sold you the Fremont fund, they wouldn't get paid. How can you find funds like this, and other ways to significantly reduce your costs and find the best funds? Use Morningstar.com's Quick Rank. It's free, and excellent. I'd even recommend springing for the $99 annual fee at Morningstar, as there are reports on thousands of funds. I think you can do a 30-day trial for free. Check it out.

4. Make Fewer Transactions

Look, 90% of fund managers can't beat the market. If the market averages 12%, fund managers on average return 10%. Why is this? You're getting the return of the market, minus their fees and their cost of doing business (commissions, spreads, office space, etc.). What's more, these guys are supposed to be professionals, and they can't beat the market. What edge do YOU have that they don't? What makes you think you can beat them? When you understand what I'm trying to say here, you can see that the cost of doing business is a big hole in your wealth bucket. The more transactions you make, the bigger the hole. So trade as little as possible, and you'll probably end up better off in the long run.

5. Pay Attention to Capital Gains Taxes

As you're likely well aware, here in America if you hold a stock for over a year and then sell it, your tax rate is substantially lower than if you hold it less than a year. So if you need to raise cash, but there's no absolute reason to sell the stock right now and you're close to the one-year mark, then you ought to wait. You could save yourself thousands of dollars.

6. Take Maximum Advantage of Tax-Deferred Retirement Programs

What's the easiest way to save $3,500 in taxes? Stuff your 401k (or similar retirement program) to the max. This is the BEST way for you to save money today. If you put the maximum of $11,000 into your 401k, and you made $100,000 this year, the government only taxes you on $89,000. So in effect, you're saving yourself a huge amount in taxes. Keep your money out of the government's hands by stuffing your retirement plans. This one is important!

7. Use Margin Sparingly—Or Not At All

This probably isn't a problem today, as you're probably not using margin. Margin is money you borrow to buy stocks. If Warren Buffett is right, and we can only expect 6-7% a year in stock returns for the next decade or so, then it's just plain stupid to borrow money at 6% or more to put in stocks. Simple as that.

8. Eliminate "Hidden" Margin Costs of Your Debt

Why anyone has money in the stock market AND tens of thousands in credit card debts, used car loans, etc., is beyond me. The math here is simple: The COST of money in these debts is much higher than your potential RETURN on your money in the stock market. The solution? Sell stocks (which may only return you 6-7%) and use the proceeds to pay off credit cards and used car loans. Whenever your COST of money is higher than your potential RETURN on money, you need to get out of that situation.

Using these eight ways, you should be able to save yourself from throwing away 2% or more in potential return. And that 2% is actually a lot—it can mean the difference between doubling your money in 10 years, or doubling it in 20 years.

If Warren Buffett is right about stocks returning just 6-7% over the next decade, then it's really important that we watch every nickel, as those nickels really add up over the long run.

Originally published in Investment U

To sign up for Dr. Sjuggerud's free Investment U service, go to: www.investmentu.com.

A Model for Predicting Good Entry Prices

By Porter Stansberry

I'd like to do something that might be a waste of your time. But I'm going to try anyway. What I'd like to do is give you a very basic template with which you can measure the value of any stock fairly. Using the tools I'll explain below, you should also be able to easily derive a "bottom basement" price for any operating company's stock.

The model I'll give you here has limitations, like all models. But it can serve as an objective starting place as you determine what investments to make, and at what price. You have to look for value.

Hearing about the importance of looking for value in your stock buys from me undoubtedly sounds funny to many of my long time readers. After all, I'm the same guy who—only a few short years ago—explained why such fundamental metrics didn't apply to the best companies in the marketplace and why it was impossible to determine reliable entry prices.

But the mood of the market changes, as we've all seen. For long stretches of time investors will prefer growth and future earnings rather than value and proven earnings. These "speculative" phases of the market are when the really big money gets made in stocks. During such periods, fundamental metrics won't help you.

On the other hand, when the market retrenches and lots of money is being lost, investors prefer proven earnings, and won't pay much of a premium for growth.

Not long ago, I picked seven small cap "value" stocks in an attempt to prove that during bear markets these are the only stocks that perform well. I picked the following stocks:

COMPANY	(SYMBOL)	[TOTAL RETURN]
Teekay Shipping	(TK)	[-12%]
Blair Corp.	(BL)	[28%]
Tommy Hilfiger	(TOM)	[-12%]
Gerber Children's Wear	(GCW)	[-4%]
American National Insurance	(ANAT)	[-2%]
Ampco-Pittsburgh Corp.	(AP)	[4%]
Worthington Industries	(WOR)	[17%]

The average total return for this very focused portfolio (only seven stocks) was 3.0%, which you might think is a very poor return for a four-month period. Actually, though, if these returns continue at a similar pace for the year, that's not bad at all. With dividends, you'll probably make 10% or a little more. Ten percent probably sounds meager compared to the rocket ship returns of the past, but please, before you dismiss these results, consider that in the same four months that we made 3% in this portfolio, the S&P 500 lost 25%. So, while the broad market was experiencing its worst four-month period in a very long time, we were still making money. That's impressive. And, our portfolio was remarkably free of volatility. In fact, we've only stopped out of one stock—Tommy Hilfiger.

Besides this experience, there is plenty of academic evidence (see *The New Finance: The Case Against Efficient Markets*, 2nd Edition, by Robert Haugen) to suggest value stocks outperform the market by a wide margin over any period longer than a few years. And, in contrast to established financial theory, the same research shows conclusively that the least volatile stocks actually return the most money for investors. If this proves to be true in the future, it would throw a monkey wrench into the theory behind index funds.

(Current financial dogma holds that it is impossible to beat the market's average return in the long run. The market, it is widely believed, is efficient, meaning that investors get paid a return based on the risk, or volatility, they're willing to accept. Smart investors, according to this theory, should always own a fund that represents the market as a whole, because it's impossible to pick stocks that offer a higher return for less risk.)

Interestingly, out of the seven "value" stocks I picked, three were "extreme value" picks. These three: Blair, American National, and Teekay Shipping, traded at less than .75 of fair book value and paid impressive dividends. Not surprisingly, these three stocks combined outperformed the whole portfolio, nearly doubling the overall average gain. They also outperformed the broader market by nearly 30%, in only four months. This is in line with what academic researchers have found over the last forty years: The more extreme the value, the better the return.

Looking at the mood in the market and the evidence for small cap value, I suggest that investors begin to pay considerably more attention to value and look outside of the familiar big cap names. Value alone doesn't equal a good investment, but starting from a value position will help you select from a pool of opportunities, that on average, is better than the market as a whole.

I'd like to show you the model I've been using to evaluate value and a fair price for shares. I can't say for sure yet that my model works, but the early results are interesting.

Here it goes. Marty Whitman, the famed value investor at the helm of Third Avenue Value Funds, says you should never pay more than ten times peak earnings for a company. But, in today's market, I think you have to look more closely at earnings to know what you're really getting. To be conservative, let's take out capital expenditures too. In this way you'll pay only 10 times cash flow, which is a more reliable—and cheaper—figure.

Here's how you do this. Take the last five years of net income (available for free from Yahoo! Finance), and subtract capital expenditures. Let me show you—it isn't hard. I'll demonstrate with Blair, the best performing stock out of my small cap value portfolio. Blair is a direct mail retailer that sells brand name clothing to mostly retired customers. Here are Blair's figures, in millions:

	'01	'00	'99	'98	'97
Net Income:	9.30	21.10	15.30	22.30	13.30
Capex:	4.90	2.90	3.80	1.00	0.10

So you can see that in 2001, Blair had about $5 million in positive cash flow from operations. Not a great year for a $190 million retailer. On the other hand, to allow for ups and downs, we're going to judge companies by the sum of their five-year results. On this basis you see that Blair made $58 million in operating cash flow in the last five years, roughly 38% of its current market cap. That's excellent cash generation from operations.

For my model to predict accurate entry prices, companies must generate at least 15% of their current market cap in cash over five years. How did I come up with that figure? Well, you can get 3% a year return—risk free—in government bonds. I figure that if a company isn't earning a higher cash return on its operations than I could get in government bonds, it doesn't qualify as a value stock.

Next, I want to verify that the company isn't diluting its stock in an effort to avoid reporting compensation costs. I check on this by going to the balance sheet and looking at how many shares are outstanding. I measure dilution by looking five years back. In my opinion, 1% dilution per year is acceptable. Blair, because of its excellent cash flow, is actually reducing the total shares outstanding significantly. In the last five years the total number of shares outstanding has decreased 11.5%. (This is unusual, and we'll have to adjust the prices my model spits out for this significant share buyback.)

Finally, I determine my "market bottom" and my "buy below" prices by looking at peak cash earnings and dividing by the number of shares outstanding.

Like Marty Whitman, my model is willing to pay 10 times peak cash earnings. For Blair, peak cash earnings occurred in 1998 when the company generated $21 million in cash flow from operations. Multiply that by ten and you get $210 million, or a little bit more than the company is valued today. You can get your per share "buy below" price by taking 1998 results, multiplying by ten and then dividing by the number of shares. You get a "buy below" price of $23.91. You have to adjust this upwards by 11% to account for the decrease in shares. When you do, you end up with $26.54, almost exactly where the stock trades today. In other words, when we bought Blair at $19.00, we bought at a very good price. Today the price is fair, but not nearly as attractive.

Here's what's really interesting: If you look at a long-term chart of Blair, you can see that the stock has hit a firm bottom in price on several occasions at around $13.50. Look at the average "buy below" prices my model generated over the last five years and you end up with $13.61. My model predicts almost exactly where the stock should bottom at, and where it actually does. Thus, this five year average number is my "market bottom" number. If you were hunting extreme value stocks, you'd want to find stocks where the share price is at or below my model's "market bottom" number.

There's only one caveat to the model. It concerns evaluating high tech companies. Our current system of accounting was designed for industrial companies. Capital expenditures don't count against annual earnings because they're expected to add value to future results. But, as you saw, I take out capital expenditures to generate my cash earnings figure. On the other hand, research and development costs do count against net income, but for high tech firms, research and development does lead to higher future earnings. So, when I'm evaluating high tech firms, I add back research and development costs. In other words, I use an adjusted cash flow number that rewards companies for research and development costs while penalizing them for capital expenditures. I do this because I believe that today's infrastructure—PCs, desks, chip labs, etc.—doesn't warrant 30-year depreciation, while R&D items—like new drugs, new software, and new computer chip designs—do.

Originally published: July 17, 2002 by Stansberry & Associates Investment Research

For more information on Porter Stansberry, go to www.stansberryresearch.com.

The World's Strongest Buy Signal

By Dr. Steve Sjuggerud, PhD

There are a million reasons why a corporate insider would sell, but only one reason why a corporate insider would buy. It may just be an outstanding buy signal for you and me when corporate insiders are buying. When you find a stock that looks good fundamentally (is "cheap"), that looks good technically (is starting to move up), and that has heavy insider buying, chances are very good you've got a big winner on your hands, according to Alexander Green, editor of *The Insider Alert*. (Alex wrote the following for the **DailyReckoning.com** on 6/19/02.)

When Insiders Buy, We Should Buy

"...Insiders are the officers who run a company, the directors who oversee the officers, and 10% beneficial owners of the stock who are presumed to be more than ordinarily well-apprised of the company's business and future prospects.

"These individuals know virtually everything that can be known about the company they run. They know the pace of sales day to day. They know of new products in development. They know whether the company is a takeover candidate... or is already getting unsolicited offers. In short, they know everything that reasonably can be known about their company's business prospects, employees, customers, suppliers, and competitors.

"In short, **they have an unfair advantage** when they go into the market to trade their own company's shares. After all, they not only know all the public information about their company... they know a great deal of non-public information as well.

"For this reason, the U.S. government requires all insiders to report their transactions to the SEC within two days.

"My philosophy is straightforward. There are plenty of reasons an insider would sell his own company's stock that have nothing to do with its business prospects. He may be diversifying his portfolio, buying a big house, putting his kids in private school, or—for all I know—paying for the upkeep on his mistress. (Or, in fact, the company outlook may be lousy. Witness the $1.1 billion in insider sales at Enron in the 12 months before they filed bankruptcy.)

"But, in my opinion, there is only one reason that multiple insiders back up the truck to buy their own company's shares. Based on their 'unfair advantage,' they think their shares are set to soar.

Not A Foolproof System—But Pretty Close

"And while no system is foolproof, I've found more often than not they're right.

"Volumes of independent research validate this point of view. In fact, just a few weeks ago, *Business Week* ran an article highlighting the same conclusion:

A study by researchers from the University of California at Los Angeles and New York University shows that a group of insider buyers, most from tech and pharmaceutical companies, beat broad market indexes by an average of 9.6% in the six months following their purchases.

"Two important points here. First, 9.6% is just about the market's average annual return over the past 100 years. Yet insiders are earning 9.6% <u>more</u> than the market's return in just the first six months after their purchases. And, secondly, remember this is merely the <u>average</u> gain after an insider purchase. What if you restricted your purchases to just those companies that were fundamentally sound, had a major catalyst for positive change AND heavy insider buying too?

"This is a question I've been researching for several years and my answer is: Good things will usually happen.

"Let's [look] to Tyson Foods for a moment. I know selling headless Rhode Island Reds is not as exciting as seeking a breakthrough in cancer treatment or the development of the next generation of semiconductors. But, damn, it can be profitable.

Bullish On Chickens

"In fact, according to *Investor's Business Daily*, the U.S. company showing the second-largest increase in profitability in the second quarter was—you guessed it—Tyson Foods. In fact, its earnings per share in the latest quarter were up more than 350%. And the stock has soared 84% in the last nine months.

"Who could have known in advance there were such huge profits to be had selling chicken? The insiders at Tyson Foods, for starters.

"A little over a year ago, directors Joe and Wilma Starr bought 15,000 shares. Then last summer, as the stock languished in the single digits, other insiders started lining up at the trough. First, director Leland Tollett bought 25,000 shares. Then director Donald J. Tyson bought a few thousand shares. Shelby Massey, another director, picked up 10,000 shares. In September, officer Greg Huett bought 9,437 shares. And so on.

"Let me remind you that this became public information not long after they made their purchases. No hindsight was necessary.

"Investors who followed in their footsteps have seen the stock rise more than

80% since the September lows. And now that the stock has skyrocketed, insiders are no longer buying. In fact, the only insider transactions in the last three months are sells. Time to move on.

"...I spend several thousand dollars a year to subscribe to a service that allows me to monitor the daily electronic filings at the SEC. I then spend hours more each week looking at each insider's track record and doing a thorough fundamental and technical analysis of each stock that looks interesting.

"I wade through an avalanche of meaningless information, like small purchases from new officers or directors who are just trying to show they're a 'member of the club.' Or insider purchases that are made solely because of option compensation.

"That's not real insider buying. Real insider buying is multiple insiders buying a large quantity of the stock with their own money at current market prices.

"That kind of information can give you a promising lead. And some of these leads have turned out to be quite rewarding. Despite the swan dive on the Nasdaq and S&P 500 year-to-date, so far this year a trading service I run, *The Insider Alert*, has already locked in double-digit profits in New York Community Bancorp, US Oncology, Bio-Reference Labs, Household International, Capital Bancorp and others. Every one of these stocks had sound fundamentals and, of course, heavy insider buying before we made our purchases."

Originally published: April 25, 2003 in Investment U

To sign up for Dr. Sjuggerud's free Investment U service, go to: www.investmentu.com.

When To Sell Value Stocks

By Dan Ferris

Warren Buffett is the greatest investor who has ever lived. Since 1965, he's averaged annual returns of about 22% per year. For every $1,000 invested back then, he and his investors today are sitting on $190 million, an unparalleled investment achievement.

There's obviously a handsome payoff for anyone who can successfully imitate Buffett's investment style. We often hear about Buffett buying stocks. In recent years, he's invested in companies like H&R Block, Nike, Yum Brands, and Liz Claiborne, just to name a few.

What you don't hear much about is when Buffett likes to sell. That would be a great bit of insight to possess, wouldn't it? Then you'd know how to maximize your investment profits as a value-oriented stock investor.

During his entire career, Warren Buffett has sold large blocks of stock on only two occasions. The first time was in 1969 after a bull market that lasted for most of the 1960s. Buffett told investors in his partnership that there were no suitable opportunities available for value-oriented investors. The market became manic in 1971 and 1972, and collapsed in 1973 and 1974.

Stocks were trading at more than 50 times a single year's earnings when Buffett sold in 1969. By 1973-1974, they fell to less than 10 times earnings.

The second time Buffett sold out in a big way was in 1998. Again, many of the stocks in his portfolio had risen to historically high price-to-earnings ratios, well in excess of 50 times earnings.

To figure out how Buffett knows when it's time to sell, take a look at just one of the stocks in Buffett's portfolio. Let's use Coca-Cola, a long time Buffett favorite. (Buffett drinks the stuff for breakfast, often with a bowl of peanuts or a dish of ice cream with chocolate sauce.)

In 1998, Coke earned $1.42 per share. Earnings had been growing 12% a year for ten years. If you bought one share of Coke that year and held it for ten years, your share of Coke's earnings would total about $24.88 by 2008.

No matter what price you paid, $24.88 is what you could expect to earn. But back in 1998, you'd have had to pay $88 for that share of Coke. That's a total return of about 28% after ten years. (That's $248.80 on every $1,000 invested.)

If you'd put your $88 to work in a corporate bond paying 6%, you would have earned a total of $52.80 after ten years, a much better deal than Coke. That's a total return of 60% after ten years, or $600 on every $1,000 invested. Bonds were making investors 200% more on their money than stocks.

You can use the same thinking as the world's greatest investor to figure out when to sell value stocks to make the highest possible profits.

First, figure out what you can expect a company to earn for the next ten years. There are many different sources for this type of information, if you don't know how to calculate it yourself. Value Line is one place where you can get it. Your broker should also be able to get you some research that tells you this. What I did was to look at the last ten years worth of earnings, calculate the average annual growth rate and extrapolate the next ten years.

If this method seems imprecise, that's because it is. Nobody has a crystal ball. Or, as a long-time investor I know who has made millions in the market has been saying for years, "I've got two balls, but neither one is crystal."

Once you get the ten years worth of earnings, you're practically done. All you have to do now is compare the stock's total expected ten-year earnings to what you'd make over the next ten years investing the same amount of money in AAA corporate bonds at the current rate.

Let's say the Moody's AAA corporate bond yield forecast for this month is 6.56%. (It's a forecast because this month isn't over yet.) That rate will pay you $65.60 every year for every $1,000 invested. After ten years, that's a total of $656 per $1,000 invested, or about 66%.

When a stock gets too expensive, it will fail the bond yield test. That tells you it's time to sell.

You'll generally find that stocks trading between 15 and 25 times earnings won't pass the bond yield test when they get above 40 times earnings. They generally won't pass the test again until they've fallen back to between 15 and 25 times earnings. But put them through the bond yield test. That's the only way to be sure.

Originally published: October 18, 2002 in Extreme Value

For more info on Dan Ferris' Extreme Value service, visit www.stansberryresearch.com online, and click on "Extreme Value."

3 Signs of a Short-Term Rally

By Porter Stansberry

If you have a trading account, you might be interested to know my three indicators for short-term rallies.

The MOST IMPORTANT indicator of short-term market action is sentiment.

There's one very good indicator of the emotions of the marketplace. This indicator is a direct measure of uncertainty. It goes up when uncertainty—fear—goes up. I want to buy stocks when they're scared and selling in a panic.

The indicator is called the Market Volatility Index (^VIX on Yahoo! finance). It's maintained by the Chicago Board Options Exchange. The index measures how much the time premium on stock options costs. The more traders are willing to pay for time, the more volatile they expect the markets to be in the future. Thus, this index is a measure of how scared the market is about the future. The VIX rarely registers readings above 50.

Black Monday in October 1987 was one such exception, as was the market panic in October 1998. Following both periods was an excellent time to be a buyer of stocks.

My second market-timing indicator is momentum.

The VIX—How to Know When Investors are Afraid
By Dr. Steve Sjuggerud, PhD

The VIX Index is a measure of market volatility. (Specifically, it's the Chicago Board of Options Exchange Volatility Index.) It's what I call the "fear gauge." There's an old saying among options pros that goes like this: "When the VIX is high, it's time to buy, when the VIX is low, it's time to go."

If you were to buy when the VIX is high, you'd be doing exactly what the best speculators do— they buy when nobody else is willing to buy. The VIX tells us when investors are extremely jittery. Speculators that have the courage to step up and buy in times of high volatility are often handsomely rewarded.

In the last five years, we've only seen highs above 40 on the VIX in October of 1998 and after September 11th. In both cases, stocks had no problem jumping significantly (20% or so) in a relatively short period of time (say, three months).

When the VIX hits 40, it's time to start paying attention to it. And once the VIX finally peaks (it reached a high of 57 after September 11th), it's time for risk-takers to take a risk. (You can follow the VIX on Yahoo! Finance (www.finance.yahoo.com) very easily, the symbol is ^VIX— don't forget the ^ sign!)

Regardless of what I personally think about the market (bullish or bearish), momentum in the market tends to be self-reinforcing. Individual stocks can buck the trend—but not the market itself. Investing on the right side of the major trend is key to short-term success. A big move higher on bad news could only happen if the momentum inside the market was bullish. Stocks can rally despite bad news (e.g., anthrax scare).

My third market-timing indicator is the availability of credit. All market analysts recognize the importance of credit to the overall trend in the market. The reason is simple: The more money that's available in the economy, the more money is likely to end up in the stock market.

But, I think that most market watchers attribute too much power to the Federal Reserve. My credit growth indicator isn't a committee of men. My credit indicator is the "risk spread" between 10-year government bonds and 10-year corporate bonds rated "A" by Moody's (a top credit rating agency). The risk spread is the difference in yield, or in other words, the difference in the interest rates on government debt versus corporate debt. When the bond market is charging higher interest rates for corporate debt than government debt, it means that corporations will have a very hard time raising money.

Originally published: October 12, 2001 by Stansberry & Associates Investment Research

For more information on Porter Stansberry, go to: www.stansberryresearch.com.

Chapter 4

Hard Assets: Gold, Silver, and Currencies

The "Max Yield" Strategy: How to Make a $220,000 Profit on the Decline of the U.S. Dollar

By Chris Weber

Unless you're one of those rare Americans who have opened a foreign bank account or bought a modest amount of foreign currencies or securities, everything you own is in dollars.

Right now, that could be incredibly detrimental to your financial well-being. Why? Because for the last three years, the U.S. dollar has been losing steam. In fact, over the last two years, the dollar has lost 25% of its value against the world's major currencies.

Think about it. If everything you own is in dollars, and the dollar has lost 25% of its value, even if you did nothing at all with your money, your net worth is just three-fourths of what it was in June 2001 relative to what it could have been if you diversified. But it gets worse if your investments are all denominated in dollars and you've fared no better than the average investor (who's seen the S&P 500 lose about 15% on average the last two years)—then your portfolio could actually be down 50% or more!

Cash Out on the Dollar... And Cash In on the World

So what's the solution? Get out of the dollar, obviously—by using the Max Yield strategy.

It's simple. With Max Yield, you'll be investing in the strongest and best-performing currencies in the world, year after year. In fact, this strategy can help you grow a $50,000 initial investment in cash into more than $220,000 almost 10 times faster than if you'd placed your capital into super-safe one-year U.S. CD's (at today's rates). **Best of all, this strategy has averaged a double-digit return on cash for 33 years,** and it has done so with all of the safety and security of having your money in the bank.

Take the First Step: Get Past Any Mental Blocks You Have

For too many American investors, the thought of diversifying outside of the dollar almost smacks of treason. But the reality is, if you don't diversify outside of the dollar, and your legacy continues to be whittled away, the real betrayal will be against your family and your heirs.

Still, others haven't diversified into alternative currencies because of the often-confusing nature of conversion rates, incredibly high denominations, or the look of that "funny money." So they stay in dollars, thinking that they're avoiding all of that potential consternation. But consider this: Even if you've never owned any currency except U.S. dollars, you have been and still are a currency investor. Because—whether you realize it or not—by holding dollars you have, in effect, chosen *not* to hold yen, marks, pounds, or Swiss francs.

Every time you put money into your savings account, buy a CD at your bank, or buy stocks or bonds from your broker, your investment immediately becomes dependent upon the integrity and value of the currency it is denominated in—the U.S. dollar.

And if, for the past 20 years, everything you own has been in dollars, that may not have been the best thing for your financial health. If your savings are in dollars, and the dollar's value falls against other currencies—something it has done for the last three years, let alone at various times throughout history—then your standard of living has unnecessarily fallen along with it.

We Americans need only look at our declining savings rate over the past generations to understand what has been happening to the dollar. And when we seek to earn interest on our savings—either in a bank or through the purchase of bonds—we'd be wise to consider currencies other than our own.

How to Use The Max Yield Strategy in Your Portfolio

For American investors, the Max Yield strategy is a chance to profit in two ways at the same time:

You can earn higher-than-stateside interest rates, and...

When you convert your pounds, marks, francs, and yen back into American money, you will sometimes find that they have earned an additional 25% to 50% in currency conversion.

Consider this story:

Max Yield threw caution to the wind, and beginning in 1970 invested $10,000 U.S. in the major currency that offered the best performance against the dollar (the currency that paid the highest rate of interest).

Thereafter, every year on January 1, Max surveyed the global economy and sank the proceeds from that previous year into what he saw as the new best-performing currency against the U.S. dollar.

If the best-performing currency hadn't changed, Max simply rolled over his investment.

If you, like Max, chased after the highest-yielding major world currency from January 1970 to May 2003, you'd have chosen U.S. dollars only two years out of the 33. The other 31 years, you would have chosen other major world currencies:

The $10,000 Max started with was worth $280,073.52 at the start of 2003.

At the end of it, its value had vaulted to $370,537.26, a rise, again, of 32.3%.

At the start of 2004, the New Zealand dollar is once again the Max Yield currency. It pays 5.48% for a one-year deposit. Interest rates have not fallen by much down there: Last's year's rate was 5.76%. If you don't want to open a bank account to get a one-year deposit, you can buy the short-term New Zealand government bond that matures in February 2005. The coupon rate is 6.50%, but the price is about 101.1, giving you a current annual yield of 5.48%. Of course, you would be selling it a month or so before maturity at the end of 2004, and moving on to the next Max Yield play.

You can buy this bond through Jeff Winn, at International Assets. It is always better to buy the actual paper from the various Max Yield governments than it is to go through more middlemen.

To put Max Yield's strategy to work in your portfolio, I recommend you contact:

Jeff Winn
International Assets
300 South Orange Ave.
Suite 1100
Orlando, FL 32801
Tel: 800.432.4402 or 407.254.1522
Fax: 407.254.1505
E-mail:jwinn@iaac.com

Originally published: January 2004 in the Weber Global Opportunity Report

At age 16, Chris Weber took $650 in paper route money and turned it into $60,000 by investing in gold coins. Over the next decade, he built a $1.8 million portfolio—simply by seeking out the world's best investments. Chris has never held a 'real job' in his life. He spends his time now writing about investing and traveling the world in search of the next great investment opportunity. He owns homes in Florida and San Francisco, and lives in Monaco, on the Mediterranean Sea. He still manages all of his own money today. For more information on Chris Weber's Global Opportunities Report, go to: www.weberglobal.net.

The Secret Currency—
How the World's Wealthiest Families Make Money Even When Stocks, Bonds and Real Estate Lose Value

By Dr. Steve Sjuggerud, PhD

One investment—which most Americans know nothing about—is one of the secrets behind some of the world's richest families. We call this investment a "secret currency" because it is beyond the reach of any government or corporation. And because many of the world's wealthiest families have used it for generations to grow dynasties.

The secret currency is a form of gold. But it's not your typical gold investment.

It has nothing to do with mining stocks, mutual funds, options, futures, or bullion. Instead, this is a kind of currency used for centuries by the richest families to profit on financial windfalls created by governments around the world. This secret currency is not old-fashioned or obsolete. In fact, look through the rolls of the richest people in the world and you find dozens of families using this investment to both grow and safeguard their wealth. For example…

- The Rothschilds (At one time, the wealthiest family in the world)

- The Onassis family (Greek shipping magnate Aristotle, married Jackie Kennedy after JFK died)

- The Hunt family of Texas (H.L. Hunt made his billions as an oil wildcatter)

- The DuPonts (whose descendants today run the 2nd biggest chemical company in the United States)

- The Morgans (JP was one of the richest railroad men of the last 100 years)

- The Adams family (famous for producing two U.S. Presidents)

This investment is like gold, only better—with the potential for much higher returns.

The last time the Salomon Brothers brokerage firm included this vehicle in its annual investment survey, the secret currency ranked #1 over the prior 20 year-span, with an annual return of 17.3%. In other words, <u>it was the single most profitable thing you could do with your money over the previous 20 years</u>.

It beat stocks, bonds, gold, silver, artwork, diamonds, U.S. Treasury bills, real estate, and oil, according to an article in the *Chicago Tribune*.

I believe you could double your money with this investment. <u>A 5-times or 10-times return wouldn't be surprising.</u> The last time the conditions were even close to this good (in 1987), investors made 665% profits.

Here are the details…

The Secret Currency of Rare Coins

The investment I want to tell you about is a way to invest in rare gold coins.

Before you dismiss this idea, remember that this is an investment the most powerful and wealthy families in the world have used for generations.

But it's not just any coins I want to show you how to invest in… it's a very specific group of gold coins.

Let me explain…

Before Franklin Delano Roosevelt, there was Teddy. Teddy had a thing for coins. He passionately hated America's coins, calling them *"artistically of atrocious hideousness."* America had become the most powerful nation on earth. And the President felt that our most valuable coins should be a reflection of our status. So he sought out the foremost sculptor of the day, Augustus Saint-Gaudens…

"Dear Mr. President…" Saint-Gaudens replied to Teddy. *"Well! Whatever I produce cannot be worse than the inanities now displayed on our coins, and we will at least have made an attempt in the right direction…."*

In poor health, Saint-Gaudens delivered. He designed the gallant $20 "Double Eagle" gold piece, a design that today is nearly unanimously considered to be the most beautiful coin of all time. It was Saint-Gaudens last work. He died and never saw the fruits of his labor.

The coins were minted from 1907 until 1933, when Teddy Roosevelt's cousin Franklin Delano Roosevelt made it illegal for individuals to own gold and melted down many of these gorgeous coins. After gold ownership was banned in 1933, private ownership of gold was not allowed in the U.S. until 1974.

While the entire 1933 series of Saint-Gaudens Double Eagles was supposedly destroyed by FDR, ten of the coins somehow sneaked out of the mint. Over the years, nine have been recovered and destroyed by the Secret Service. The government seized the 10th coin in New York and made arrests, but the government case fell apart and a compromise was met. The coin would be auctioned, with the proceeds split half and half between the government and the other party. This 1933 Saint-Gaudens $20 Double Eagle sold for $7,590,000, the highest price ever paid for a coin.

Before 1933, we had Double Eagles ($20 gold pieces that contained nearly an ounce of gold), Eagles ($10 gold pieces with nearly a half ounce of gold) half-eagles ($5) and so on. A Saint-Gaudens $20 dollar gold piece would have an intrinsic value of about $392 dollars today, since it contains nearly an ounce of gold, and an ounce of gold is worth about $392.

Of course, coin enthusiasts will always pay more than meltdown value for Saint-Gaudens $20 gold pieces—as they are considered to be the most beautiful coins in the world. But right now, these Saint-Gaudens gold coins are selling for their smallest premium over the price of gold in recorded history. We can own a piece of history, and we can own real money with real gold, for a small premium over the meltdown value.

What Kind of Upside Potential Are We Talking About?

"With modest investment in the right coins in the early 1970s you could cash out and buy a house by 1980, and many did."
~ David Hall, Collectors Universe

Rare coins have experienced a few roaring bull markets since gold ownership became legal again. Coin prices (as measured by the CU 3000 Index) were up 1,195% in the 1976-1980 bull market in coins. In other words, a $10,000 investment would have risen to $129,500 in value.

In the 1987-1989 bull market, coin prices (as measured by the CU 3000 Index) rose by 665%. Coins like the Saint-Gaudens in pristine "Mint State" condition (coins graded "MS65" by the coin grading service PCGS) were big winners.

Then in 1989, the bottom fell out. Coins were in a horrendous bear market for the next 14 years, which brought the Saint-Gaudens to ridiculous bargain levels. As you can imagine, after fourteen years of misery, there were a lot of bitter people in the coin business. After 14 years of people getting burned, it reached the point where the word "investor" was a dirty word…

I flew out to visit the headquarters of the largest coin dealer in America recently, and stated my intentions… to learn about their business as a potential coin investor and to potentially tell thousands of potential investors about them. The dealer wouldn't see me. The next week I went to one of the country's major coin shows, and again I approached the same coin dealer, again genuinely stating my intentions to invest in coins. Yet again, they wouldn't see me, as an "investor." How ridiculous is that?

Our Investment Prospects

When it comes to gold coins, there are basically two types… rare ones and common ones.

The common gold coins are called *"bullion coins,"* because a one-ounce gold bullion coin generally sells at about the same price of (or at a small premium to) an ounce of gold. Famous bullion coins include South African Kruggerands and Canadian Maple Leafs. If gold is $392, you might buy these for $420.

The rare gold coins are called *"numismatic coins."* These coins trade based on their rarity, scarcity, and collector demand. Though gold may be at $392, a rare and highly prized one-ounce gold coin can easily fetch tens of thousands of dollars.

Then there is a bit of a third type of gold coin… The *hybrid coin,* I call it. And this is what I like. These have characteristics of both of the types above, but they're not really either. The typical Saint-Gaudens is a prime example of these…

Saint-Gaudens dating from 1924-1928, for example, have a high collectible value, yet they are easy to buy and sell. Like bullion coins there are enough of them to go around, plus they contain just under an ounce of gold. I expect these will likely be the first coins snapped up when people discover how cheap the coin market is right now.

Mint State Saint-Gaudens coins (graded MS-63 by PCGS—if you're new to coin-lingo visit www.PCGS.com) from these dates are currently selling for around $630 each. The MS-65 coins are currently selling for about $1,175, or about a 200% premium to the current price of gold.

Buying at the Best Possible Price

There are many ways to buy these coins. Since these coins have been graded and sealed by the grading service PCGS, it is okay to buy them sight unseen. So you can buy them through your local dealer, or try your luck on eBay (I typed "Gaudens" into eBay today and 350 items came up).

The question is, what is the right price? There are many coin price guides out there. And for each price guide, you'll find a wildly different price. Price guides fall into two categories: "retail" price guides, and "dealer" price guides.

"Retail" is the asking price, like what a car dealer would ask for a used car. "Retail" is generally a pipe dream for a dealer… particularly when it comes to easy-to-find coins like the 1924-1928 Saint-Gaudens.

When I first recommended the St. Gaudens coins, Paul Montgomery, of Bowers and Merena, was filling all of the orders.

In the past year, the Generic Gold Coin Index that I use as a benchmark (it's a sub-index of the CU3000 Index, available at www.PCGS.com) is up over 19%.

The question is can it last? How much more can be made in gold coins? And what's my risk?

I'm willing to pay a 50% premium above the price of gold for the MS63s, 80% above the price of gold for MS-64s, and a 200% premium above the price of gold for the MS65s.

Again, we'll pay:

• 50% premium above the price of gold for MS63 St. Gaudens
• 80% premium above the price of gold for MS64 St. Gaudens
• 200% premium above the price of gold for MS65 St. Gaudens

How do you determine what the current premiums are above the price of gold?

It's easy.

1) First, go to www.gold.org. There, you'll find the price of gold, updated every minute. As I write this, it's $392 an ounce.

2) Next, multiply the price of gold times our allotted premium for each coin:

• For the MS63 St. Gaudens, we'll pay a 50% premium above the price of gold. ($392 x 1.50 = $588). So our buy-up-to price as I write this for the MS63s is $588.

• For the MS64s, we multiply the price of gold times 80% ($392 x 1.80 = $705). So our buy-up-to price as of this writing is $705.

• For the MS65s, we multiply the price of gold times 200% ($392 x 3 = $1,176). So our buy-up-to price as of this writing is $1,176.

3) Then, all you have to do is contact a coin dealer (we recommend three good ones we've worked with on the next few pages), and find out if you can buy these coins below our buy-up-to prices.

IMPORTANT NOTE: The buy-up-to prices will change as the price of gold changes. You can check the price of gold in the newspaper or on-line (www.gold.org is one good resource). Remember, don't pay more than the buy-up-to price as outlined above.

Another Coin Recommendation: Liberty Double Eagles

If you have trouble buying the St. Gaudens at our buy-up-to prices… or if you want to make another coin investment, I'm also recommending **Liberty Double Eagles** from the turn of the century.

Specifically, the Liberties I'm recommending are in what's called "About

Uncirculated" (AU) condition, minted between 1891 and 1907. They call these "Type 3" Liberties, and they are works of art (though they are not as gorgeous as the Saint-Gaudens Double Eagles that replaced them starting in 1907). Think about this… they're not making any more of these 100-year-old coins… and chances of finding a big stash in uncirculated condition are pretty slim.

I ask you, what should a coin like this be worth? Again we're talking about 100-year-old gold coins that contain just under an ounce of gold (0.9675oz), in About Uncirculated condition.

These coins can be bought for about a 20% premium over the price of an ounce of gold. So at current prices, it's like you are buying raw gold, almost *at cost*. The fact that you're owning a 100-year old piece of U.S. history—they can't "make more" 100-year old coins—is completely ignored at current prices.

These are 100 year-old works of art—pieces of history. No one is making any more of them. And you can buy them for a tiny premium over the current price of gold, with a downside risk guarantee. Your upside is unlimited, and your downside is limited to 20%.

I recommend buying these coins now. Buy them up to a 25% premium over the current price of gold.

• For the Liberty Coins, we multiply the price of gold times 25% ($392 x 1.25 = $490). So our buy-up-to price as of this writing is $490.

Here are the specifics of what you want to buy: "Raw" Liberty Double Eagles, Type 3, AU50 grade (or similar, within $20 either way).

Where to Buy Our Recommended Coins

The rise in the gold price and the increased demand for the Saint-Gaudens coins has bumped up the price since I first recommended the coins.

Here are three dealers I feel comfortable recommending. They came highly recommended to me. I personally sought them out and spent time with them. I've known most of them for years. And I believe they'll treat you right.

Van Simmons, President
David Hall Rare Coins
P.O. Box 6220
Newport Beach, CA 92658
Tel: (800)759-7575
In California: 949-567-1325
Fax: 949-477-5874

E-mail: van@davidhall.com

Website: www.davidhall.com

Burt Blumert at:

Camino Coin

P.O. Box 4292

Burlingame, CA 94011

Phone: 800-348-8001 or 650-348-3000

Fax: 650-401-5530

burtblu@hotmail.com

Rich Checkan or Glen Kirsh at:

Asset Strategies International, Inc. 1700 Rockville Pike #400

Rockville, MD 20852

Phone: 800-831-0007 or 301-881-8600

Fax: 301-881-1936

rcheckan@assetstrategies.com

These dealers have good reputations and decades of experience.

MY RECOMMENDATION: Call or email one of these dealers, and tell them you'd like to buy two MS-63 graded Saint-Gaudens and one MS-65 graded Saint-Gaudens from the 1924-1928 mintage. Make sure they're graded by either PCGS or NGC.

In addition, or as a substitute for the MS-63 Saint-Gaudens, buy the Type III Liberty $20 gold piece. At the time of your order, ask the dealer which of those he thinks is a better deal. And also ask if he believes it's a better deal to replace the MS65 Saint-Gaudens with a highly-graded Type III Liberty, like an MS64.

My recommendation is to buy two MS63 Saint-Gaudens coins and one MS65 Saint-Gaudens. Buy as many as you'd like in that ratio, with up to 4% of your investment portfolio.

Originally published: April 2004 in True Wealth

For more information on Dr. Sjuggerud's True Wealth advisory service, go to: www.stansberryresearch.com, or call (888) 261-2693.

9 Things You Need to Know to Invest in Rare Coins

By David Hall

EDITOR'S NOTE: If you are going to invest in rare coins, here are nine "facts of life," from one of the leading coin experts in the world. This material is reprinted from David Hall's book: A Mercenary's Guide to the Rare Coin Market.

#1: *THERE ARE NO BARGAINS.*

Bargains ("rips" in the lexicon of the numismatic insiders) are a seldom encountered exception to the day-to-day reality of the rare coin marketplace. I'm defining a bargain as a purchase that can be immediately resold for a profit of more than 20%. I'll use myself as an example. Throughout the 1970s I attended most major coin shows. I was usually among the first to hit the bourse floor, which I faithfully scoured for "rips." Even though I knew rare coin values just about as well as anybody, and even though I was a very aggressive buyer, I was lucky if I found one or two "bargains" per show! In other words, once or twice per show I bought a coin for $200 and sold it for, say, $300. Most of my dealer-to-dealer coin show sales consisted of buying a coin for $200 and selling it for $225. I concentrated on buying coins at slightly under fair market prices and selling them for a little more than I paid.

Now compare your situation with mine. You probably have neither my expertise nor my exposure to the marketplace. If it was, and still is, difficult for me to find bargains, it's probably impossible for you to "rip" one. You will have enough trouble receiving fair value, i.e. buying a $100 coin for around $100. If you are offered a $100 coin for considerably under $100, there is a good chance the coin is being misrepresented (possibly counterfeit, more probably overgraded) especially if you remember: THERE ARE NO BARGAINS.

#2: *RARE COINS ARE OFTEN OVERGRADED.*

Misrepresentation is a problem in most collectible fields (coins, stamps, art, antiques, baseball cards, etc.). In the rare coin field, the two basic forms of misrepresentation are counterfeiting and overgrading. Counterfeiting is a fringe problem. "Reputable" dealers do not knowingly sell counterfeit coins; unfortunately, some of them do knowingly overgrade. The quality of a coin has a tremendous bearing on its price. Very minute differences in quality often mean large differences in price. Many dealers yield to the temptation to grade optimistically. The problem is particularly acute in the area of Mint State (uncirculated) coins. I estimate that over 50% of all coins represented as Mint State in advertisements and auctions are overgraded.

Your best protection against buying overgraded coins is to learn to grade accurately. However, grading is a difficult skill to master. Still, you can be aware of the basic grading concepts. Carefully examine every coin you purchase. Notice how sharply the details of the design stand out. Take note of all major and minor marks. Now compare the coin with another, preferably of the same type. The coin with the greatest detail and least marks is logically the better coin. Consult with friends. But, as a practical manner, you should seek professional assistance, because RARE COINS ARE OFTEN OVERGRADED.

#3: *MOST DEALERS HAVE A LIMITED KNOWLEDGE OF THE RARE COIN MARKET.*

When I started traveling the coin show circuit, one of my most startling revelations was when it came to actual rare coin values, many of my previous "idols" weren't all that sharp. They were good businessmen, tough negotiators, and many had great marketing expertise. However, as I began doing business with the major dealers, I soon realized that many of them could not grade accurately. Even more of them could not tell you what a particular coin was worth without reaching for the latest copy of the Greysheet (*Coin Dealer Newsletter*).

I now feel that there are approximately 100 people in this country that truly know U.S. rare coin values. The other dealers are limited by their own prejudices, limited perspective, and/or lack of knowledge. All of their limited points of view are reflected in their advertising, both printed and spoken. So be wary of all you read and hear. Trust your own instincts because MOST DEALERS HAVE A LIMITED KNOWLEDGE OF THE RARE COIN MARKET.

#4: *AUCTIONS ARE A GOOD DEAL FOR AUCTION COMPANIES.*

Auction companies offer you an avenue to buy and sell rare coins. After looking at a couple hundred thousand auction lots, sitting through countless hours of auction sessions, and consigning coins to most of the major auction houses, I've come to the conclusion that there are better ways to buy and sell coins.

On the buying end:

Buying coins at an auction is incredibly time consuming. You can probably do better on the bourse floor or on the telephone, if you are a dealer, or by paying for someone else's time and expertise if you are an investor.

With the rare exception of catching a "sleeper," if you buy a coin at auction, you have probably paid absolute top dollar. You've certainly paid more than any dealer, collector, or investor in attendance would pay.

If you are not 100% sure of the value of a coin, there are several traps awaiting you, including: Dealers who consign coins to auctions and then bid them up themselves, and coins owned by the auction company that have high opening bids.

On the selling end:

You have no control over prices realized.

All auction companies charge a 10% to 20% commission, though some of them disguise part of the commission by calling it a "buyer's charge."

Dealer collusion is blatantly practiced at most major auctions.

It takes too long to sell your coins, three to six months from the time you consign them until you receive your settlement check. Many firms offer cash advances, but they usually charge interest on the money advanced.

It is much faster and more efficient to sell your coins yourself by offering them to a willing buyer.

In short, AUCTIONS ARE A GOOD DEAL FOR AUCTION COMPANIES.

#5: *VALUE IS RELATIVE.*

Coins do not have absolute values. Coins have relative values that are constantly changing. Consider the following stumbling blocks to accurately assessing a coin's value:

Price guides do not buy or sell coins. The common mistake is to say, "This coin is worth $500," when all you are really saying is, "This coin catalogues for $500."

Mintage is not always relevant. The number of coins supposedly made of a particular issue (mint records are sometimes inaccurate) often has little bearing on its value. The number of surviving specimens is the important consideration. Disregard mintage and concentrate on availability.

Prices can be determined

Don't Buy Coins Unless You Get the Right Grading Guarantee.

Look for a guarantee that ties your coins' values to a specific price. The dealer should be willing to offer you a cash buy price at any time in the future.

There are two more comments that must be made about grading guarantees. First, there are some firms that offer financially unsupportable guarantees. These are the guarantees that promise to pay 15% per year or 20% over purchase price at any time. Besides being financially unsupportable, these guarantees also violate the securities laws. Avoid any firm that offers a guaranteed profit or a guarantee of no loss. Also avoid firms that claim their clients have never lost money. The coin market is a free market. Prices go up and down. In my opinion, any firm that claims none of its clients has ever lost money is probably lying to you about other things as well.

only when coins are on the market. It is very difficult to pinpoint prices of unavailable coins. This lack of accurate pricing information is often reflected in price guides and dealer/collector/investor thinking. Often, more common coins are priced higher than ones that are more rare because recent transactions provide a frame of reference.

Look for coins that are difficult to purchase at current prices. Compare relative prices within a series. In the rare coin market, VALUE IS RELATIVE.

#6: *PRETZEL LOGIC IS THE PREDOMINANT MODE OF THINKING AMONG RARE COIN BUYERS.*

Most coin buyers, both dealers and public, buy high and sell low. The gold bullion market offers a perfect example of this "pretzel logic." At $250 an ounce, everybody wanted to buy gold; at $200 an ounce it didn't look as good and they became sellers. Common date BU Walking Liberty half dollar rolls were available at $275 for two years. Then they got hot and went to $600 in about six months. I began to get calls along the lines of, "What do you think of these Walking Liberties? They seem like a good investment." I'm not saying that BU Walkers are a bad deal at $600* per roll. I'm just wondering where these people were when Walkers were at $275 a roll. Fight the psychological forces that keep you from buying underpriced coins and selling overpriced ones. Remember, PRETZEL LOGIC IS THE PRE-DOMINANT MODE OF THINKING AMONG RARE COIN BUYERS.

Note that the pricing time frame was January, 1979.

#7: *HIGH QUALITY COINS INCREASE IN VALUE FASTER THAN OFF-QUALITY COINS.*

Now this certainly seems logical. The best quality is in the greatest demand, and therefore, prices of high quality coins increase more rapidly. So, buy the best quality. If you cannot afford to buy Gem gold, buy Gem Mercury dimes. If you cannot afford to buy Gem Mercs, buy Gem Roosevelt dimes. Do not settle for less than the best. It will be much easier for you to confront fact #8 if you remember fact #7: HIGH QUALITY COINS INCREASE IN VALUE FASTER THAN OFF-QUALITY COINS.

#8: *YOU MUST SELL YOUR COINS.*

When a coin reaches its full price potential, it should be sold. Two stock market sayings help illustrate this fact:

"Bulls make money, bears make money, pigs don't."

"The only people that buy at the bottom and sell at the top are liars."

Consider the following advantages of occasionally selling. You will be able to convert paper profits into real profits. By selling coins now and then, you can become familiar with the mechanics of the selling side of the rare coin market. This could be a great help should you ever need to sell quickly. You will also find out for sure who has been selling you properly graded coins at fair market prices. Once or twice a year you can weed out the weak parts of your portfolio. Don't be afraid to take losses on mistakes—consider it tuition. Move into areas with more potential. Learn about the selling side of the rare coin market, because eventually, YOU MUST SELL YOUR COINS.

#9: *THE SECRET TO SUCCESSFUL RARE COIN INVESTING IS PAYING A FAIR PRICE FOR PROPERLY GRADED COINS*.

The easiest thing to do in the rare coin market is spend money. It's not quite as easy to receive fair value. If you are lucky, you are buying coins from a dealer who marks his coins up 15% to 30% above his cost. Many dealers mark coins up 50% to 100% above their cost. Some telemarketing firms use mark-ups of 200% to 300%, even 500%!!! The following will help soften the blow of excessive dealer mark-ups:

Be aware of the price you are paying for coins. Study and compare coin prices.

Ask for buy-backs. Find out at what price a dealer would buy his coin back. Get it in writing.

Learn how to grade or get a grading guarantee that is very specific about the buy-back process and price.

To participate in all the fabulous rare coin profits you read about, you must realize: THE SECRET TO SUCCESSFUL RARE COIN INVESTING IS PAYING A FAIR PRICE FOR PROPERLY GRADED COINS.

Originally published: *A Mercenary's Guide to the Rare Coin Market*

David Hall sold his first rare coin in 1961. He has been a major force in the rare coin industry since 1972. David has handled virtually every type of rare U.S. coin, and today is considered one of the world's top coin experts. David's coin business, David Hall Rare Coins, is a division of the publicly traded company Collector's Universe.

To buy or sell rare coins, contact Van Simmons of David Hall Rare Coins by e-mail: vsimmons@davidhall.com, or toll-free phone: (800)759-7575.

The Top 10 Rare Coins

By David Hall

EDITOR'S NOTE: David Hall is one of THE world's leading experts on top quality rare coins. Below, he outlines the all-time Top 10 rare coins. This material is reprinted from David Hall's book: <u>A Mercenary's Guide to the Rare Coin Market</u>.

There are several thousand United States rare coins that are appropriate additions to any portfolio being built for maximum profit potential. But what are the best coins in this group? What are the 10 very best coins to have in your portfolio?

I have compiled a list of the 10 coins that I feel represent the rare coin market's ten best bets for short-term, medium-term, and long-term potential. I call it "The Top 10 All-Time Rare Coin List." These are the top 10 quality examples from the five most active, most liquid, most popular, and best performing areas of the rare coins market. Here are the criteria I used:

Past Performance. A coin's past performance is a great barometer of its future potential. If buyers have been attracted to the coin in the past, it is a good bet the demand would be high for the coin in the future.

High Liquidity. Liquidity is an important, but often overlooked consideration for coin buyers. The "back door" is just as important as the "front door." Consequently, these are not highly esoteric issues of interest only to a few specialists; these are coins that are among the most popular and most actively traded issues in the rare coin market.

Availability. It doesn't do any good to recommend coins that no one can buy. The coins I have picked for this "cream of the crop" list are ones you can actually go out and buy quickly and easily.

Fundamentals. For this very specific portfolio strategy, <u>the coins must be fundamentally important U.S. coins</u>. They are classic numismatic issues.

So, with that in mind, here are the 10 coins that belong in every portfolio. Note: This list has at least one coin from each of the five major areas of the market: type coins, rare gold, silver dollars, 20th Century singles, and silver commems. I've also included coins in three price groups: inexpensive coins ($50 to $1,000 for Gem quality examples), moderately priced coins ($1,000 to $10,000), and expensive (or, "Big Boy") coins (over $10,000). As usual, all recommendations and prices apply to

MS 64 or better quality coins <u>only</u>.

St. Gaudens ($3,200). While the coins to follow are not in any specific order, I decided to put the $20 St. Gaudens first because it is probably the world's best known coin. It is also one of the most beautiful coin designs in numismatic history. This coin has it all: beauty, popularity, rarity (in top condition), good past performance, and don't forget, it's almost exactly one ounce of "Oro Puro!" MS65 St. Gaudens is also one of the few coins that didn't flop in price during the 1980-82 bear market, even though the price of gold bullion and MS 60 and MS 63 St. Gaudens tumbled. I have said it before, but it's worth repeating—EVERY PORTFOLIO SHOULD HAVE AT LEAST ONE MS64 OR BETTER QUALITY ST. GAUDENS!!

Price Group One: Inexpensive coins…

Texas Commemorative Half Dollar. There are many excellent silver commemorative issues, but the Texas was an easy choice for number one commem on the "All-Time List." Between 1934 and 1938, approximately 150,000 Texas Centennial half dollars were minted. Probably 60% to 80% of those survive today. Of these, approximately 50% grade MS65 or better. So, this is not a truly rare coin, just a scarce coin. The thing that sets the Texas apart is the beauty of its design and the coin's extreme popularity. In fact, no other U.S. issue is associated with as much regional chauvinism (i.e. support) as the Texas half dollar.

Walking Liberty Half Dollar. Like the $20 St. Gaudens, this is one of the world's most beautiful coins. It is also extremely popular with coin buyers. Again, I've used the "most affordable" concept, though these coins are certainly not easy to find in top condition. And all five of the 1941 to 1945 Philadelphia issues make the list—proof Walking Liberty half dollars are also great. They were only minted from 1936 to 1942, and they are a little more expensive than the circulation strikes.

Mercury Dimes. Mercury dimes and Walking Liberty halves represent the ultimate in 20th Century numismatic beauty and importance. Though the Mercury dime series stretched between 1916 and 1945, proofs were made only between 1936 and 1942. Circulation strike Mercury dimes circa 1940 to 1945 are very reasonably priced, with Gems selling for less than $50. The proofs are a little more expensive.

Price Group Two: Moderately-priced coins…

1917 Type One Standing Liberty Quarter. Though this is one of the truly beautiful U.S. coin types, it was made for only two years. The exposed breast of Ms. Liberty caused such an uproar that they radically changed the design halfway through 1917. Since the 1916 is a five-figure rarity, this coin is effectively a one-year-only type coin. It is beautiful, popular, important, and rare in top condition.

Barber Half Dollars. Barber halves were minted between 1892 and 1915. They are one of the coin market's most important issues. They are collected both by date and by "type" collectors. They are the rarest of the 20th Century silver type issues. They are beautiful and important rare coins and both Gem quality circulation strikes and proofs are wonderful.

Twenty Cent Pieces. This odd coin was only made for four years—1875 through 1878. The coin looked too much like a quarter to catch on with the public, and there really wasn't a commercial need for the denomination. Today, twenty cent pieces are highly prized collector's items. The design is the beautiful Liberty Seated type, and all twenty cent pieces are rare in top condition.

Price Group Three: "Big Boy" coins…

Liberty Seated Dollars. This is one of the most beautiful coins ever made and one of the rarest of the major 19th Century U.S. types. Both circulation strikes and proofs are very rare. This coin is the number one favorite of my business partner, Van Simmons.

Early U.S. gold coins. From 1795 to 1834, the U.S. minted $2.50, $5, and $10 gold coins. In 1834, the gold content of our coins was lowered slightly, and most pre-1835 gold coins hit the melting pot. Today, these early treasures of American financial history are rare in all grades and super rare in Gem condition.

Proof Gold. Today the Mint strikes millions of proof coins a year and sells them to collectors all over the world. In the 19th Century, the Mint struck a few thousand proof coins each year and only a handful of proof gold coins. Proof gold coins are the caviar of the numismatic marketplace… the beachfront property of rare coins. They are expensive, but they are super rare and demand is always sky high in both good and bad markets.

Originally published: *A Mercenary's Guide to the Rare Coin Market*

To buy or sell rare coins, contact Van Simmons of David Hall Rare Coins by e-mail: vsimmons@davidhall.com, or toll-free phone: (800)759-7575.

Gold You Can Fold and Carry in Your Pocket

By Michael Checkan

Every seasoned investor knows the value of holding precious metals. I believe that gold is the best store of value available. Nothing else holds its worth or is as easily converted as gold. In moments of need or crisis it can aid and protect you and your family anywhere in the world.

For the Stansberry & Associates Investment Research, the problem has always been how to store and secure your gold. How can you be sure that your nest egg is not only completely safe, but that you can access it at a moment's notice?

Now there's a way you can own all the gold you want. Gold that holds its value better and is more easily realized than any other asset. Gold that cannot be stolen by thieves or confiscated by greedy governments. Now you can fold up and carry a thousand ounces of gold, even a million ounces, around in your pocket.

Sound too good to be true?

There is now an ideal way to own gold and other precious metals. It's called the **Perth Mint Certificate Program (PMCP)**. It's incredibly simple. All you have to do is buy a Perth Mint Certificate.

This document represents—and gives you title to—whatever quantity of precious metals you choose to invest in (above a certain minimum). Your gold is stored at the Perth Mint in Perth, Western Australia. Your certificate is registered to you, and referenced by both client name and certificate number. The Perth Mint also records a client number to ensure total confidentiality and security.

Your gold can be held in two ways. First, in unallocated storage, which means that your gold is held as part of a larger pool of precious metals. The beauty of this method is that you hold your metals under government guarantee, but your ownership is absolutely free of storage charges. This is clearly the most attractive option for most private investors.

Second, you can also choose to hold you gold or precious metals in allocated storage. This means that your gold is placed in a sealed box that is specifically assigned to you via the Perth Mint Certificate.

A Perth Mint Certificate is non-negotiable. However, ownership is transferable. You may sell or transfer your title to your precious metals. You may do this at any time and to anyone you choose.

Investing For Security... But How Secure Is Your Investment?

The Perth Mint offers one of the most secure locations for hard asset storage worldwide.

Australia is one of the most politically and economically stable countries. The Perth Mint itself is a division of Gold Corporation (GC). GC is wholly owned by the Western Australia Government. The Perth Mint refines 8% of annual world gold mine production. The Perth Mint has been dealing in precious metals since 1899. It is the world's oldest mint continuously operating from the same location.

The Perth Mint Certificate is the only government-guaranteed precious metals certificate in the world. The Western Australian Government has a Standard & Poor's AAA investment rating. The bullion bar products of the Gold Corporation Group are accepted by all serious international institutions. The London Bullion Market Association (LBMA), The New York Commodities Exchange (COMEX), and the Tokyo Commodities Exchange (TOCOM) all welcome its products.

Complete Security and Total Flexibility

So how much do you need to invest? The minimum requirement for the Perth Mint Certificate Program is US$10,000. Any further investments must be made in increments of no less than US$5,000.

A wide variety of precious metals are available under the **Perth Mint Certificate Program**. The **PMCP** offers investors the option of holding all the major precious metals: gold, silver, platinum, and palladium.

The Perth Mint Certificate offers unrivaled security and accessibility. There is also another superb feature for the private investor. There are no set certificate sizes to which your holdings must conform (aside from the minimums). This entirely flexible program allows you to tailor your precious metals purchase to whatever amount suits your individual needs.

The Perth Mint Certificate is available to individual, private investors through an Approved Dealer network maintained and certified by the Perth Mint. Your certificate may be purchased and liquidated very simply. I'll show you how to purchase your certificate in just a moment. First let's take a look at how easy it is to sell your gold.

You can liquidate your certificate easily and free up your cash quickly in two ways. The first and most convenient way is to simply sell the certificate back to an Approved Dealer. The second is to take physical delivery of the precious metals represented on the certificate either at the Perth Mint, or arrange for physical delivery at a variety of locations worldwide.

If you want, you can also surrender just a portion of the precious metals on the certificate. This aspect is another of the program's distinct advantages. You can surrender any part of your certificate, as long as you continue to meet the established minimums. A new certificate is issued for the remainder of your precious metals, for which you are charged a small additional fee.

How do you know for sure how much gold you have? Or how pure is it? Well, the Perth Mint warrants the precise unit or interest held in each certificate. It also warrants the quantity and authenticity of bullion coins. Likewise, the hallmark, purity, and weight of bullion bars are guaranteed. The gold you buy in certificate form will come directly from Gold Corporation's own refinery. The other precious metals are all produced at the Mint under an exclusive agreement with the Australian Commonwealth Government.

The fees to purchase a Perth Mint Certificate are very low. Besides the purchase price of the precious metals, there is only a US$50 certificate fee. That is what you pay regardless of how large the amount of the certificate. For allocated storage only, there is an additional prepaid storage fee. This works out to 1% for gold and platinum, 2% for silver, and 2% for palladium per annum. The only other fee is the Approved Dealer's commission. There is no charge for unallocated storage at all.

Not only is the PMCP simple, but it is economical to use as well. There are also some excellent tax advantages for non-residents holding precious metals in Australia. There are no Australian duties on the import, export, or domestic purchase and sale of high purity precious metal bars or bullion coins.

International clients are only required to pay capital gains tax if they are residents for tax purposes. Clients should consult their taxation advisers for specific taxation advice.

Gold You Can Hold—But Can't Lose

Earlier, I said that you could fold your gold up and carry it around with you. That's exactly what I meant. If you wanted, you could go down to the supermarket or go out to your favorite restaurant with it.

What if you lose your Perth Mint certificate or it's stolen? You simply get a replacement certificate. You just file a lost certificate declaration form with the Perth Mint, and pay a small certificate re-issuance fee. No one can use your certificate without the specified ID and authorized signature that you gave when you purchased it.

I believe that the **PMCP** is the only way to make the most of the desirability of precious metals. It combines the flexibility and accessibility that the smart investor requires from his assets—security and freedom in one package.

Originally published: *Investing in Gold,* **2004**

Michael Checkan is the president of Asset Strategies International, Inc. ASI specializes in precious metals, foreign currencies, and overseas wealth protection. For more information on the Perth Mint Certificate Program *contact: Michael Checkan, President, Asset Strategies International, Inc., 1700 Rockville Pike, Suite 400, Rockville, Maryland USA 20852 toll-free (800) 831-0007 or (301) 881-8600; fax (301) 881-1936; e-mail: rcheckan@assetstrategies.com.*

4 Hidden Asset Classes You Should Consider

By Dr. Steve Sjuggerud, PhD

I spend most of my time discussing stocks, bonds, mutual funds... as well as "other" asset classes, such as real estate or gold. But there are still other asset classes out there. These are things that nobody talks about—the "**hidden**" assets that will provide good diversification to your portfolio—assets I recommend you invest in with no more than 5% of your investable funds.

But the truth is—these types of investments are not for everyone. If, however, this investment class interests you, and you're ready to further diversify by exploring some opportunities that you may not have considered before—then this list of investments may be very helpful to you.

Now then... let's take a look at "**4 Hidden Asset Classes You Should Consider**"

1. Hedge Funds or Commodity Trading Funds

These are big "secret" funds for wealthy investors. According to *Barron's*, the 25-largest hedge funds have ***returned 12.3% a year*** annualized over the last three years, an excellent return in comparison with the markets. Though 2002 wasn't quite as exciting (up an average of 4.46%), this was still better than the markets, fulfilling the funds' promise of "***absolute returns***"—positive returns in any market.

Hedge funds are not allowed to advertise. They are not regulated by the SEC (or anyone), and information about them is hard to come by. Minimums can be $1 million or more. Please do a ton of due diligence before even considering investing in hedge funds, as they are not appropriate (or even affordable) for most investors. If you are interested, places and people to start with include John Mauldin (www.johnmauldin.com), Eric Roseman (www.eas.ca), and www.hedgeworld.com. Also, make sure you read the (somewhat one-sided) article at: www.forbes.com/2001/08/06/070.html. It details the "worst-case scenario" of an unregulated entity. Don't miss the sidebar called "The Money Vanishes."

2. Coins

The coin market looks good right now, for the first time in many years. For some perspective, here's why coins look good...

In brief, rare coins as an "investment" really came into their own in the late 1970s (ownership of gold was restricted until 1975). Gold coins (South African Krugerrands) became hot immediately. Gold soared into 1980, and coins did even better, tripling in value in the 12 months that ended January 1980. Coin values then doubled over the next 12 months. Yes, six times your money in two years. (The exact returns are debatable, but we can all agree that coins went up a heck of a lot.)

Prices continued to rise until 1986—sort of. At the time, coin industry insiders call what happened "Gradeflation" (a story for another day), where coins weren't *really* worth what they were *quoted* to be worth. This led to the creation of independent grading services, like PCGS, in 1986.

Then the really big boom came—1988 to 1990. Now that there were legitimate independent graders of coins, *Wall Street was going to start offering mutual funds of rare coins.* $100+ million was supposed to be invested by Wall Street firms, and this anticipation drove coin prices through the roof, doubling in the 12 months that ended with June 1989. The outbreak of the Gulf War and a 500-point fall in the stock market abruptly halted Wall Street's plans, and the coin market went into a tailspin.

The coin market didn't actually find a bottom until 1994-1995. Since then, it has only been a shadow of its former self. Prices have been slowly rising since then. I think that 1994-1995 was the worst it could possibly get, and that's a nice "support" level for coin prices... the BOTTOM, as this chart shows: www.pcgs.com/images/graphs/indexallgraph.gif.

3. Interest-Paying Foreign Currency Investments

I recently had lunch with Frank Trotter, CEO of Everbank (www.everbank.com). Everbank's World Markets division offers foreign currency CDs that are easy for you (in the States) to do. I will say that it was the first time I'd met Frank, and liked him. The lunch meeting gave me even more confidence in his company's products. You can earn 5% or more in interest in some foreign currency CDs. And if the currency strengthens (or weakens) by 10% versus the dollar, you can either make (or lose) an additional 10%.

Another option is someone like Howard Goldstein (hgoldstein@pfmail.com), who shares his outstanding income ideas with me regularly. He called me this week with a floating rate Australian income investment, where if interest rates go up, your principal won't fall. Howard and I have been good friends for a decade now (his assistant is my cousin Alison, actually). Howard and Alison will take great care of you. They can handle it all, but he's particularly good at international income investments.

4. Fine Art

I find this area intriguing. "*While art does have the disadvantage of being illiquid and lumpy, its high long-term returns and low correlation with stocks may justify serious attention from institutional investors as an alternative investment class,*" says an e-mail I received today from an NYU professor.

"*The last five years yielded a 12.9% annualized return for art versus no increase for stocks,*" it continues. Over the last 50 years, stocks and art have apparently both returned about 11% annually. The full story is available for free (though you have to register) at www.meimosesfineartindex.org.

Originally published: February 20, 2003 in Investment U

How to Evaluate a Small Mining Stock

By Rick Rule

Successful speculation in junior gold stocks has to solve one riddle: How do you anticipate exploration successes before the financial community reacts to them?

The 12-year bear market in gold has given you one leg up. The bear dismantled the research and information infrastructure for precious metal stocks. In the late '70s and early '80s, the big Wall Street firms employed hundreds of brokers who specialized in gold stocks, and dozens of 'hard money' newsletters thrived. Since nobody gives medals to yesterday's heroes, most of those gold experts long ago moved to greener pastures.

Here's another leg up: A successful speculator builds a diversified portfolio. Placing all your eggs in one basket often breaks your basket. Always prefer a group of intelligently selected speculations to one large bet, no matter how compelling the story. A contrarian, counter-cyclical orientation helps as well.

In exploration and speculation, one thing never changes: Success favors the trained observer. Luck follows those who use the best tools with consistent discipline. Here are some other tools. The right answers to the following ten questions can help you decide if you even want to bother following, much less buying, the stock.

Look For Value

Question 1. "What is the current liquidation value of your company versus the market capitalization?"

Compare the company's actual value, if auctioned off tomorrow, against the value the stock market places on all of its shares. If the market cap outweighs the liquidation value, there may be a rat in the feedbag.

Speculation can't stand on one leg alone. You have to forecast both the upside and downside. When promoters are trying to sell a stock, you'll hear how precious metals will soon soar, how exploration will soon hit the Mother Lode, and how their promotion will boost the stock's price. That's all great, but we have to weigh that side against our possible downside, and value is the scale we use. Nothing reduces risk like plain, old value. If a mining company is not a viable business, there's no reason to buy it.

A mining company is only worth what it owns. Add up all the current assets (like cash), subtract the liabilities, and add the liquidation value of the company's mineral projects. Liquidation value means what the projects would bring as is.

What's the market cap? For a rough estimate, multiply outstanding shares by the current market price. With 10 million shares outstanding quoted at $2.50 a share, the market capitalization is $25 million. If this company has $5 million cash and no debt, its net financial assets are 20% of market cap.

Assume the company has four exploration properties. With a cold and steely eye, assign a value to each of them. Now let's add it up. Net financial assets of $5 million and say, property assets of $12.5 million for a "guesstimated" liquidation value of $17.5 million, versus a market capitalization of $25 million. If the management can answer other questions, this could be a sensible speculation. More often, however, we find market capitalizations of $100 million and liquidation values of $2 million.

Look For Personnel

Question 2. "Tell me about your management and directors, especially about their past successes in mining and markets."

Past winners are more likely to be future winners. Why do we need to understand the track record of the technical team, the directors, and the dominant shareholders? Most successful mines are made, not found. It takes technical prowess to unlock the deposit's geology to production. It takes financial prowess to unlock the capital crucial to mining, so the management team must include experienced, proven fundraisers.

Do their skills fit the job? If the team cut its teeth strip mining oxide gold deposits in Nevada, it may break those teeth on an underground silver, lead, zinc sulfide deposit in Peru. Be particularly leery of exploration teams with little production experience who are out to build and operate a mine, rather than to sell the deposit to someone more experienced. The reverse can hold true as well: Mine *operators* are often poor mine *finders*. The tasks don't resemble each other, and what's successful in one field is often unsuited to the other.

Look at the controlling shareholder's track record as well. Has he made money for investors in previous deals? Sorry, it's not enough to make a mine—we want to make money. Be picky here, too. Can the dominant entrepreneur transfer his experience to the project at hand?

Look For The Means

Question 3. "How are you going to make me money on this deal, and when will I make it?"

This is the question the promoters want you to ask, but make sure you control the conversation so they actually answer it. I once heard a stockbroker explaining a venture capital investment in a technological process. One potential investor asked, "How does the process work?" The broker replied, "It works fine!" Beware of such answers.

Make the promoter explain in detail how the company's exploration activities will increase both shareholder value and stock price. Why? We want to understand what sequence of events management believes will occur over that time, and how that will affect share prices. We must assign probabilities to the outcomes forecast, and understand their timing and sensitivity. If management doesn't have a plan outlined, it's probably too early to buy.

If the company refuses to keep us informed, or if they promise but don't deliver, we must consider selling the stock. If management doesn't have a geological theory with a plan to explore and prove it, it's probably too early to buy. If the results achieved are below what we've been led to expect, we should sell the stock.

What Are The Goals and Strategies?

Question 4. "What are the company's goals, and how are they going to reach those goals?"

Thousands of public companies specializing in precious metals exploration litter the investment landscape. The vast majority has always failed. Many "penny miners" have, at best, only sketchy goals. Most have none. Small wonder they couldn't achieve anything—they didn't set out to!

When a company expresses goals, make them get specific. Ask about intended results on a per-share basis. What do you care if cash flow doubles and issued shares increase tenfold? Will the company's expressed goals increase share prices? Some entrepreneurs simply seek to increase the assets they're managing to secure their own cash flow.

Do the company's goals seem reasonable? Will they raise share prices if they bear fruit? If the answers are "yes," then ask if the company's strategy fits its goals. Many companies look like Don Quixote on his battle-mule: Their goals sound grand, but they have no clue how to reach them. Measure their goals against the backdrop of the people. What is their track record for meeting their goals? Have they succeeded in similar endeavors? Are their backgrounds suited to their strategies?

Where's The Money?

Question 5. "How much money do you have, how much money do you need to make me rich, and how are you going to get it?"

Watch the white-leather-shoe boys blanch when you pop this question on them. Mineral exploration is a capital-intensive business: No capital, no business!

Start with current assets (cash, treasuries, bank deposits, inventories, prepaid expenses and the like) and deduct current liabilities. This should give you a rough idea of the net working capital. Get a detailed description of monthly "burn rate." What does it cost for rent, utilities, salaries, promotion expenses, professionals fees, listing expenses, etc.? Then superimpose projected exploration expenditures on a monthly basis. If the company has any debt, make sure to add in interest and principal payments.

This exercise narrows the playing field fast. Many small public-exploration companies with less than $1 million in net working capital spend $600,000 annually on non-project overhead, while they need to spend several million on exploration to meet goals (and make us money).

Finally, where will they get the money they need? Years ago at a gold mining conference, I spoke to an erstwhile promoter who didn't know my face. I asked him where he would solve his working capital problems and he informed me that a "hot" west coast broker named Rick Rule would raise all the money he needed at much higher share prices. Imagine his surprise when I identified myself and explained the likelihood of his phantom financing!

When companies detail their financing plans, ask what conditions apply to the receipt of funds. Decide for yourself whether the companies will receive the necessary cash infusions and on what terms. If possible, get the names and phone numbers of their financing sources, then telephone those sources and verify that the capital is available. See if the preconditions and terms match the company's own understanding.

Where Is The Owner?

Question 6. "Who owns this company? How much did they (or will they) pay for it, and when can they sell it?"

Make the company explain its capitalization history to you. If there were escrow or founders shares (shares issued for $0.01 to early insiders), who got them, for what service, and when will they be free to trade them? Determine at what price every financing has taken place. Is the stock from those financings already free trading, or can it hit the market later to depress share prices? How many options and warrants are outstanding? At what price can holders exercise them?

What About Promotion?

Question 7. "Who else will you tell this story to, how will you tell them, and when?"

Promotion often makes the difference between success and failure. Promotion is crucial in capital-intensive businesses because it raises subsequent financing with less dilution and increased liquidity and share prices. Since exploration companies seldom pass out gold watches to thirty-year shareholders, you want increasing share prices.

Make the company (preferably its promoter) detail its promotional plan. Who is the audience? What is the message? Who is the messenger? Do the three mix? What is the promotional budget? Is that sufficient? How will the promoter raise additional capital? At what price, and from whom?

Companies must budget at least $150,000 annually for promotion. Sad, but true. At least two management road shows through Toronto, New York, and London should be scheduled annually and one yearly tour of the company's focus properties for analysts. North American companies that don't appear at the "gold shows" are almost automatic losers.

Institutional investors finance exploration, but retail investors provide market liquidity. Promoting to only one constituency is a flawed strategy. Promoting to retail investors should take into account that Canada has 27 million people, and the U.S. has 260 million. Will they spend their money in markets that have the money?

Most Canadian companies know almost nothing about U.S. securities regulations. Promoting in the U.S. is against American regulations and will get rougher and tougher. Make sure that the promoter knows and complies with federal and state laws. If the promoters are not aware of these regulations and don't have concrete plans for complying, forget about their stocks. In fact, if they don't have plans to list on NASDAQ or AMEX, greatly discount the rest of their promotional plans.

Where Can It Go Wrong?

Question 8. "What can go wrong, how can I know what is going wrong, and what will you do if it goes wrong?"

If company management can't name at least three things that could go wrong, they haven't thought through their enterprise. Make them describe the three worst fears for you as a minority shareholder.

Make the promoter describe specifically how you as a shareholder will get negative information and warnings. Ask what telltale signs you should look for and how you will get information (by fax is the best answer) to help you assess these risks day-by-day.

Who Is Your Promoter?

Question 9. "Who's buying the beer?"

If a company has answered these questions in reasonably good form, get to know the promoter personally. No company will answer every question perfectly, but candor and reasonable responses will tell you whom to spend more time with. As you build a bond with the promoter, get him to tell the real story. Because your interrogation took control of the promoter's spiel, you have helped him order his thoughts about his company. Now let him lapse into "streams of consciousness," and listen carefully for tidbits of information you would never get from his canned spiel.

Where's The Dope?

Question 10. "Where can I learn more?"

If you are still interested, this could be a great company. Get their annual and quarterly reports as far back as you can. Read what they hoped to accomplish, and compare that to what they did accomplish. Get newsletter write-ups, securities analysis' reports, and news releases as far back as you can. One final trick: Summarize your understandings in writing and see if you can get the promoters to accept your memo as true and correct. Hold them to their representations.

Most of you will skim this article and say, "I'm glad Global Resource Investments does this so I don't have to." Relying on our opinion with your money increases your risks. Many of you will choose to take that risk, but one word of warning to those who won't do the work: If you want a broker to answer these questions, don't even think about asking, "How do your commissions compare to Charles Schwab?"

Originally published in December 2003

Rick Rule is principal shareholder and senior analyst for Global Resource Investments, Ltd. Rick began his career in the securities business in 1974, and has been involved in natural resource security investments ever since. He is a leading analyst specializing in mining, energy, water, forest products, and agriculture. Rick is a regular speaker at investment conferences and resource investment forums throughout the world. Global Resource Investments provides investment advice and brokerage service to individuals, corporations, and institutions worldwide.

For more information on Global Resource Investments, contact Rick Rule and his team—call: (800) 477-7853 or (760) 943-3939; write to Global Resource Investments, 7770 El Camino Real, Carlsbad, CA 92009, or go to: www.globalresourceinvestments.com.

To read Rick's free reports on investing in junior gold stocks, go to: www.gril.net.

Chapter 5

Real Estate

3 Secrets to Successful Real Estate Investing

By Dr. Steve Sjuggerud, PhD

"Buy land—they aren't making any more of it."
~ Will Rogers

I'm sure you know a person or two that have made a lot of money in real estate. What was the secret to their success? Did they do something special? Or do you think real estate prices just keep going up, and they were in the right place at the right time?

Do you feel like real estate prices are now too high to even consider real estate investing? How do you know?

Well, I've asked you a lot of questions. Now it's time to get to some answers grounded in facts, not myths (as myths are the usual ways real estate investment advice is passed around).

The first important fact that will probably surprise you is that housing prices have only risen by about 2% a year since the 1960s, adjusted for inflation. I know you're thinking "that can't be true," but it is. The reality is that home prices have risen about 6% a year, but inflation was about 4% over that period.

So the people you know who have made a lot of money in real estate probably didn't just make it on overall market price appreciation alone. They must have known something. And that something, I'd be willing to bet, is one of the three principles to success in real estate we'll cover in just a moment.

When it comes to real estate, no matter what you're looking at, there are only three things you need to understand (and no, it's not "Location, Location, Location!"). Once you understand these things, you can apply the principles to all kinds of real estate investments, from houses to bigger opportunities—REITs and commercial properties.

Investment Rule #1: Don't Pay Too Much for the Earth

The first rule of successful real estate investing is: **Don't pay too much for the earth**.

This may seem obvious. But many people fall in love with a particular property and are willing to pay any price. If you're not buying for investment purposes, but for touchy-feely reasons instead, think again.

Buying at what you can determine is at least a 10% discount (AFTER estimated closing costs and estimated renovations) to what you can determine is the true market value of the property is an important part of the investing in real estate puzzle.

Personally, I've been very successful buying homes this way. I've been fortunate enough to buy at discounts of about 20% to the market value based on comparable sales per square foot in the area.

The keys for me, I believe, have been that:

1. I was willing to walk away from the deal (it didn't *have* to be *that* house).
2. The houses I bought showed terribly but were fine structurally.
3. The owners lived out of state and didn't have a strong emotional attachment to the house.

These keys have worked for me. I think they are all extremely important, and I could go on about them. For the sake of space, please just read them again and think about each one and how it can improve your chances of buying at an attractive price. But ultimately, the point is, don't ever overpay. There are plenty of other properties to choose from.

In addition to buying at a discount, another thing to keep in mind is that there's another way to size up the property.

Don't pay too much for the business.

What do I mean by "the business?" Well, I'm talking about a rental house or other investment property here. A simple rule of thumb would be you want to earn a 10% yield or more, and I'm talking net rental yield.

If you can net a return of 10% or more on rent, after estimated expenses, chances are, you'll probably do pretty darn well. But 10% net rental yields are hard to come by.

Rule #2: Don't Fight Interest Rates

When the Fed is hiking rates, when mortgage rates are rising, or when interest rates have been rising in general, housing prices suffer. It makes sense. People can afford a particular mortgage payment. If interest rates go up, the amount of house they can afford for the same mortgage payment goes down.

You can think of mortgage rates like the tides. The tide is going to come in—there's no holding it back. Housing prices will suffer under rising interest rates. If the tide is rising, don't fight it.

Fortunately, the tide eventually goes out. Interest rates eventually start falling again.

A good rule of thumb is, if the most recent 10% move in mortgage rates is against you (rates going up), there's no hurry to buy. Fortunately, housing prices move glacially. However, once mortgage rates have moved 10% in your favor (lower), prices will start moving higher.

The best place to follow mortgage rates on the web is www.bankrate.com.

Have your homework done ahead of time, and be ready to act swiftly when the interest rate environment improves.

Rule #3: Don't Fight the Price Trend

My parents-in-law bought two oceanfront lots in Florida for $20,000 back in the 1970s. After owning the lots for 20 years, they sold one and built a house on the other and still live there now. Today, the lot they sold is probably worth a half a million dollars or more. Unfortunately, they sold in the early 1990s for $70,000 or so.

One of the keys to making money in real estate is not selling too early—to let the price trend run its course. Another key is pulling the trigger without hesitation when it's time to sell.

For most people, as soon as they see a profit in their home, they immediately consider selling it to get something else.

The problem is people don't really think about the fact that every other house in the neighborhood has probably risen by about the same percentage. So instead of really making money, due to all of the transaction costs involved, people end up losing money in the deal.

Transaction costs can kill great returns in the short run. If your house has appreciated by 15% since you bought it a year ago, and you sell it today, nearly all of your gains will probably be eaten up by transaction costs that you paid going in, coming out, and going in again.

The Profit Cycles of Real Estate

Again, like interest rates, real estate moves in waves. "Cycles" is probably a better way to describe this phenomenon.

The bottom of the cycle is DEPRESSION in the property markets. This is generally characterized by low prices, no new construction, high vacancies, low rents, etc. Eventually, the depression bottoms out when you start to hear things like "nobody will ever make money in property again."

Then the RECOVERY miraculously materializes out of thin air. Prices are no longer falling. Neither are rents. Occupancy rates start to rise. Yet there's still no new construction.

Next, optimism takes over, and the BOOM sets in. Construction cranks up at a furious pace. Prices and rents rise rapidly. You know the top has arrived when everyone thinks real estate is now "a sure thing."

Then, out of nowhere, the DOWNTURN arrives. All the overbuilding started to get carried away, and some generally bad ideas are hatched in the midst of all the frenzy. Returns on real estate start to shrink.

Then we start all over again. It's amazing how it's all common sense. Yet the same sequence seems to play itself out every four to six years.

Summing up the three rules:

Rule #1: Don't pay too much for the earth OR for the business.
Rule #2: Don't fight the interest rates.
Rule #3: Don't fight the price trend.

Originally published: February 2003 in True Wealth

For more information on Dr. Sjuggerud's True Wealth, go to www.stansberryresearch.com, and follow the "True Wealth" link in the middle of the page.

The Key to Real Estate Investing: Know Your Risks

By Dr. Steve Sjuggerud, PhD

There are smart reasons to invest in real estate, and there are dumb reasons. The truth is, for example, that we can't know for sure whether what's happening in real estate right now (in 2003) is the formation of a "bubble." But if you're investing for the "right" reasons—and you know your risks—chances are your investment will be a good one.

While the topic of real estate is just too big to cover in one short note, I'll cover some of the major points that you've got to keep in mind.

1. Speculating vs. Investing:

Buying a chunk of land and hoping it goes up in value is SPECULATING. Buying a property to collect high income in the form of rent is INVESTING. When you compare investors who speculated in Nasdaq stocks in 2000 (and lost it all) to those who invested in bonds and smartly collected income, the difference in risk between speculating and investing is obvious. Investing is a much safer (and smarter) way to go.

2. "Property Will Always Go Up in Value:"

Don't believe this dangerous myth! Property prices in Japan have fallen by 75% over the last decade—about the same amount that Nasdaq stocks have fallen since 2000. Hoping for—or worse, expecting—a price rise is speculation. Make sure the investment makes great sense from a positive cash-flow perspective first. Then if the property falls in value, you're still "right side up" on your cash flows. Consider any appreciation to be simply icing on the cake.

3. Start With Residential Property:

It's easier to understand, purchase, and manage than other types of property. If you're a homeowner, you've already got experience here. And you're the boss. Start close to home, so you can stay on top of things.

4. Don't Believe Everything You Hear or Read:

Sellers and real estate agents ultimately want you to buy the property they're showing. So what they're telling you is most likely the rosy scenario, not the actual scenario. If the property has been a rental, ask the seller for his Schedule E from his taxes. It'll show his ACTUAL revenue and expenses, or at least the ones he reported to the government. What you can expect to earn is somewhere between what he reported to the IRS and what he's promising you.

5. Where to Buy:

There is—as you probably know—a widely held belief that the three most important factors involved in real estate success are "Location, Location, Location." But real estate expert John T. Reed (www.johntreed.com) actually says there's MORE profit in less desirable locations. Reed looks for what he calls a "double-digit cap rate." As an example, if you net $1,000 a month in rent on a $100,000 investment, that's $12,000 a year, or 12% of $100,000. That's a double-digit return that year, or a double-digit cap rate. The catch is that this is NET rent or rent AFTER expenses. My parents have had rental properties for decades. And off the top of his head, my father suggests that 5-10% is close to what really happens,

One Investor's Secret to Finding Good Tenants

By Mike Palmer

A friend of mine, who makes his living entirely with real estate, recently told me one of his secrets for finding good tenants. If you own rental real estate, you might want to try the same thing.

Other than the obvious things, such as checking credit and business references, as well as other landlord references, my friend recommends that you do the following: Be willing to rent to people with kids or pets.

Most landlords shy away from these tenants because of the extra wear and tear on their properties. But the truth is, such tenants are usually not only more responsible... they tend to stay longer than individuals or couples because they know they'll have a hard time finding a new place. All you have to do is charge a larger security deposit.

even after doing your homework. (Conclusion: There are no get-rich-quick schemes here.)

6. Check Out Your Potential Renters Thoroughly:

You know all the horror stories here. But with the Internet, there's no excuse for not investigating potential renters. For next to nothing, you can know everything about someone: Check references, police reports, employment/credit histories, past occupancies, everything. This occupant is your sole source of income from this property. Do what you can to keep him or her from being a liability.

For more information on True Wealth, go to www.stansberryresearch.com and follow the "True Wealth" link in the middle of the page.

7 Rules for Buying Investment Properties

By Michael Masterson

I know Delray Beach pretty well. I own homes here and have bought and sold more than a dozen properties in my neighborhoods. I have been able to observe firsthand the growth in real-estate prices since the mid-1990s. And I know a good number of people who are active in the real estate market.

The big secret about real estate that I have learned (at least for making money in the short term) is to buy good property at or below market value. And no matter what the popular books tell you, you won't be able to do that on a regular basis unless you take the time to get out there and find the best deals yourself.

These are the rules I have set for myself:

1. Don't own real estate from afar.

2. Buy only in proven, up-and-coming neighborhoods, or those that border on the same.

3. Never buy a house for rental that, when improved, will have cost more than $125,000. I've found that it's very hard to rent out a home consistently if the monthly rental is more than $2,000, which means you can't hope to get a good rate of return on your money. In the $125,000-plus range, I buy homes to spruce up and "flip."

4. Figure out how much you're paying on a square-foot basis, trying to keep it as close to $100 per square foot as possible. That number is relative to the particular market. In Delray Beach, for example, nice homes in nice neighborhoods sell for $200 per square foot. I'd rather be down around $100 to leave room for improvements and margins for commissions.

5. Buy only homes where you can get a $2 to $4 return on every $1 you spend fixing them up. This is actually easier to determine than you might think. The trick is to buy a house priced considerably under the market and then redo it as cheaply as possible.

6. Spend money improving the house, but only where it matters. Paint. Put up cheap shutters and awnings. Replace cabinet doors and carpeting. Put ceramic tile on countertops. And landscape the entryway. Those are the main upgrade opportunities. Everything else you might do—including plumbing and electrical work—will

probably not be a good investment.

7. If possible, have a renter for your house before you buy it. If you let the word out sufficiently often, your friends and colleagues will think of you when they meet someone who is looking for a place to stay.

That said, there is still much that is nebulous about determining value.

For example, is the two-bedroom ranch house that I saw on 13th Street and Seacrest worth the $150,000 being asked for it? In my judgment, it is. But I think virtually the same house one block away on 12th and Seacrest is overpriced at $120,000.

You can't answer those kinds of questions unless you have a very good feel for the neighborhood. And, as I said, you can't have a very good feel for a neighborhood unless (a) you limit your investing to a particular area—preferably in your own hometown—and (b) you are willing to drive around that neighborhood and ask questions.

If you can do those two things, real estate can work for you.

Think about it. And start looking.

Originally published: April 25, 2002 in Early to Rise

Michael Masterson is a multi-millionaire who has started, run, and sold literally dozens of businesses—everything from jewelry and art shops to vitamin and publishing businesses. He writes the daily business and investing coaching service called Early to Rise. If you want to learn the secrets of a very successful businessman and investor, go to www.earlytorise.com.

How to Determine the P/E Ratio of your House

By Dr. Steve Sjuggerud, PhD

When I'm considering real estate VALUE, whether it's a real estate stock or a property, there are two value rules: ***Don't Pay Too Much for the Earth and Don't Pay Too Much for the Business.***

"Don't pay too much for the earth" is simple. For a real estate STOCK, I don't pay more than a 10% premium to the market value of the properties. And when it comes to buying a house, you'd better think long and hard before you'd consider paying a 10% premium to comparable values in the neighborhood. I much prefer to buy at a 20% discount. If you're not too picky, it's actually not hard to do (if you're willing to do a little sprucing up after buying).

"Don't pay too much for the business" is simple as well. Just like a stock, look at the P/E ratio… "The P/E ratio? Of real estate?" You're probably thinking I've lost my mind. I haven't. A lot of real estate out there has "earnings"—it's called rent. While real estate prices can fluctuate anywhere in the short run, in the long run, property prices are significantly driven by rental values. *If you look at the "Price-to-earnings" ratio of your property, you can learn about your home's true "intrinsic" value.* As a good rule of thumb, net rents in real estate (by "net," I mean after expenses) have averaged about 1% above Treasury bonds (that's the way it's been with real estate stocks since 1990).

The Treasury bond is at 5.15% as I write, so we might guess that the nationwide average net rent is 6.15%. *(EDITOR'S NOTE: 6.15% is the "earnings-to-price" ratio, so we need to find the inverse of it for the P/E of your house. To find the inverse, we simply divide the percentage into 100, or 100 ÷ 6.15, which equals 16.)*

If that "1% above Treasuries" rule is correct, that means the "fair" value for a home now, based on net rental earnings, should be a price-to-earnings ratio of 16. Where I live, that means the big gains in real estate so far have just brought us up to FAIR value now—there's still plenty of room to run before things get overpriced.

How can you figure the P/E for your property? *Forbes* suggests the only real way to know: "To get rental data for homes comparable to the one you're buying or selling, check with the relocation department of big real estate agencies." You've got to know what the comparable net rents are to your property. This is all a very rough guide. Once you've figured your P/E, it may be very different from the current nationwide fair value P/E guess of 16. If your P/E is low, you may have gotten a good deal, or you could collect high rents from your place. If your P/E is twice as high as 16, you ought to consider selling.

The tricky thing about selling real estate is that real estate is not liquid. Unlike stocks, where we have the luxury of being able to sell whenever we want and the luxury of trailing stops to get us out exactly when we want out, determining when to sell real estate is not so easy. You, unfortunately, need to be a good guesser, because you actually need to sell into an "up" market, and buy in a down market. While this can't be done successfully on a regular basis, you can improve your chances considerably by doing what works in the stock market as well. I found that you *never* make money in stocks over the long run when the P/E of the market is above 17. While I don't have the data on homes, the numbers may be very similar. So if you live in

Boston, or Silicon Valley, now may be a time to get out close to the top.

Originally published in True Wealth, May 28, 2002

For more information on True Wealth, go to www.stansberryresearch.com, and follow the "True Wealth" link in the middle of the page.

How to Make Sure You Always Get a Fair Price

By Justin Ford

I'm going to describe one technique that will help you quickly determine how much a property is worth. Use it and you'll never have to rely on a broker's potentially inflated figures or worry about overpaying.

It's best to determine your own property values, because your broker has a significant conflict of interest. He makes a commission as a percentage of the sales price, so he tends to prefer estimating the worth of a property as high as possible. As a buyer, on the other hand, you want the property valued as low as possible.

By learning how to do your own, quick "comparable-sales analysis," you can get a very good idea of the current market value of any property you're thinking of buying—giving you leverage when negotiating and helping you quickly spot below-market values.

What Your Neighbor Paid for His Home

By Mike Palmer

If you're looking to buy a house, here's a valuable tool you'll want to use. The folks at Motley Fool have put together a website database of purchase prices for more than 20 million homes recently sold across the United States.

You can use it to find out what just about any home sold for recently.

It's a great way to compare prices. Your real estate agent can do the same thing through the Multiple List Service, but this database allows you to quickly do your own research.

You can search the database by street, price range, or by a specific address. The site claims to cover "over 84% of the top metro areas in the country, and 80% of the U.S."

The only problem with this database is that you'll have to wait at least six weeks from a house transaction's closing date to see the price appear. It's free, by the way. Go to http://fool.homepricecheck.com/.

So how do you do it? The same way your county's property appraiser finds out how much tax to charge you—primarily by looking at recent sales of comparable homes in your neighborhood (which are a matter of public record).

A very important note, however: Make sure you're looking only at actual sales values, not at "appraised values," to use as your guide for determining market value. The difference, for tax purposes, can be significant because of special exemptions given to homeowners.

The Secret Home-Repair History of Any House

By Mike Palmer

Most people don't know there's a way for you to do a background check on any house you're thinking about buying.

It's called a C.L.U.E. report, which stands for Comprehensive Loss Underwriting Exchange. This database is made up of more than 90% of the companies that insure homes. These reports will give you the details on any homeowner's insurance claims filed on a particular home.

Although you can't order a C.L.U.E. report on someone else's property, you can ask the seller to provide one for you. The price of the report varies, depending on where you live. In my home state of Maryland, and in a handful of other states, it's free. Elsewhere, a C.L.U.E report rarely costs more than $8.

A C.L.U.E. report can help you in two ways:

First, it will let you know if there's a history of significant damage, such as roof problems or flooding.

Second, if you see a history of high claims, you'll know that it may be hard for you to get a good deal on homeowner's coverage. You may be able to use that information as a negotiating point. For more information, go to **www.choicetrust.com**. Click on "home," and scroll down to "C.L.U.E. Personal Property Report."

In some counties, these records are completely accessible online. In others, however, you have to physically visit the office of the Tax Assessor or Property Appraiser. Also, some counties allow access to these records free of charge, while others may charge a nominal fee.

To find out which office you need to contact, call your county government and ask which office is in charge of the "property-sales-tax records." You should also be able to find the appropriate department in the "blue pages" (government listings) of your local phone book. When you connect with the right place, ask if they have an online database that displays property tax and sales records.

Whether you're collecting your data in person or online, there is certain information you need to watch for and specific techniques you can use to make your research more efficient.

With most databases, you can search for a property by

using such criteria as an address, parcel number, subdivision, or even the owner's name. Begin with the property's address. Look for—and jot down—information like the property's sales history and square footage. And make a note of the parcel number, subdivision, and owner. This type of information can help you take advantage of more sophisticated and super-efficient search techniques.

But you can quickly take the first step in the property-investment process by using the easily accessible records made available by your local tax assessor to quickly compute the average square-foot prices in your area. Do this now and you'll have the numbers you need, at your fingertips, to make sure you're always buying local real estate at a good value. This is crucially important, because the secret to making money in real estate is to buy right in the first place.

Originally published: January 26, 2004 in Early to Rise

Justin Ford is the author of Main Street Millionaire, a step-by-step program on how to make real estate investing as profitable and low-risk as possible. For more information, go to: www.agora-inc.com/reports/XRE/WXREDWEB/.

Investing in Real Estate: Buying and Selling Fixer-Uppers

By Michael Masterson

Buying and selling fixer-uppers may be the best-known way of making money in real estate. The no-money-down real-estate gurus tend to focus on this area because the numbers can look very good, especially when you get into low-income housing.

It's not as fast and easy as some say, but it can work. First, I'll tell you how to buy properties in "bad" neighborhoods. Then, I'll tell you what to do once you've built up enough money to invest in better properties.

Getting Started

If you're on a tight budget and want to start with inexpensive properties, you'll be buying houses in the poorest part of town. That will make you (from some perspectives) the worst kind of capitalist pig—one who "gentrifies" ethnic neighborhoods.

Poor neighborhoods are generally ethnic neighborhoods, so, unless you are of the group you are "exploiting," you'll probably be categorized as some sort of local robber baron.

You'll know how ridiculous such thinking is. But your neighbor—the woman who went to Vassar and makes a living promoting rich-lady wine-tasting tours in Tuscany—will secretly despise you. Oh, well.

Meanwhile, you will be busy:

* Studying the neighborhood before you buy into it
* Buying a cheap house, even by local standards
* Fixing it up to sell it fast
* Selling it to the first person who buys, regardless of race, creed, or color. (That's the part that will make people think you're un-American.)

In order to make this a part-time business, you'll have to develop a network of workers—reliable tradesmen who won't overcharge you—to take care of all the fixing up.

From what I've learned, there are two things you should do to make this type of investing profitable:

1. Don't hunt and peck for houses. Target a specific area and plan to eventually buy up many if not most of the homes in that area. That way, you will get the benefit of having a neighborhood go up in value along with the individual units you are buying.

2. If you can, select a target area that has at least one border on the outside. By "the outside," I mean a better neighborhood. Giving your potential buyers the feeling that they are buying into a section of a neighborhood that has a corridor to safety will increase—significantly—the value of every house in that section. It will also give you a wider market. (This is where you'll be accused of gentrifying.)

What you look for in terms of structure in a buy-and-sell situation is very different from what you look for when you are buying rental property. When you are going to be a landlord, you want to buy a property that has no significant structural problems—roofing, plumbing, etc.

For a buy-and-sell home, you simply want to make sure everything is working now and will be working for another year or so. The more important consideration—at least from the profit angle—is how much "under market" you can buy it for.

What you'll want to do is buy a $60,000 home in a neighborhood where most of the homes sell for $75,000, make it look 100% better for about $5,000, and then sell it for $73,000 in less than three months.

Sometimes, you'll be able to do better than that. But you don't want to hold onto a property for more than 90 days if you can possibly avoid it. Even if you make a smaller profit—say $5,000 to $10,000—it's better to get out of a slow-selling house and into another that will sell quickly.

In the buy-and-sell real-estate business, it's all about moving quickly.

That also pertains to the fixing up you'll be doing. Don't take on anything that might require long-term renovation. Avoid bad roofs, serious electrical problems, and "issues" with sewage or flooding.

Spend your money on quick-and-easy stuff like painting, landscaping, and carpeting. If you can't make the property look considerably more valuable with such "cosmetic" changes, you probably shouldn't buy it.

Buying Properties in Not-so-Bad Neighborhoods

But you don't HAVE TO start at the bottom. If you have more money to invest, you can do all of the above in a better neighborhood. In fact, if you can, I'd advise it.

The higher the level of fixer-upper you can buy, the more money you're going to make. Neighborhoods tend to be priced within certain price ranges. But those ranges are determined by percentages, not absolute numbers.

Generally speaking, the range is about 30%. That means that in a neighborhood of homes with a mean selling price of $90,000, the vast majority of individual homes would be priced between, say, $75,000 and $105,000. A neighborhood of homes with a mean selling price of $60,000 would have a range between $50,000 and $70,000. And one with a mean selling price of $400,000 would have a range between $340,000 and $460,000.

Rule of thumb: The more expensive the fixer-upper you do, the more money you'll make from it. So start where you need to and graduate to more expensive properties as you go.

My brother-in-law's experience illustrates this. Since he got into this business two years ago, he's made a decent living with his "bad-neighborhood" investments. He turns over an average of three or four a year at a $20,000 profit for each. Recently, however, he fixed up a $170,000 house that he moved into. When he was offered $275,00 for it a year later, he happily vacated.

Buying Properties in Really Good Neighborhoods

I know a lot of builders. And many of them play the musical-home game. It goes like this: They buy a relatively inexpensive home in a pricey neighborhood (say, a

$550,000 home in a $700,000 neighborhood). They move in and use their resources to fix it up over a period of time—usually six months to a year. They can't really afford to live in such an expensive home, but everything is a write-off. Plus, they have plans.

Soon after everything is finished, along comes a buyer—and they are "forced" to sell their home for a $150,000 profit. They invest that money in their next home—a $750,000 home in a $950,000 neighborhood.

One of these guys just moved into my neighborhood. He has put—as near as I can tell—about $1.7 million into a house that could easily fetch $2.7 million. He hasn't told his neighbors that it's up for sale, but I know two brokers who are showing it privately. This is a guy who was living in a $65,000 townhouse 10 years ago.

Originally published: July 26, 2001 in Early to Rise

For more details on Michael Masterson's daily business and investing coaching service, go to www.earlytorise.com.

One Investor's Secret: Buy on the Fringe

By Dr. Steve Sjuggerud, PhD

I know a guy named Gene who's been a full-time real-estate investor for the last nine years. Because of real estate, he has never really had to get a regular job. After graduating from Brown University, Gene went to the University of Florida for a master's degree. But a funny thing happened along the way. He discovered that he could make more money as a real-estate investor than he could ever possibly make in his chosen field. In fact, when he finished his master's, he didn't even bother getting a job in his field.

You see, while in school, Gene bought up a few tiny little properties in Gainesville (where the University of Florida is located) in what he thought were good deals. He spruced them up himself. And he either sold them or rented them out—for truly extraordinary profits.

At that time, it seemed easy—too easy. He felt that he must have been lucky. So he started ordering every course out there on real estate to find out what works. He tried foreclosures, auctions, high-end properties, and low-end properties. He tried them all. But none of them worked nearly as well as his initial instinct. Nine years later, he's learned a lot on the way and is still learning. But he's sticking with his core premise.

Here's what he does: He buys middle- to lower-class properties on the fringe of good neighborhoods. He only buys at what he considers to be a 20% discount or more to the market value of the property. And he only buys when he can net at least 8% a year in rent. That's it. After trying all the hype, that is what works for him.

I asked, "Why middle-to-lower-class properties?" He said, "Look, the lower-class rents are nearly as high as the middle-class rents [I don't remember exactly what Gene said—let's say $600 a month vs. $750 a month]. But the middle-class properties generally sell for twice what the lower-class properties sell for or more. So buying middle-to-lower-class properties, right on the fringe of good neighborhoods, I earn twice the income."

Makes good sense.

He buys right on the fringe of good neighborhoods, where his properties can potentially get swallowed up by expansion of the good neighborhoods and potentially earn him a large profit. But he doesn't count on that. The rents have to be there first.

There's a difference between speculating and investing in real estate. Speculation is buying a chunk of earth and hoping it goes up in value—without considering the rental income. Investing is making sure you get a nice return on your money. Gene only <u>invests</u> in real estate—he only buys properties that will give him a great return on his money now, through rent.

He says a lot of sensible things. For example, when I asked him about economic downturns, he said, "There will always be a demand for the properties I buy. In an economic downturn, middle-class folks move down to these so they can pay rent. And in an economic upturn, lower-class folks will move up."

I asked him about rent collection and property destruction, both of which might be issues in a lower-class neighborhood. He says he gets a huge security deposit and his leases are written such that the residents know that if they screw up, they lose their deposits. Also, Gene makes sure that every deal he does makes sense even if up to 40% of the rent he collects goes away due to expenses or bad tenants.

Gene told me he tried more expensive homes but the return wasn't there. He said that many "investors" own such homes just to say that they own them. But the real money to be made is in properties that nobody else is willing to take a chance on. He quotes Warren Buffett's margin-of-safety concept, figuring that if you can make a sound enough investment at a low enough discount to the property's underlying value, and get paid handsomely, there's enough margin of safety that you should be fine, regardless of what happens.

After listening to Gene, I started looking at rental properties myself.

Originally published: September 4, 2002 in Early to Rise

For more information on the Early to Rise dialing business and investment coaching service, go to: www.earlytorise.com.

How to Own the Biggest Office Building in Town for $10

By Dr. Steve Sjuggerud, PhD

Commercial real estate has been excellent over the past few decades, with only one down year in the last 25. And the volatility has been much less than stock prices as well. That's why commercial property deserves a place in your portfolio.

But most of us can't go out and buy a big office building, much less a handful of buildings to get some diversification. And most of us wouldn't want to do this even if we could. Buying buildings in our hometowns wouldn't provide us much diversification, and we aren't professional property managers.

You should buy real estate listings on the stock market instead, even though they aren't exactly regular stocks. Yes, for as little as $10 a share on the New York Stock Exchange, you can buy a share of a billion-dollar-plus property portfolio that's professionally managed.

These are just perfect for us. The returns have been comparable to stocks. And with little correlation to the stock market, they provide excellent portfolio diversification.

According to Ibbotsen (a highly respected stock market analysis firm), the correlation of real estate stocks (REITs) to the stock market (the S&P 500) has been 0.25 since 1993, which is basically non-existent. And the correlation of real estate stocks to government bonds has been even less, at 0.16.

If REITs are so good for me, why haven't I heard of them before?

REITs have been the redheaded stepchild of the stock market. As they sometimes say with problem children "if it ain't one thing, it's two things."

Stock investors have traditionally shunned REITs as "boring real estate investments." Real estate investors have traditionally shunned REITs as "risky stock investments." Funny how these are exactly opposite beliefs. The truth really is somewhere in the middle.

REITs haven't been around that long, and the path to get to where we are today has been a rocky one. But this rocky past has now been behind them for years. More and more investors, including institutional investors with very deep pockets, are discovering them every day.

It's nice that REITs trade on the stock exchange. When you want to get out of the real estate business, all you do is sell your stock. It won't take months, and there are no closing costs.

So by investing in REITs, we have a hassle-free way to invest in the best properties in America, with professional management to boot. And you collect healthy dividends from rental income. When REITs offer good values, these dividends can increase by 8% a year or more. Compare that to bonds, which pay you less in income, and have no appreciation potential. Even better, while bonds have no inflation protection against a falling dollar, with real estate you own the land, which can't be eroded like paper investments.

Unlike stocks, the REIT business is fairly predictable. Analysts who follow REITs can generally forecast quarterly results, within a few cents.

When you buy a REIT, you own two things: the real estate, and the business.

Generally, REITs don't have much short-term debt; so short-term moves in interest rates can affect them less than other investments.

The Redheaded Stepchild—The History of REITs

Congress created REITs in 1960, though the first REIT didn't appear until 1963. The law was intended to allow individual investors to invest in real estate with the same tax advantages as the big boys.

The tax advantage of REITs is one of their big selling points. REITs are not subject to corporate income tax. But they must pay out 90% of their earnings to shareholders. Of course, we as shareholders must pay taxes on our REIT dividends.

Only 10 REITs of any size existed during the 1960s. However, from 1968 to the mid-70s, the REIT industry's assets flew from $1 billion to $20 billion. Since REITs were unproven, they were hammered by high interest rates in 1973-74.

REITs fell even further out of favor by 1981, as the "can't miss" investments of real estate limited partnerships came into full swing with Congress's Economic Recovery Act of 1981. REITs were forced to compete for capital with limited partnerships that didn't even have to show a positive cash flow. These limited partnerships would pay outrageous prices for real estate, because it didn't matter, they didn't have to make money.

This all came crumbling down in 1986, with the Tax Reform Act, as Congress changed those laws and crushed the real estate limited partnership tax benefits. By the late 1980s, due to overbuilding and no regard for the bottom line, the real estate market was in trouble.

So the overbuilding of the late 1980s led to the real estate "bear market" that ended by 1991. REITs had now been officially in existence 30 years, and with the exception of a few fleeting moments, had never caught a break.

In 1991, REITs finally hit their stride. As REITs were able to buy at "depression prices" 1991-1993 returns averaged 23.3%. They bought from bust banks, limited partnerships, and the RTC, which had been organized by Congress to acquire and liquidate real estate and real estate loans.

This is what caused what became known as "The REIT IPO Boom" in the early 1990s, and REITs haven't looked back since. At the end of 1990, the value of all publicly traded equity REITs was $5.6 billion. By the end of 1994, it was over $38.8 billion.

1994 is when REITs truly came into their own. In my opinion, there was finally a big enough universe to come up with some valid valuation techniques. In 1993-94, over $30 billion was raised in REIT IPOs. This gave us more choices to invest in. And it gave us a big enough universe to do a proper investment analysis.

Now we can invest in apartments, manufactured home communities, malls, neighborhood shopping centers, outlet malls, offices, industrial properties, hotels, self-storage facilities, hospitals, golf courses, assisted-living facilities, and even prisons.

Of course, after the boom comes oversupply. It's inevitable. The hot money disappeared—it ran off to chase tech stocks.

The REIT market shook this off quickly. A new bull market started in 1996 and equity REITs returned 35%. The universe of companies to choose from is simply much better. The REIT market bottomed again in 2000.

I think that REITs really didn't become an "acceptable" investment until the early-to-mid 1990s. So I think of REITs as an incredibly young asset class. And if the rest of the investment community is doing its homework, it may come to the same conclusions shortly—that REITs provide similar total returns as stocks with little correlation to stocks. So I expect the "big money"—the pension funds and other institutional investors to start taking notice, where they never have before.

Originally published in 2002 in True Wealth

For more information on True Wealth, go to www.stansberryresearch.com and follow the "True Wealth" link in the middle of the page.

How to Profit from the Inefficiencies of Foreign Markets

By Lief Simon

Non-U.S. real estate markets are highly inefficient. (We can debate the efficiency of the U.S. real estate market another time.) There are no multiple listings, no sales histories, no comps, sometimes no real estate agents, and often no agents you can trust.

Sellers find buyers or buyers find sellers almost by chance, and they agree on a price based on how they feel that day. There doesn't have to be a reason why the price is $10,000 more today than it was yesterday. If you are a "gringo buyer" looking at property in Latin America, the asking price is going to be higher than it would be if you were a native, based on the color of your skin... partly because the seller assumes you don't know the local market and partly because the seller assumes you have more money to spend (aren't all North Americans millionaires?). If you accidentally insult the owner, he may not sell to you at any price.

With these inefficiencies come opportunities, even in areas that have seen tremendous recent appreciation. The hotter the market, the greater the challenge, and the more legwork required. But it is possible, even in markets where prices are rising monthly (we know some), to get an amazingly sweet deal.

How?

Start with the local realtors, if there are any, to get an idea of the general market. Ask them what's for sale at what price. Treat this information as what it is: a starting point.

Then hit the streets. Literally. Walk around until you identify the areas or neighborhoods you're interested in. Look for "For Sale" signs. Stop in the local bars and speak casually with whomever will speak with you. It helps if you speak the local language. And it really helps if you have a reliable local contact to act as your front person, someone who can make initial inquiries for you, to be sure you're quoted local market prices, not gringo market prices.

I just went through this process in Granada, Nicaragua. This is a very hot market. Prices for the old colonials in this town have risen tremendously in the past few years, and asking prices increase almost monthly. I looked around with local realtors and was disappointed by the prices quoted. Then I made more discreet inquiries with the help of a local friend. After several visits... he helped me find the house I think I'm going to buy (which is, I must say, an amazingly sweet deal).

Yes, a lot of work. A big investment of time. But the payoff can be tremendous.

Originally published: April 17, 2002 in International Living

Lief Simon lives and works in Ireland and the United States. He has an MBA in International Management from Thunderbird, and has worked for a CPA firm, an international oil company, and as the chief financial officer for a hospitality design and consulting firm that renovates hotels around the world.

He's owned real estate in Europe, Central America, and North America, and he's lived on five continents. Lief is still involved on a day-to-day basis with projects in both Panama and Nicaragua. He manages International Living's real estate investments, oversees International Living's network of offices in The Americas and Europe, and is the editor of Global Real Estate Investor, a small group of the world's savviest real estate investors.

For more information on Lief Simon and International Living, go to: www.internationalliving.com

Chapter 6

Secrets of the World's Greatest Investors

The Five Secrets of Building Wealth

By Michael Masterson

Anybody can get rich. It doesn't take genius. Nor are special talents required. You don't need to be lucky. Becoming rich is a matter of making certain decisions and practicing certain skills, none of which are difficult or complicated. Viewed from this perspective, becoming rich is simple. You can acquire a multimillion-dollar net worth by doing just five things:

1. Get to work an hour early.
2. Develop and then perfect a financially valuable skill.
3. Use that skill to earn an above-average income.
4. Spend less than you earn.
5. Invest your savings smartly.

By practicing the five behaviors identified above, you can become just as rich as the richest Internet promoter, just as quickly as the latest lottery winner, and with a lot less legal and moral danger than the best known Wall Street shyster.

I know because I've used these secrets myself and have coached countless friends, colleagues, and protégés to do the same.

Secret #1: Get to Work an Hour Early

To get rich, you have to give yourself an edge over everybody else. And the best way I know to do that is to get to work early. By getting to work early, you can do all the little things that put you ahead of the pack. You can make extra contacts, learn useful skills, take time to write an impressive memo, polish off a report, etc.

There is no better time to collect your thoughts and plan your day than early in the morning when the office is quiet. Not only are you undisturbed by phone calls and interruptions; but also, ahead of you is the potential of an unopened day.

And if you do it right, this will be the most productive part of your day. Start it with your weekly to-do list. On a sheet of paper, jot down anything you need to get done. Make sure you give primary attention to your top goal that day, and get it done.

Use your extra time to get at least one positive thing done before you start doing all the regular things. The regular things will give you a regular life. The extra things will give you all the extras—including the extra millions.

Secret #2: Develop and Then Perfect a Financially Valued Skill

To make more money than the guy sitting next to you, you've got to be able to do something that is worth more money to someone else—your boss, your business, your customers.

Selling is a financially valued skill. So is producing profits. So is creating growth. Other skills—making things run smoothly, eliminating mistakes, balancing books, etc.—are valuable to a business, but not as highly valued when it comes to dividing up the money pie.

What successful businesses mostly need—and value—are employees who stimulate sales, increase customer retention, boost customer spending, and bring in a bigger profit. The marketing jobs, selling jobs, and the merchandising jobs are the ones that contribute to the bottom line.

You can add to the bottom line and become a financially valued employee by gradually developing sales, marketing, and profit-building skills. Study the sales and marketing programs that are currently working. Learn from existing masters. Keep at it until you are confident you know how to create more wealth for your business. Then communicate your ideas to the powers that be. Do everything you can to help your boss produce a better bottom line.

If you work at this long enough and with intelligence, people will take notice.

Secret #3: Make an Above-Average Income

You don't have to earn a ton of money to become a millionaire, but you do need a higher-than-average income. To get wealthy while you're young enough to enjoy it, you need to make about $75,000 or more. If you are making less than $75,000 a year now, it's almost certainly because you have not perfected a financially valued skill. Go back to Secret #2.

When you have learned to produce profits and have put yourself into the business of helping your business grow its profits, then the first and most important thing you need to do is ask for a raise. You can simply ask for more money—as I did when I first made the transition—or you can ask for some kind of incentive-based remuneration tied into the financial rewards you are producing for your business.

Or you can also apply your financially valued skill toward developing a side business. (See Secret #5 below.)

Plying a financially valued skill toward a business you work for or a business you own (or both) will definitely produce wealth. Part of that wealth should go to you. Ask for it.

Demand it.

Secret #4: Spend Less Than You Earn

It isn't easy to make a lot of moolah, but it's very, very easy to spend it.

The Millionaire Next Door made and proved the point clearly: Most millionaires become wealthy not by making a ton of money, but by saving and investing modest amounts over time. That's precisely why I believe you can become wealthy when you earn as little as $75,000 a year.

To make sure you spend less than you earn, use this powerful money-management trick. It's something I began doing many years ago. It has allowed me to get richer in good times and bad, when my ideas were working and when they were not, when the economy boomed and when it stalled.

One day, I took out a sheet of paper and tallied up my net worth. Despite earning $50,000 more than I had the previous year, my net worth was less than $10,000.

I made myself a simple promise. I said that from then on I'd recalculate my net worth once a month and that I'd do everything I possibly could to make sure that each month's total would be larger than the month before. It was as easy as that. I decided simply to get richer one month at a time.

By calculating my net worth, I saw that many of my habits (including some of my spending habits) were financially unhealthy. It also gave me, at times, the panicked energy I needed to do something drastic—to start something new or end something that had gone wrong. Plus, it gave me an underlying determination to get a little bit richer every day—and this, as Robert Frost said, has made all the difference.

Don't dismiss this little technique because it's simple. All the best and most powerful things in life are simple. This *will* make a difference. Do it.

Secret #5: Invest Wisely

Investing wisely means doing two things:

1. Create a second, active income, and keep it growing.
2. Invest your passive income in a sensible, conservative fashion.

Part One: Creating a Second Income

I believe in "chicken entrepreneurship"—starting out slowly and learning about a side business while you have the safe and steady income of your main job. By a "side business," I mean something you can run on weekends or weekday evenings. It is something that won't take your attention away from your full-time job. It should be something you enjoy and are willing to stick with.

Start with your financially valued skill. You are using that to create your first income, but now use it to create the second. Don't do anything underhanded like compete with your boss (or primary business), but figure out how you can leverage the skill (and all the resources and connections that skill gives you) for a second income.

Just stick with your strengths—your strongest skills, your smartest contacts, your most devoted supporter—and you'll succeed.

Part Two: Investing Your Second Income

Finally, take the extra money you make from your main business and the extra money from your side business (by extra, I mean the money you can't reinvest in that business because you simply don't need it) and put it into an investing program that is reliable, safe and productive.

The best such program I know has been developed by Dr. Steve Sjuggerud and appears in his newsletter "True Wealth."

But for today, to get started on the road to wealth, do all of the following:

1. Set your alarm an hour earlier.
2. Identify the financially valued skill you are going to develop.
3. Commit to spending less than you earn.
4. Think about a second stream of income.

These are the steps that have worked for me and dozens of others I've personally coached. They will work for you too. You can start them today or you can wait a year or two or ten and wish you had started today. It's up to you.

Michael Masterson is a multi-millionaire businessman. He's run, by his own estimate, more than 35 businesses. Today he's still a partner in a $100 million business, and runs a dozen smaller operations. He provides a free daily e-mail coaching service called Early to Rise. For more information, go to www.earlytorise.com. This piece originally appeared in his Early to Rise service.

How Do You Compare to the "Average Wealthy American?"

By Dr. Steve Sjuggerud, PhD

I t's time to see how YOU measure up. Are you doing things right? Or is it time to make some serious changes? That's what I'll address here, as we examine the makeup of the "Average Wealthy American." (I'll explain how we came up with the figures for this "Average Wealthy American" in just a moment.)

I think two of the big questions going through our minds about our money today are: "Where does it all go?" and "How do I measure up? (Am I doing things right?)."

After crunching a ton of numbers, I've come up with what I believe is a pretty accurate picture of the Average Wealthy American. (I used data from the Federal Reserve's Survey of Consumer Finances, which contains interviews with thousands of Americans across all income, wealth, race, and regional areas.)

So we'll use this data to help us answer these two truly important questions: "Where does all our money go?" And, "How do I measure up? (Am I doing things right?)."

First, consider the "picture" of the Average Wealthy American that I've provided below, and think about how you measure up. But as you're doing so, you should keep in mind two things:

1) Just because someone is wealthy doesn't mean they've done things exactly right.

2) They *are* wealthy, so they're as good a guide as any to what people have done right.

The Results May Surprise You

The Average Wealthy American (based on the numbers I crunched) has $1,000,000 in assets, and $200,000 in debts, for a net worth of $800,000.

Of that million in assets, only about $400k is in financial assets, the other $600k is in non-financial assets, like property.

Of the $200,000 in debt, 80% of it is on properties. (For those of you who still have significant credit card debt, you should know that the Average Wealthy American has just 1% of outstanding credit card debt.)

That's the basics. Now let's take a closer look...

Do You Have Too Much in Individual Stocks?

The Average Wealthy American only has 11% of his assets in individual stocks. Far more of his money—36%—is in retirement accounts or mutual funds, where (for better or worse) somebody else is managing it. Here's the exact breakdown of financial assets, which are 40% of the Average Wealthy American's total $1,000,000 assets:

21% Retirement accounts
15% Mutual funds
12% Cash earning interest (and CDs)
15% Bonds
11% Stocks
4% Life insurance cash value
22% Other (savings bonds, partnerships, etc.)

Said another way, that's:

$84k Retirement accounts
$60k Mutual funds
$48k Cash earning interest (and CDs)
$60k Bonds
$44k Stocks
$16k Life insurance cash value
$88k Other (savings bonds, partnerships, etc.)

Instead of spending all of your time trying to pick the big stock winner, you ought to spend time on allocating your assets. Are your retirement plans stuffed to the gills? Do you have a healthy enough cash reserve? These are the types of questions that you need to ask yourself on a regular basis.

Among investors I hear from, I find that most are pretty close to this table, with one major exception: Most have too little in bonds and bond-type investments. How do you measure up? If you've got way too much in stocks, or way too little in bonds, you may want to make some changes.

Your Home... And Your Second Home... And Your Third???

There were many surprises in the breakdown of non-financial assets, which include things like homes, jewelry, and cars, basically anything that's not a piece of paper.

First of all, I was surprised to find that wealthy folks have nearly the same amount in real estate outside of their homes as they do in their homes. Literally, the

Average Wealthy American has a home worth about $200,000 and other investment properties worth $200,000. Now, of course, there are numbers well above and below this number, but this was the median.

The other third of the $600,000 of non-financial assets was significantly made up by equity in private businesses. The statistics for wealth for the self-employed are dramatic. The numbers really suggest that this is the way significant wealth is generated in America. Here are the specifics:

NON-FINANCIAL ASSETS:

32% Home
28% Equity in own business
18% Second residential property
13% Non-residential property
3% Vehicles
5% Other (jewelry, artwork, antiques, etc.)

Said another way:

$192k Home
$168k Equity in own business
$108k Second residential property
$78k Non-residential property
$18k Vehicles
$30k Other (jewelry, artwork, antiques, etc.)

One last note: Take a look at the total value of vehicles—it's just $18K. That's the median value of the sum of all vehicles they own. As a rule, wealthy people don't drive rich. The fancy car that depreciates in value will only SLOW your wealth creation. (But, of course, it is fun to drive...)

What About Debt?

I was amazed to learn that the median home mortgage is just under $100,000. I thought it'd be higher. But people do have on average an additional $60,000 borrowed for other residences. The usual killers of the middle class—car loans and credit cards—don't make a dent. Wealthy folks generally seem to not live above their means. Car loans and credit card balances among the wealthy are almost non-existent.

If you're dogged by credit cards and car loans, I hate to break it to you, but you may be living beyond your means. Or at the very least, you're not living by the same principles of people who have successfully generated wealth. They don't drive rich. And they don't sit on high interest credit card balances.

Other Interesting Facts About the Average Wealthy American

The self-employed are the wealthy folks of America. The average net worth of a family where the head of a household works for someone else is $52,400. When it comes to the self-employed, the average net worth is $248,100.

All the wealth in America is concentrated among homeowners (two-thirds of Americans own their own homes). The difference is stunning. The average home-owner's net worth is $132,000, while the average renter's net worth is a measly $4,200.

Lastly, it turns out that education is valuable. The net worth where the family head DID NOT graduate from high school is only $21,000. Meanwhile, the net worth where the family head DID graduate from college is $146,800. (Grad school was not part of the survey.) An investment in a college education could provide a return greater than you could even expect in the stock market!

So what—if anything—should you do with all the figures I've given you about the Average Wealthy American? Well, first, you should take a look at your assets and see how you stack up. Now is as good a time as any to roll up your sleeves and examine your own financial picture.

While it's true there is no "magic formula" that works for everyone... it's also clear that the wealthy in this country spend more time on asset allocation than you might think. The Average Wealthy American also does not live beyond his means, which means NO credit card debt—and passing on that expensive sports car.

I urge you to take this opportunity to see just how you compare. It may be an eye-opening experience... or you may be pleasantly surprised. But don't be afraid to make those difficult decisions if you need to.

Originally published: January 27, 2003 in Investment U

For more information on this educational series, go to www.investmentu.com.

What America's Millionaires Have in Common

By Dr. Steve Sjuggerud, PhD

Y**ou** should read *The Millionaire Mind*—how millionaires in America REALLY think—so you can size yourself up in relation to America's most financially successful.

You probably know *The Millionaire Next Door,* the best-selling book by Thomas J. Stanley, which describes how millionaires in America really live. *The Millionaire Mind* is Stanley's much larger follow up. After interviewing more than 1,300 millionaires, the following are the author's conclusions…

The Eight Important Elements of Economic Success

Take a moment and consider your own opinions on each of these points and how you size up to the millionaire's perspective. And think about whether or not you need to start making some changes in your life.

1. Understand the key success factors that our economy rewards: Being honest with all people, hard work, integrity, and focus. [We were amazed to learn that the top of the list was "being honest with all people"—even above hard work!]

2. Never allow a lackluster academic record to stand in the way of becoming economically productive. [Can you believe that the average millionaire graduated college with a 2.9 GPA—and that's if he even graduated!]

3. Have the courage to take some financial risk. And learn how to overcome defeat. [Handling defeat is a big key in investing. The most important—and toughest—thing to do is to *cut your losers*.]

4. Select a job that is not only unique and profitable; pick one you love.

5. Be careful in selecting a spouse. [People who are economically productive married men or women who shared the characteristics that are most compatible with success.]

6. Operate an economically productive household. [Many millionaires prefer to repair or refinish rather than buy new.]

7. Follow the lead of millionaires when selecting a home—study, search, and negotiate aggressively.

8. Adopt a balanced lifestyle. Many millionaires are "cheap dates." It does not take a lot of money to enjoy the company of your family and friends.

Contrary to the popular wisdom about the "rich," we were pleased to find that millionaires in America generally are honest people. They value their marriages. And they value the company of their family and friends over expensive "stuff." What a refreshing revelation—that these are the core values of achieving true wealth.

If you're interested in learning more about how America's most financially successful people think, check out the book *The Millionaire Mind* by Thomas Stanley.

Originally published in Investment U

For more information on Dr. Steve Sjuggerud's free Investment U educational service, go to: www.investmentu.com.

How the 2nd Richest Man in the World Made 45% When Stocks Dropped 25%

By Dan Ferris

In the spring of 1956, 26-year old Warren Buffett was already flush with cash. He had turned $9,800 into $140,000 while working for Ben Graham in New York City.

Buffett wanted to do two things next. Move back home to Omaha. And work for himself. So on May 1, 1956, he started his first independent investment operation, Buffett Associates, Ltd., with $105,000 raised from seven friends and family members.

From 1956 to 1969, Buffett Associates *never had a single losing year*. During that time, he earned an average annual compounded return of 29.5%. More money was raised, but that original $105,000 became more than $3 million, *multiplying investors' money more than 28 times*. By 1966, the partnership was worth $44 million. The rest, as they say, is history.

To this day, the Buffett Partnership's perfect record is a feat unparalleled in financial management.

Back in the days of Buffett Associates, Warren Buffett wasn't buying stock in Gillette and Coca-Cola. He was buying cheap, undervalued companies. But he was doing something else, too. He had to. In 1982, the stock market fell 25%. Buffett's regular long stock positions were underwater, just like everyone else's.

But Warren Buffett had a secret weapon. Poof. No more losses. There aren't many widely publicized examples of the little-known strategy Warren Buffett used to pull financial rabbits out of his hat year after year. But if you look on page 256 of Mary Buffett's excellent book, *Buffettology*, you'll find one spelled out in intimate detail.

In February 1982, Warren Buffett bought 5.7% of the Bayuk Cigar Company's outstanding shares for $572,907, or $5.44 each. He bought them because he knew he was going to make 45% on the deal.

The way he knew it was simple. On February 13, 1982, Bayuk Cigars Inc. announced that it had approval from the U.S. Justice Dept. to sell its cigar operations to American Maize Products Co. The buyout price was $7.87 per share, a 45% premium over Buffett's buy price.

Buffett didn't have any inside information. He didn't know anyone at the company. He simply read the news and knew that Bayuk's takeover was imminent, fully approved by the U.S. government's anti trust investigators.

Buffett simply saw Bayuk's shares trading at a huge discount to the price it had accepted. So he just bought and waited, knowing that it was some of the safest money he'd ever make. It didn't require him to make any guesses about the future. He didn't study the cigar industry and predict a consolidation. All Buffett had to do was subtract the buy price from the market price, and that's how much he knew he was going to make.

Buffett is also known to have bought RJR Nabisco shares when management announced its intentions to take the company private. Over the years, he's held stock in companies like Texas National Petroleum, Lear-Siegler, Allegis, Federated, Marine Midland, and Southland after mergers were announced.

Buying the shares of acquisition targets after the announcements have been publicly announced is called *mergers and acquisitions risk arbitrage,* or risk arbitrage for short. Buffett learned risk arbitrage from his mentor, friend, and former boss, Ben Graham. Graham had pioneered the technique, using a special equation he developed during the days of the Graham-Newman partnership (which earned investors *80 times their money* by the time it folded in 1956). Graham had read about arbitrage in the 1931 classic, *Arbitrage in Securities*, by Meyer H. Weinstein. He then wrote his own ideas down in the 1951 edition of his massive tome, *Security Analysis*.

I won't rehash Graham's math, since the techniques have changed somewhat. But

I will tell you that Buffett and Graham's secret weapon is still used today.

In the days of Buffett and Graham, all you did was buy the acquired stock and waited. Today, the arbitrageur also sells short an equal sized position of the acquiring company. *Buy the acquired company; sell short the acquirer.* That's it. That's what risk arbitrage is all about.

In the case of Bayuk Cigars, Buffett turned his initial investment of $572,907 into $828,819 (a 45% gain) in less than one year. Any time you can do that in less than a year, you're probably outperforming every major stock index and 99.9% of all investment managers.

The Sage of Omaha has used risk arbitrage throughout his career. At any given time, he might have 20 arbitrage positions open, or he may have none at all. Bottom line is… when the chips were down and Warren Buffett needed to make things happen, when he needed to bring investment profits in the door for the partners who'd trusted him with their capital, Warren Buffett was bailed out by *risk arbitrage.* Without that technique, the Buffett legend might not be what it is today. Buffett's bank account would definitely be smaller, if only by $5 or $10 billion.

If you're interested in keeping abreast of new merger announcements, visit: www.theonlineinvestor.com/mergers.phtml

Originally published: May 2003 in Extreme Value

For more information on Dan Ferris' Extreme Value newsletter, go to www.stansberryresearch.com, and follow the "Extreme Value" link in the middle of the page.

Buffett's Secret of the 135% Dividend

By Dan Ferris

"If a man buys a security below its investment value he need never lose, even if its price should fall at once, because he can still hold for income and get a return above normal on his cost price."
~ John Burr Williams, *The Theory of Investment Value*

Warren Buffett more than doubles his money every year on his investment in Coca-Cola shares. Whether the stock price goes up or down hardly matters to

Buffett. He's making 135% on Coke, year in and year out.

Here's how he did it...

Buffett paid $5.23 a share for Coke back in the late 80s, shortly after the crash of 1987 that cut 25% off Coke's share price. (Coke's share price hit $85 in June 1998.)

But today, he makes $7.04 in dividends for each share he bought before 1990. Wait a minute, you say. Coke's annual dividend is only 88 cents a share. That's right. Today, Coke pays a cash dividend of 22 cents per quarter on each share, totaling 88 cents per year.

Buffett bought his shares shortly after the crash of October 19, 1987. Since then, Coke has split its shares 3 times, in 1990, 1992 and 1996. Each time the split gave you twice as many shares as you had before. Those who bought Coke before 1990 and are still holding today, now own 8 Coca-Cola shares for each one they originally purchased.

For every $5.23 share Buffett spent on Coke in 1988, he now receives $7.04 in dividends—every year, no matter what happens to the price of his stock. That's a dividend yield of 135%, more than doubling Buffett's original purchase price, every single year.

Don't let the stock splits confuse you. They don't change anything. Coke has a great business, and it has raised its dividend consistently. At today's prices, I wouldn't buy it. And even if I did, I'd know that I wasn't buying it for what it would pay me today or even next year. Rather, I'd be buying what it would pay me ten years from now, knowing that there's just no other way to get that kind of payout but to buy and wait.

It makes obvious sense. Buy a high quality business or asset at the moment of greatest pessimism and hold it for the long term, and you'll get rich. That's what Buffett has done his whole career. That's why he says his favorite holding period is forever. He would be a fool to sell his Coke shares, now... or ever.

So the promise in my title is simple, but perhaps not easy for the average impatient investor. You merely have to exercise a capacity that almost no investor is willing to use in a world where almost no one really thinks long term anymore: Patience.

Originally published: August 14, 2003 in Extreme Value

For more information on Dan Ferris' Extreme Value service, visit www.stansberryresearch.com, and click on "Extreme Value."

Millionaires Who Buy Only "Safe" and "Cheap" Investments

By Dan Ferris

O nly a handful of investors have ever bested the achievement of Ben Graham, the father of value investing. Ben Graham earned his clients 17% a year, on average, from 1929 – 1956.

Starting with $12,000, Graham would have made you a millionaire by the time he left Graham-Newman investment partnership, 28 years later.

As any of Graham's successful students—the likes of William Ruane, Warren Buffett and Walter Schloss—will tell you, imitating their great teacher's success is not especially difficult.

Graham was very open about his methods. He didn't care what industry he invested in. As long as he could find valuable assets at a deep discount, he was a buyer. Graham knew this gave him what he called a "margin of safety."

To Graham, a margin of safety meant that he was buying something that had an undeniable value well above what the market was presently offering.

For Graham, a margin of safety wasn't a nebulous, subjective idea. He used several easy-to-understand numerical tools to find stocks that were safe enough to buy. If you use these tools and nothing else, you'll never need any other investment strategy. If you stick with Graham's methods for a few years, it's highly unlikely that you'll want any other strategy.

For example, Graham found that stocks whose earnings yield was three times the AAA corporate bond-yield were very safe. With the AAA yield at around 6.37%, that would correspond to a price to earnings ratio of 5.

Another tool: Graham liked companies whose total debt was less than their tangible book value. He thought this meant that shareholders might still be left with something in the event of the company's liquidation. If the worst happened, he reasoned, investors would still be okay. They might even make a little money. If something less than the worst happened, they would surely profit.

Henry Oppenheimer, professor of finance at the State University of New York, conducted extensive research into the effectiveness of Graham's principles.

Using the two Grahamian investment tools I just mentioned produced average returns of 38% a year from 1974 through 1981. (1974 was a big market bottom, but from 1976 – 1981, the Dow Jones Industrials Average treaded water.)

With just two of Graham's tools, you'd have made over 13 times your money in 8 years. Investing in a Dow Jones index fund during that time would have earned you less than 3% a year.

Another excellent Graham idea was to buy stocks trading at a discount to net current asset value, or NCAV. Finding NCAV is easy. Just subtract all liabilities, including preferred stock, long- and short-term debt, from current assets. Current assets are things such as cash, securities, inventory, and accounts receivable, which can be converted to cash within a year.

Joseph D. Vu of St. Paul University found that if you could buy stocks trading below their NCAV, and hold them for two years, you'd average 24% a year over time. That's enough to outperform Graham's prized pupil, Warren Buffett. Buffett has averaged 22.2% a year since 1965, turning every $1,000 invested into more than $2.4 million today.

The difference between Buffett's 22.2% and NCAV's 24% doesn't sound like much. But the 1.8% difference adds an additional $1.1 million to Buffett's results. So $1,000 gets you $3.5 million since 1965, instead of $2.4 million. An extra million never hurt anybody.

A couple of researchers have used an even simpler approach, and make real money with it. Graham's style emphasized stocks trading below tangible asset values. Eugene Fama and Ken French of the University of Chicago found that one safe and very profitable way to invest is to buy the cheapest 10% of all stocks, and sell them every two years.

Fama and French's ideas have become the foundation of Dimensional Fund Advisors, Inc. They now manage a few dozen funds, several of which have beat the S&P 500 and Russell 2000 indexes consistently since their inception over 20 years ago.

There are so many voices today, coming from hundreds of media sources, all telling you what you ought to do with your money. Buck the trend of all the complicating, conflicting advice. Keep it as simple as you can, and buy only what is safe and cheap.

If you want an easy, effective way to put this admittedly general advice to specific, profitable use, you can do no better than to start by using the Ben Graham principles mentioned above.

Originally published: March 27, 2003 in Extreme Value

For more information on Dan Ferris' Extreme Value service, visit www.stansberryresearch.com, and click on "Extreme Value."

A Number the Best Money Managers Care About

By Dan Ferris

S ay you left $10,000 in a savings account for ten years. At current interest rates, you'd have about $10,500 after ten years. It's not even worth doing. Now say you gave the same $10,000 to one of the great investors of today. These men have been earning huge returns for investors, year after year, for a long time:

Warren Buffett: 22.2% a year since 1965
Bill Nygren: 17.1% a year since 1991
Mason Hawkins: 17.7% since 1988
Robert Olstein: 17.8% since 1995
Marty Whitman: 15.7% since 1990

Give your money to one of these guys, and the least you'll have in ten years, at the above rates of return, is $42,000, about $31,500 more than if you leave it in the bank. These guys rarely have a down year, so you're not taking much more risk, either.

It sure would be nice to know exactly how they do what they do. After all, investing should be like everything else in life. There's probably a single trick or secret to it that makes it a whole lot easier.

I'm not saying it's easy to earn big investment returns. It's not. But the basic method all of these super investors are using is very simple to understand. Each one is using his variation of a single, time-tested method.

The investors listed above produce high returns year after year by focusing on one aspect of the businesses they invest in: a business's ability to generate free cash flow.

There are different definitions of free cash flow, but it all boils down to the same thing. Free cash flow is money a company makes by doing business. It's not money that comes in from selling more shares of its stock, or getting a loan, or selling off assets. Free cash flow is money that comes from doing business. It's called "free" because it's cash that is left over after the company reinvests in the business to keep it running. It's money that management is free to do with as it pleases after it pays all the bills.

The basic method of calculating free cash flow is easy to do. You take a company's net income, and add back certain non-cash charges like depreciation and amortization. Then you subtract how much capital spending the company needs to do to stay in business. That's your free cash flow.

Let's use Wal-Mart as a simplified example. In 2002, Wal-Mart earned net income of $8.04 billion. It took depreciation charges for the year of $3.4 billion. You can add this back because it isn't $3.4 billion in cash that Wal-Mart had to pay anyone. It is simply the amount that its equipment and buildings lost in value as a result of age and use. Accounting rules say you have to subtract it from earnings before you arrive at net income as though it were cash.

Add those two together and you get $11.44 billion. Subtract capital spending of $9.4 billion, and you get $2.04 billion of free cash flow.

Value investors like the ones listed above earn huge returns because they buy companies that trade at discounts to the company's value as a cash generator. One company that at least three of the above investors have bought is Yum Brands. That's the owner of Taco Bell, Kentucky Fried Chicken, Pizza Hut, and Long John Silver's. By our simple equation, Yum Brands generated $193 million of free cash flow in 2002.

Knowing one year's worth of free cash flow is just the beginning of the process value investors go through. To do what our super investors do, you have to make an estimate of free cash flow for each of the next seven to 10 years. Then you have to account for the fact that a dollar ten years from now isn't worth as much today as a dollar two years from now.

It's simple to understand, but doing it can get pretty complicated. It's much easier just to give these guys your money and let them do it. That's one of the best things you can do with your money.

Originally published: February 19, 2004 in Extreme Value

For more information on Dan Ferris' Extreme Value service, visit www.stansberryresearch.com, and click on "Extreme Value."

Secrets of the World's Richest Woman

"There is no great secret in fortune-making. All you do is buy cheap and sell dear, act with thrift and shrewdness and be persistent."

~Hetty Green, in the late 1800s

How to Buck the Odds and Become a Self-Made Billionaire

Of the 497 billionaires in the world, only 9% are women. Among those women, only three are self-made billionaires: Oprah Winfrey, JK Rowling (author of the Harry Potter books), and Margaret Whitman.

Doris Fisher almost makes the list. Mrs. Fisher and her husband opened the first Gap store in San Francisco in the late 1960s. But that makes the Fishers "team billionaires" to us. The rest of the billionaire women on the *Forbes* list of the World's Richest People either inherited money or inherited businesses.

So why are there only 3 self-made woman billionaires in the world? We've had "equal opportunity" for 20 years now. And we've had women as Chief Executives for some time now as well. What's the secret? How can a woman generate extraordinary wealth? And can her secrets be applied to all people?

The answer to these questions lies within the story of Hetty Green.

The Wicked Witch of Wall Street

Hetty Green was 82 when she died in 1916, leaving an estate that, in today's dollars, was worth about $2.5 billion. She became the richest woman in the world without any help from anyone. She was eccentric and tough as nails, both of which contributed to her nickname: "The Wicked Witch of Wall Street."

Green's road to wealth was always an uphill battle. You've got to remember, this was a *woman* on Wall Street in the 1800s. Women had few rights back then—even voting was still decades away. Green was quoted as saying; "I wish women had more rights in business. I find men will take advantage of women in business in ways they would not attempt with men. I have found this particularly so in the courts, where I have been fighting all my life." But she didn't let the fact that she was a woman stand in the way of becoming a billionaire.

Four Secrets of Hetty Green's Success

There are four "secrets" to Hetty's success that we can learn from. First is her "Millionaire Next Door" miserliness. The traditional view of billionaires is probably something like Donald Trump—living the high life. Well, Hetty Green in her day was *wealthier* than Trump is today. But unlike Trump, Hetty lived on the cheap, often in a $14-a-month apartment in Hoboken. (She had no permanent residence.) She didn't even have an office—she regularly sat on the floor at Chemical Bank during the business day—for 25 years. Instead of the finest fabrics, she generally dressed in black, often wearing hand-me-downs. Hardly Donald Trump.

Second is her investment strategy. It wasn't anything novel—she bought quality assets on the cheap. "There is no great secret in fortune-making. All you do is buy cheap and sell dear, act with thrift and shrewdness and be persistent," she said. "When I see a thing going cheap because nobody wants it, I buy a lot of it and tuck it away. Then when the time comes, they have to hunt me up and pay me a good price for my holdings." Warren Buffett isn't doing anything new—he's only doing what Hetty Green did 100 years ago.

Third, Hetty was unbelievably shrewd about minimizing her taxes. In a time before the Federal income tax (imagine that!), Hetty was able to slide around state tax laws with remarkable ease. With no permanent address, she shuffled between New York, New Jersey, and Vermont. Among her many tax tricks, was this one: In an unspoken agreement with the NYC comptroller, Hetty acted as the bank for the city of New York. She would hold New York bonds, allowing the city to pay her less than market interest rates, effectively giving the city cheap loans in exchange for the New York taxman looking the other way.

Fourth, hard assets were key. She bought real estate and railroads on the cheap, and rarely sold. She didn't want mansions. She wanted paying properties and rails in the boomtowns, which at the time included Denver, St. Louis, and Cincinnati. A typical move was to buy on the outskirts of town, and wait for the city to grow to her—a seemingly sound investment strategy throughout the history of the United States.

Hetty's Four "Simple" Secrets taken to the Extreme

Here's a quick review of Hetty Green's secrets:

1. Live miserly
2. Buy what nobody else wants
3. Minimize your taxes
4. Overweight your holdings in hard assets that pay

None of Hetty Green's secrets sound very novel. Yet her real "secret" appears to be that she took all of these to the extreme.

As a woman on Wall Street in the late 1800s, the cards were truly stacked against her. But by following these four secrets, Hetty Green became three times as wealthy as Oprah Winfrey—the wealthiest truly self-made woman—is today.

We sure don't have the obstacles in front of us today that Hetty faced back then. So if we follow her secrets, we shouldn't have a problem achieving her success . . . right?

Originally published in Investment U

For more information on the free Investment U e-mail service, go to www.investmentu.com.

How to Grow Rich by Doing Nothing: Lessons From the Bull Market

By Chris Weber

I just finished the best book that I have read on finance and investment in years. It's called *BULL! A History of the Boom, 1982-1999,* and subtitled *What Drove the Breakneck Market—And What Every Investor Needs to Know About Financial Cycles.*

Written by journalist **Maggie Mahar,** and published by Harper at $27.95, it is 486 pages. This seems like a lot, but I can understand when people say that they want to read it at one sitting, or can't put it down. It's that gripping.

I want to relate some of the choice passages, at least for me, and maybe give a little of my own thoughts. I learned a lot from it.

On the Paradox of Making Money From Investments:

Mahar points up something that I have noticed all of my life:

"Another of Wall Street's ironies: professional investors who are obsessed with money—or the idea that it makes life secure—are often less likely to succeed. When they are wrong, they have a hard time cutting their losses. Those who realize that investing is a game have the edge. They know that they cannot be right all of the time: The future is, by definition, unpredictable. This makes it much easier to ride a bull. You know that, from time to time, you will be tossed over his horns—and gored. It is part of the game."

I would only add that if you see the investment arena as more of a piece of theatre in the classic sense, the Greek sense, you get the same advantage as seeing it as a game. *But if you grimly enter the investment arena with the prime view of needing to make money, the cards are stacked against you.*

On Those Investors Who Can't Sit Still:

I am a firm believer that the best way to invest is to identify a bull market in an asset class, be it bonds, stocks, gold or a currency, take a big position, and then just sit back and wait. Do not be swayed by what "everyone" else is saying or doing. Don't worry if you are "only" making 10% when "everyone" else is making 40%." Don't worry about "zigging" when everyone else is "zagging." It is hard, but the smartest thing to do is to buy and hold as long as you can see a bull market.

Mahar quotes a Tweedy Browne investment report that in turn gives this great quote from the French 17th-century thinker Blaise Pascal:

"All men's miseries come from their inability to sit quiet and alone." Further from the Browne report, *"Investors… who flip stocks [do so] because they're interested in short-term results, and the illusion of control. They are like the guy you see on the turn-pike weaving in and out of lanes. He gets ahead of you. He gets behind you. He gets ahead of you. And if he's investing, he pays taxes on short-term capital gains."*

On Investors Who Crave Certainty:

Later, Mahar writes:

"Like the market itself, investors abhor ambiguity. They want a seer who comes with a system for counting the cards. Like Dorothy in Oz, investors invent wizards to give them courage. Financial gurus exist because they satisfy Wall Street's need to believe that 'the market' is rational, efficient, and above all predictable—that 'the market' is not us, but a higher, separate power, and that Wall Street's shamans are in touch with that power."

On How Gurus Invest Their *Own* Money:

I emerged from this book with much more understanding and respect for Henry Blodget, the star Internet analyst now so hated by the same world that lionized him a few short years ago. He was caught in a no-win position: He got lucky on a few calls, and then his firm, and the investment world in general, refused to see *any* ambiguities and caution. His firm wanted the fat investment banking fees from the Internet companies that were going public, so Blodget had to recommend them. **Individual investors craved certainty on the part of their gurus.**

Mahar quotes Blodget in her book: "On one occasion, a CNBC anchor asked, 'If you had $50,000 to invest, which Internet stocks would you buy?'"

The fact is that Blodget saw the inside of these Internet companies more than most anyone, and he knew that they were often bogus. His own actions, given quite candidly to *Forbes*, show this.

In fact, many of the Internet "gurus" had their own money in Treasuries during the last couple years of the Boom. They weren't dummies!

On Telling All Investors What to Buy, Sell or Hold:

I quote Mahar quoting Steven Einhorn, the great research director for Goldman Sachs until 1998:

" 'There is no one-size-fits-all advice for individuals. Even when I spoke to our 'high net worth' individual investors, I would tell them that if we were raising our model portfolio allocation from 60 percent to equities to 70 percent, that didn't mean that they should do the same. Everything depended on their age, income, how much savings they had, how much debt. I would tell them, 'If normally you hold 20 percent of your portfolio in equities, and we raise our allocation from 60 percent to 70 percent, you might want to raise yours proportionately, to, say 23 percent.' But this was never the message that the financial press wanted to transmit, said Einhorn. 'I can remember being interviewed by reporters. I tried to tell them this, and their eyes glazed over. The press wanted something simple—they wanted a single number: 60 percent, 70 percent.' "

And it is not just the press that wants a simple number: Investors do, too. That is why so few reporters and individual investors will ever be successful at investing.

Take the Long Term, Look Widely, and Do Nothing:

Mahar, again:

"The most successful long-term investors are those who avoid becoming mesmerized by the week-to-week or month-to-month action of the markets, step back, and take a longer look at the larger cycles that drive a multi-faceted global economy. While one bull market cycle is ending, another is beginning somewhere else—in another sector, in another class of assets, or in another country. There is always someplace in the world to make money."

But this does not mean that you have to be "doing something" all of the time. As Warren Buffett explained in one company report, "Occasionally successful investing requires inactivity."

What I would add: If you can identify a bull market in any asset class, anywhere in the world, take a long view, get in and then wait. Try to ride the whole of the bull cycle. This "requires inactivity." But if you can't find any bull market anywhere, and you don't see good value anywhere, well, that "requires inactivity" too. *I think most time spent as a successful investor is time spent doing nothing at all.*

But Buy and Hold is Not Always Smart:

I know this all sounds like a contradiction, but you don't want to believe the brokerage industry hype about buying stocks for the long term. Each asset class has bull and bear markets, and none of them lasts forever. The most important thing you can do is not trade in and out of a cycle, but be able to identify that long cycle, and when it is nearly over.

So you have to identify a bull market, act on it, and then be able to stay with it (that is, be prepared to do nothing), and then decide when it is over.

This is not easy.

For instance, I was lucky enough to identify the birth of the bull market in bonds in 1980. And I have stayed with it ever since. Of course, I have changed currencies a few times since then. I started out in the U.S. dollar, went into other currencies in 1985, back into the dollar, and so forth (now I am nearly totally out of the U.S. dollar), but the global bull market in bonds from 1980 to 2003 has been breathtaking.

I could go on... this book is great. Showing the corruption, the greed and the hype that pervaded the bull market in all of its aspects, from mutual fund companies to stock brokerages, to analysts, to individual investors, the job Mahar does is not only a history lesson, but makes you think of how you can be a better investor.

Originally published in the Weber Global Opportunity Report

For more information on Chris Weber's Global Opportunities Report, *go to:* *www.weberglobal.net.*

Legendary Investor Adopts Our Trailing Stop Strategy

By Dr. Steve Sjuggerud, PhD

Mark Mobius became a legend in the early 1990s, when he racked up triple-digit returns in a year in his Templeton Emerging Markets Fund. He is a hero of mine, one of the few independent thinkers in the investment world. Now, it seems, Mobius is impressed with my exit strategy.

Mark is extremely careful in his buying and selling. You don't become known as one of the great value investors unless you really buy on the cheap, as Mark does.

I remember when I brought a broker friend from Shanghai to Templeton's offices. The Templeton Asia folks basically told my friend: "We don't really care who you are, as we do our own research. Here is a list of the stocks we want to buy and the prices we want to pay (which were 20% less than the price in the market). If you can quietly get us shares at these prices without moving the markets, we'll do business with you. Otherwise, don't call on us." Wow.

My friend Van Tharp was in Korea last week, speaking to Mobius and the Templeton team. Van sent me this email:

"Met Mark Mobius in Korea. He was impressed enough with my talk that he's ordering 30 home study courses for people in Templeton. He wants me to speak at their next semiannual meeting. In addition, I had enough influence on him that he's going to put in a 25% stop loss policy in Templeton (at least the part he controls). First time I've had that much influence over a portfolio manager. He seems very nice."

I was proud when I read this email—it was validation from yet another independent thinker that an exit strategy is crucial, and that ours is sound. It was also a clear indication that Mark is an independent thinker, as other portfolio managers agree with Van, but say they're helpless to change their policy.

As a trading coach, Van has interviewed thousands of traders. Out of all the strategies Van has heard in his decades in the business, he recommends the 25% trailing stop he learned from me as the most useful exit strategy for long-term stock position. It is an important part of his regular speech. Van is an independent thinker operating in the real world. He only concerns himself with what works. And our simple exit strategy, he has independently determined, works.

He gave his regular speech to Mobius and crew. Mobius has been famous for making money around the globe for decades now. But it seems even an old dog can learn a new trick. Independent-thinking Mobius recognized the benefit of unemotional exiting with a 25% trailing stop when Van presented it.

These days it seems that nobody uses an exit strategy. It's not taught in the academic world, and it's not taught in the real world. But I'm convinced that if you have no exit strategy, you really have no strategy at all—what you've got is "buy and hope" or "buy and guess when to sell," which is generally "never" when a stock is going against you.

Two great independent thinkers—Van Tharp and Mark Mobius—clearly understand the value of limiting your downside risk. For me, it is a feather in my cap that Mobius is implementing my exit strategy. For you as an investor, it is further validation that the 25% trailing stop policy, while not mainstream, is quietly being adopted by great independent-thinking investors.

Originally published: July 15, 2003 in True Wealth

For more information on Dr. Steve Sjuggerud's True Wealth advisory service go to: www.stansberryresearch.com, or call (888) 261-2693.

Chapter 7

The Truth About Investing in Options

The Truth About Options

By Dr. Steve Sjuggerud, PhD

The truth about options needs to be told. We are absolutely overloaded with financial information these days. It's too much. And when it comes to options, the quantity of information out there is tremendous—you've got books, courses, fancy expensive computer programs, and more. <u>But nearly all of it is garbage</u>.

Most of it is incredibly confusing. These things are never in plain English. They're full of weird charts and diagrams. And way too many numbers. Even worse, much of it just contains bad logic, which will ultimately lead to bad losses in the markets.

I don't know how there can be so much *information* out there on this topic, and so little imparted *knowledge*.

The worst sin of all is that nobody is telling the truth.

Everybody seems to have a vested interest. Whether you're at an investment conference, watching CNBC, or reading an investment magazine, there's always somebody promoting options trading. But then you talk to your broker about it, and he *always* talks you out of it. Why is that? The reality is, your broker doesn't want to waste his time following your option trade all day long. He'll never tell you this, but the truth of what he's thinking is *"this is way too much hassle for way too little commission."*

I don't care if you trade options or not. But I think my experience can help you decide whether or not options are right for you… and help you become a better trader if you decide to get in the game.

So without further ado, it's time for **The Truth About Options.**

This chapter is all you need to know about options. It is short, but it is complete. How can it be short and complete? Because 99.9% of the stuff out there about options won't help you make any money. I'll explain why in the pages that follow. But first:

Truth #1: Most Options Are Recipes for Disaster

As a general rule, I must say, I don't particularly care for *most* options *most* of the time. You've probably figured this out so far.

Most people lose money by trading options. The primary reason they lose money is because they follow "limited upside, unlimited downside" strategies.

This, as a general rule, is dumb.

Think about it. Here's the sales pitch: "Hey buddy, how about this—you've got the chance here to make a profit of 10% if you do this trade and it works perfectly. If it doesn't work out right, you could lose all your money—and then even owe some."

Now why would anybody invest in such a strategy? I have no idea. But that's the way most people trade options. They just don't realize what they're doing. You should never trade in "limited upside, unlimited downside opportunities." Calling them "opportunities" is a misnomer. **You should only invest or trade in unlimited upside, limited downside opportunities.**

The problem with most options is that nearly all of them *don't qualify* as unlimited upside, limited downside opportunities. But this is good for you. It means that you don't have to learn any of the exotic options strategies that are taught in books, trading services, and software programs out there. **They're all useless, limited upside, unlimited downside strategies that are doomed from the start!**

THE TRUTH ABOUT THE MAJOR OPTIONS STRATEGIES

UNLIMITED PROFITS, LIMITED LOSSES	LIMITED PROFITS, LIMITED LOSSES
Buying calls	Bull spreads
Buying puts	Long butterfly
Long straddle	Long condor
Long strangle	Long iron butterfly
Backspreads	
UNLIMITED PROFITS, UNLIMITED LOSSES	LIMITED PROFITS, UNLIMITED LOSSES
None	Selling calls (aka "writing" calls)
	Selling puts
	Covered calls
	Short straddle
	Short strangle
	Ratio spreads

I can't stop you from doing the options trades that are not in the shaded area if you want to do them. But I know that in both investing and trading, you really make your money on the few big winners—your triple-digit moves. And if you limit your upside, you'll never profit from these moves—ever.

So for 99.9% of us, we'd be shooting ourselves in the foot by employing limited upside strategies. If you do your homework, you might find that these losing strategies somehow sound good on paper. But in the real world, they just don't work out over the long run. I'd say, for most people, don't waste your time with any strategies outside the shaded area.

The Truth About the Major Options Strategies

Looking at the strategies in the shaded box, two of them (straddles and strangles) aren't relevant to our strategies—they're bets on the *volatility* of a stock, not *which way* a stock will move. So you shouldn't bother with those. Don't worry about learning anything about these unless you're interested in making a bet on the future volatility of a stock. These are best left to professional traders.

And one of them, backspreads, *would* be applicable, but quite frankly, it's really not worth explaining. The idea is far too complicated. That leaves us with **buying puts** and **buying calls**.

These are easy to understand and explain. And they accomplish exactly what we're trying to accomplish—unlimited upside, limited downside ways to profit on the direction of a stock price.

Let me start by explaining **buying calls** with a little story...

Truth #2: The Easy Way to Understand Options

There's a piece of land on the beach that I've had my eye on for some time. Empty lots on the water are hard to come by around here—they rarely go on the market. And when they do, they're snapped up pretty fast.

---

3 Major Factors That Determine The Price of Options

Distance of the Strike Price from the Market Price - For out-of-the-money options, the closer the market is to the option's strike price, the more valuable the option will be.

Time Until Expiration - The longer an option has to work, the more expensive it will be. A homeowner's policy that is good for one year costs more than a policy good for six months.

Volatility - The more volatile the market, the more expensive the option will be. Because the probability that the option seller will have to meet his obligation rises in direct proportion to volatility, he will demand more money. Hurricane insurance will always cost more in Florida than it will in Chicago.

I drove by it around dusk one day on my way to a dinner party and saw an old man on the property. I got out of my car to strike up a conversation. It turned out he was the owner. I asked him if he'd ever consider selling the property. "Sure" he said. "A million firm."

Right on the spot, I tried to work a deal. I thought a million was actually a good price for ocean-front around here, but I didn't want to tell him that. And I needed a little time to do my homework and get my finances together.

Here's the deal I offered: "I'll give you ten thousand dollars right now—that you can keep—if you can give me a piece of paper giving me the right to buy this property for a million dollars anytime in the next 30 days. If I decide not to buy it, you keep the money."

"You've got yourself a deal right there," he said, happy to pocket the no-risk $10,000.

I headed out to the dinner party. At the party I met some folks who'd been looking to buy on the ocean for months, but nothing had come on the market. They mentioned that they'd snap up the first thing available, even over $1 million.

Long-story short, I sold them the old man's oceanfront lot for $1,050,000.

I made a profit of 400% basically in a few hours, by selling an asset that I controlled, but didn't own, for a higher price than I could buy it for myself.

I could have completed the transaction two ways:

I could have exercised my right to buy the land and gone through all the paperwork hassles, taxes, and fees, only to turn around and go through all that again. Or...

I could simply sell my "right to buy" piece of paper to the couple for $50,000.

For $10,000, I had the "option" to buy this land over the next 30 days. I could either buy the land, or sell my right to buy. That's exactly what an option is.

Okay, I confess, this isn't a true story. But it is a perfect example of buying a **call** option.

A call option is the right (but not the obligation) to buy something. That's pretty much it. I paid $10,000 to the old man for the option to buy his property. I

A BRIEF OPTIONS GLOSSARY

The Underlying Stock: What you have the right to buy and sell.

The Premium: The amount you pay when you buy an option.

The Expiration Date: The date that the option expires. It is important to know the expiration date because time until expiration is a major factor in determining an option's fair price. An option is known as a "wasting asset." It loses value with the passage of time.

The Strike Price: The price at which you can "exercise" your option. This price is based on the underlying instrument. Call option buyers have the right to buy the underlying stock at the strike price. Put option buyers have the right to sell at the strike price.

In-the-money: Calls are "in-the-money" if the price of the underlying instrument is HIGHER than the strike price. Puts are "in-the-money" if the price of the underlying instrument is LOWER than the strike price. (For example, a $20 put is "in-the-money" with the stock at $19.)

At-the-money: When the price of the underlying instrument is identical to the striking price. Same for both puts and calls.

Out-of-the-money: Calls are "out-of-the-money" if the price of the underlying stock is LOWER than the strike price. Puts are "out-of-the-money" if the price of the underlying instrument is HIGHER than the strike price. (A $25 crude oil call is "out-of-the- money" if crude is at $20.)

paid $10,000 for a call option.

A call option has an **expiration date**. In this case, in 30 days, it would expire—worthless. Options are worthless after their expiration date. You'd better either **exercise** your option by buying the property, or **sell the option** to somebody else before it's expired.

For stock options, you have the same options as I did with the couple. I could either **exercise** the right to buy the stock at a certain **agreed upon price** (like the $1 million price), or I could **sell the option** to somebody else through the options market, basically just like the New York Stock Exchange. Only it's the options exchange. And it's in Chicago.

The reality is that nobody goes through the hassle of exercising the right to buy, just like I didn't when it came to the land. I didn't want the land transferred to me before I sold it to the couple. And the same is true for stock options. Because there is an options exchange, people are trading these options all the time. I just sell the option.

And the "agreed upon price" in options parlance is called the **strike price**. There's probably a good reason why it's called the strike price. But I don't know it.

That's the basics of a call option. Now let me cover the basics of a **put option**.

Using Your Homeowner's Policy To Understand Puts

Every time you buy an insurance policy you are essentially buying a put option.

Take your homeowner's policy as an example. When you sign on the dotted line and write your check, you are essentially **buying the right to sell** your house back to the insurance company *for a certain value, under certain conditions, for a limited period of time.* By accepting your money, the insurance company has taken on an obligation to buy your house back from you under the same terms. The longer your policy has to run, the more the insurance company will charge you. A six-month policy obviously costs less than a 12-month policy, etc. It works exactly the same way with put options. The longer it's good for, the more it costs.

As put option buyers we have two big advantages over insurance policy holders. First of all, most options are not subject to the terms and conditions of many insurance policies. A disaster is not necessary for them to "pay off." In the case of put options, the stock has to go down. That's it.

Secondly, unlike the insurance policy holder, buyers and sellers of options are free to offset or add to their positions at any time. If you change your mind about a position for any reason, you can exit by simply selling it in the market.

For the most part, options are as easy to buy and sell as stocks are. This makes them an ideal investment for investors who wish to take advantage of big moves, as it can be done without the expense and risk of buying or selling huge chunks of stock.

In short: **Buyers of call options want the stock to go up. They only make money if the stock goes up.**

Buyers of put options want the stock to go down. They only make money if the stock falls.

Truth #3: Why Options are the Riskiest and Most Rewarding Game on Wall Street...

Options master Victor Sperandeo racked up a nominal rate of return of 70.7% without a losing year between 1978 and 1989 (according to the liner notes of his 1994 book, *Trader Vic II: Principles of Professional Speculation*).

With his astounding track record, we'd be foolish not to pay attention to what he has to say:

*"Options are, many say, the riskiest game in town. Certainly they are by far the most challenging, flexible, and potentially profitable financial instruments available. But if you **trade them prudently**, if you **apply sound principles of money management**, trade only when the risk/reward ratio is highly in your favor, and **execute your trades with diligence and patience**, then in all likelihood you will be profitable over the long term. I can say, conservatively, that at least 40 percent of all the returns I've made in my life have been with options."*

Truth #4: Why You Need to Watch Your Losers When You Invest in Options

To succeed in trading options, you really need to limit your trading to opportunities that have a minimum of a 3-to-1 payout. A 5-to-1 reward-to-risk ratio of course, is better. But at minimum, you want to have the potential to pocket three dollars in return for every dollar you risk.

You accomplish many things by forcing a minimum 3-to-1 discipline on yourself. For one, it forces you to think in terms of reward and risk, which is extremely important. Most failed options traders, even ones that may have had good trading systems, fail because they didn't pay enough attention to risk.

If you're willing to lose 50% on a position, you'd better be expecting a gain of 150% or more—at minimum. That's a tall order. If you're willing to lose it all (meaning have the potential for a minus—100% return on a position), then you'd better be expecting a 300% to 500% or more gain in that position.

When you see it in those terms, and you realize that 500% winners don't come along every day, you can see "risking it all" is a bad bet, in terms of risk versus reward.

I'm never willing to lose more than 50% on a position. If an option that I hold closes down more than 50%, I sell it the next day, no ifs, ands, or buts. Generally, I'll sell even earlier than that. If an option falls from $4 to $3, you only have to make up a buck in some future trade. But if it falls to $1, that means you're hoping for it to rise 300% just to get back to where you started—not good odds!

Figuring Out the Profit Potential of Your Options

Profit potential for both buying and selling options is typically figured at expiration.

However, that doesn't mean that you need to hold an option until expiration. At expiration, hard-to-figure pricing variables such as time and volatility drop from the equation, making profit calculations much easier.

To take a profit on a put or call, simply sell it. You do not need to exercise your option in order to profit from a long position. The vast majority of options are not carried through until expiration at all. Rather, they are offset at some point during their life cycles. You can also cut losses in losing positions by doing the same thing.

Here are some simple formulas for figuring risk and profit potential, based on the market price of the underlying instrument at expiration, for four possible option scenarios.

1. Buying a call:

NET PROFIT = MARKET PRICE - STRIKE PRICE - AMOUNT PAID FOR OPTION

BREAKEVEN PRICE = STRIKE PRICE + OPTION COST (The market needs to be ABOVE this price at expiration to be profitable.)

2. Buying a put:

NET PROFIT = STRIKE PRICE - MARKET PRICE - AMOUNT PAID FOR OPTION

BREAKEVEN PRICE = STRIKE PRICE - OPTION COST (The market needs to be BELOW this price at expiration to be profitable.)

Options are a lot like poker. Your hand is only a small portion of the battle. Betting appropriately for the entire game is really what's important, which leads us to...

Truth #5: Big Winners Make Small Bets

You've got to know when to hold 'em, and know when to fold 'em. But you'd sure hate to fold 'em and take a total loss with a big bet on... so don't ever put yourself in that boat! **Limit the size of your positions.** You should only have 2-3% of your risk capital *at risk* on any one trade. I really can't imagine any combination of circumstances where you'd consider putting more than 10% of your risk capital on one trade. Don't do it!

To end up like Vic Sperandeo over the long run, you've got to stick to the program. Limit the size of your positions. And limit your downside by never allowing a small loss to turn into a big loss. Traders who follow this have a chance of being winners in options over the long run. Those who don't do this will be quickly drummed out of the club, taken for literally every penny.

Originally published by Dr. Steve Sjuggerud in February 2004 for his True Wealth Trader Options Service

Dr. Steve Sjuggerud runs True Wealth, one of the most successful investment advisory newsletters in the world, with more than 60,000 subscribers. He also runs a small trading service called the True Wealth Trader, for investors who want to speculate with a small portion of their portfolio for bigger gains. For more information on Dr. Sjuggerud and his investment research, go to: www.stansberryresearch.com.

BEST OPTIONS RESOURCES

MY FAVORITE OPTIONS BROKER:

Fox Investments
Sue Rutsen or Neil Fern
srutsen@foxinvestments.com
nfern@foxinvestments.com
Toll-Free: 800-345-7026
141 West Jackson Blvd., Suite 1800A
Chicago, IL 60604

Fox Investments has been in business for 30 years. It's located inside the Chicago Board of Trade building, right across the street from the Chicago Board Options Exchange (CBOE).

Fox Investments is a subsidiary of Mann Financial. But don't be confused when you call them to set up your account, and they answer "Mann Financial" or "Fox Investments" or both. They're the same company, but Fox is the arm that handles trading.

WHO TO TALK TO: Ask for either **Neil Fern** or **Sue Rutzen** at toll-free **(800) 345-7026.**

ACCOUNT MINIMUM: Fox has a minimum of $10,000 required to open a margin account.

Options are bought and sold as **contracts**. So when you buy one options contract, you're buying 100 options. Put another way: **1 options contract = 100 options**.

Whether you decide to call your orders in yourself, or you use an auto-trade account, commissions for your trades will be the same: $50 per ticket and $5 per option contract.

To simplify, you'll pay $55 for each option contract you buy through Fox Investments.

MY FAVORITE ONLINE BROKER:

optionsXpress
Go to www.optionsxpress.com

They're *Barron's* highest-ranked online broker ever (4 1/2 stars) in their annual online brokerage review.

This broker best serves online options traders. But another reason I like optionsXpress is that you can also buy stocks and mutual funds here, too.

ACCOUNT MINIMUM:

OptionsXpress charges $1.50 per contract with a minimum of $14.95. So if you traded 1 to 9 options contracts, you would pay $14.95. Ten options contracts would be $15.00, or $1.50 per contract. Twenty options contracts would be $30.00, and so on.

Placing an order at optionsXpress takes less than ten seconds, and each order comes with the NBBO (national best bid or offer) Guarantee. That means if your trade does not receive the NBBO, they will reimburse your commission.

Chapter 8

How to Protect and Enjoy Your Wealth

The Best Place to Retire in the World—Our 12th Annual Global Retirement Index

By Laura Sheridan, Editor, International Living

For the third year running, Panama has taken top honors in our Annual Global Retirement Index. If you're looking for a place outside U.S. borders to retire, this country should be at the top of your list, as it is ours.

Panama has a lot going for it. Here, you can enjoy spring-like weather year-round, a low cost of living, safety, security, peace of mind, beautiful landscapes—mountainsides covered with flowers and planted with coffee, and cascading waterfalls, not to mention the best pensionado program in the world.

In every category in this index, Panama scores well. It has a stable economy (the U.S. dollar is its currency), favorable offshore banking laws, good infrastructure, diverse geography, cheap real estate—and still it's a relatively undiscovered paradise. Panama City is our number-one choice the globe over if you're looking for inexpensive cosmopolitan living. You'll find world-class restaurants, five-star hotels, international banks, hundreds of multinational businesses, a Manhattan-type skyline, every imaginable luxury, all at about half the price you'd pay in Miami, or any other U.S. city for that matter.

The energy here and the warmth of the people is overwhelming. Most people are surprised to learn that Panama City has just about everything that you'll find in all of the world's major cities.

Panama City is really three cities in one: Old Panama, Colonial Panama, and Modern Panama. In Old Panama, you can explore the ruins of the old city, which was ransacked and destroyed by the pirate Henry Morgan in 1671. Colonial Panama, with its narrow streets and decorative balconies, is being rebuilt. The San Jose Church's Golden Altar, the Flat Arch, the National Theater, the cathedrals, and Las Bovedas promenade are all worth a visit.

Luxury Downtown Apartment for $60,000

Property, both for sale and for rental, is extremely affordable. Since the U.S. military and Panama Canal personnel pulled out (in 1999), thousands of houses and apartments have flooded the market. Abundant supply and limited demand. Prices are cheap. You can find a three-bedroom, luxury apartment downtown—with a deck, private parking, a pool... the works—for about $80,000. Here's another bonus: Walk just about anywhere in Panama City, and you have an ocean view.

You can invest in a smaller apartment, away from the prime areas, for as little as $40,000. The real bargains will require renovation, but labor is cheap and plentiful. Workmanship is adequate to good. If you're interested in a renovation project here, it would be helpful to know a little about construction and to speak at least passable Spanish.

Prices for reconstructed apartments average around $100 per square foot.

Pacific Coast Properties

Beachfront also can be a tremendous bargain. At Gorgona, a Pacific coast resort area, for example, you can purchase beachfront apartments right now for as little as $60,000. At Lagomar you can buy a large house on the lakeshore with a swimming pool for around $150,000. At El Valle, a little town up in the hills about an hour and a half drive from Panama City, you might pay as little as $60,000.

Here is a sample of properties on offer along the Pacific coast right now:

- Gorgona: 650-square-foot beachfront apartment with two bedrooms and two bathrooms, $65,000.

- Gorgona: A new 1,100-square-foot beachfront apartment, $97,000.

- El Valle: 1,500-square-foot house with three bedrooms and two bathrooms, plus a wonderful view, $60,000.

- El Valle: four-bedroom, three-bathroom house, with terrace and gardens, $145,000.

- Lagomar: large three-bedroom, two-bathroom house on 6.6 acres with a swimming pool and a gazebo on the lakeshore, $160,000.

Where the Rich and Famous Vacation

Panama also hides some of the world's most appealing—and least discovered—island property. Though foreigners typically cannot purchase on an island, there is an important exception: the island of Contadora.

As long-time readers of International Living know, this is one of our favorite spots in this country (in fact, we have invested here ourselves). Turquoise waters, 13 white-sand beaches, secluded coves, bright red and yellow fishing boats, swaying palm and cashew trees, giant coral reefs, coconuts, mangoes, parrots, pelicans, sea turtles. This is the place where Panama's rich and famous come to vacation.

From the latter half of the 16th century until the latter half of the 20th century,

Contadora was sparsely inhabited. Then, a Panamanian named Gabriel Lewis Galindo bought the island and established the basic infrastructure—water, electricity, an airstrip, a marina, and a property division.

Now habitable, the island attracted the attention of Panama's elite—because of its sheer natural beauty and, most importantly, because of the privacy it afforded. Even today, few in the world know that this little island, part of the Pearl Island archipelago in the Bay of Panama, just 15 minutes from Panama City, even exists.

Here are the numbers behind our rankings of the top 29 places in the world to retire. See the box below for more details on where these numbers come from.

This is changing in a dramatic way.

Survivor, America's popular reality TV show, with 20 million viewers per episode, has announced that its next series is to be filmed here. Production crews are already

---

How our Global Retirement Index is scored

• Real estate. Countries where real estate prices are low and the purchase of real estate is relatively easy receive the highest scores. We use our own experiences plus reports from our contributing editors and real estate contacts around the world to rate each country. Weight: 15%

• Entertainment, Recreation, and Culture. This category considers the number of newspapers per 1,000 citizens, the number of museums and cinemas per capita, the number of university students, the literacy rate, and the variety of cultural and recreational offerings. Weight: 10%

• Cost of living. This score is based on statistics from the Indexes of Living Costs Abroad, Quarter Allowances, and Hardship Differentials, published by the United States Department of State, and on data published by Business International. We also use our firsthand experiences living and traveling in these countries. The lower the score, the higher the cost of living. Weight: 20%

• Safety and stability. This measure of unrest in each country is based primarily on Interpol data and State Department statistics. It also takes into account the civil liberties and political rights granted by each government. Our own experiences and reports from expatriates living in these countries also influence the safety scores. Weight: 5%

• Health care. Considered in this category are the cost of a typical visit to a general practitioner and the cost and coverage particulars of health insurance. Weight: 20%

• Climate. Countries with temperate weather throughout the year, moderate rainfall, and little risk of natural disaster come out on top in this category. We use data representing each country as a whole instead of favoring one region over another. Weight: 5%

• Special benefits. This category considers government provisions that make moving to and living in each country easier and more affordable for foreigners. Taken into account are property rights for foreign residents, property tax rates, duty-free imports on personal belongings, currency controls, employment restrictions, voting rights, and transportation discounts for seniors. Weight: 20%

• Infrastructure. This section considers the number of cars and telephones per 1,000 residents, the length of railroad track in usable condition, the number of airports, the quality of the country's road and highway network, and the availability of telecommunications. Weight: 5%

2003 GLOBAL RETIREMENT INDEX

Country	Real Estate	Special Benefits	Cost of Living	Culture	Health	Infra-structure	Safety	Climate	Total
Panama	85	100	75	49	55	14	100	46	72
Malta	68	65	67	62	84	31	100	100	71
Australia	81	63	23	95	82	100	100	93	70
France	81	63	8	100	100	77	100	83	69
Canada	52	63	71	80	70	75	100	57	68
New Zealand	99	36	50	84	73	63	100	80	67
Cyprus	87	76	52	51	75	30	100	14	66
Mexico	82	58	67	58	52	27	100	99	65
Nicaragua	89	68	75	47	48	12	90	45	64
Greece	68	49	58	56	80	30	90	74	63
Portugal	62	23	79	58	77	23	100	93	62
Poland	81	23	71	76	64	41	90	55	61
Brazil	100	46	79	45	32	35	86	72	60
Italy	43	68	8	76	89	45	100	84	59
Ecuador	87	31	94	42	32	7	90	96	58
Chile	100	47	52	56	48	30	100	32	58
Spain	68	49	65	64	41	23	100	68	57
Argentina	53	29	77	45	48	41	90	93	55
Belize	13	88	48	20	64	52	90	33	53
Malaysia	85	31	75	51	45	0	90	0	53
South Africa	81	23	100	49	0	18	90	99	52
Slovenia	77	46	25	64	48	34	100	68	52
U.K.	1	55	6	84	82	69	100	82	50
Croatia	62	0	58	56	59	30	90	95	49
Honduras	71	19	88	0	9	4	70	79	42
Dominican Republic	45	55	65	24	14	0	65	43	41
Ireland	0	79	0	73	36	44	100	71	41
U.S.	0	7	56	73	36	96	100	80	41
Thailand	72	1	65	42	27	4	80	32	39

in place, and the teaser footage they're showing is giving America a glimpse of what these islands have to offer. When the series airs this autumn, we predict a boom in real estate prices.

Remember what happened after *Temptation Island* aired its series filmed on Ambergris Cay, Belize? Real estate values rose more than 100% in six months. Real estate agents there couldn't field the inquiries.

The real estate market on Contadora is small and limited. Not a lot of inventory. The spike in values here could be even greater than it was on Ambergris in the wake of *Temptation Island.*

Is Panama Safe?

To set the record straight, General Manuel Noriega and his kidnapping, corrupt government have been out of power for more than a decade now. Furthermore, despite what you may read in the mainstream press, Panama's economic performance is, almost every year, better than that of just about every other country in Latin America. In fact, over the past 40 years, the country's inflation has averaged less than 2% per year, which is simply unheard of south of the United States.

> ### The benefits of being a retiree in Panama
> - 50% off entertainment anywhere in the country (movies, theatres, concerts, sporting events, etc.)
> - 30% off bus, boat, and train fares
> - 25% off airline tickets
> - 50% off hotel accommodations (Monday through Thursday)
> - 30% off hotels from Friday through Sunday
> - 25% off restaurants
> - 15% off fast-food restaurants
> - 15% off hospital bills (if no insurance applies)
> - 10% off prescription medicines
> - 20% off doctor's consultations
> - 15% off dental and eye exams
> - 20% off professional and technical services
> - 50% off closing costs for home loans

It's a very affordable place to live (a full-time, live-in maid costs $150 a month; first-run movies cost $3.75). It's the safest place in Central and South America (the Pinkerton Global Intelligence Agency recently gave Panama its highest rating for tourist safety). And it's the most developed place south of the United States (home to some of the top companies in the world, including 80 of the world's biggest banks, and other giants such as Federal Express, DHL, Price Costco, and BellSouth).

In short, Panama has its act together. Still, very few foreigners, particularly Americans, consider Panama as a travel destination, and even fewer think of it as a place worth considering for retirement. Therein lies your opportunity.

The Little (Unknown) Mediterranean Islands

Not interested in Central America? Think retirement to Europe might suit you better? The top choice on that side of the Pond, according to our 2003 Global Retirement Index, is Malta, which takes this year's runner-up spot, ranking as the world's second-best retirement haven.

Although Malta receives full marks in but one category (Safety and Stability), it scores high marks across the board. The island of Malta and her sister island of Gozo aren't mainstream destinations for North Americans, but these little isles in the Mediterranean have a lot to offer—a tranquil way of life and virtually non-existent crime, year-round sunshine, the opportunity to benefit from a considerable reduction in your tax burden, and a population that speaks English. Plus, resident retirees are entitled to certain benefits, including the tax-free importation of your personal goods.

Anyone can rent or buy a home on these islands, with certain restrictions to foreigners:

* Unless in specially designated areas, foreign buyers can purchase only one home on the islands.

* The value of the property must amount to at least $71,500 for an apartment and $119,000 for a house (at current exchange rates). However, the minimum price can include restoration costs and furnishings.

* If renting, the annual rent must be at least $4,280.

The nitty gritty—closing costs, taxes, and foreign ownership restrictions for the world's top five retirement havens

• **Panama:**

Real estate closing costs: Typically 1% to 2% of the purchase price.
Property taxes: The levied rate varies from 1.5% to 2.1% of the property's registered value. New buyers can enjoy a five- to twenty-year exemption on property tax.
Foreign restrictions: Foreigners cannot own property within six miles of an international border. By law, all beachfront properties must provide a public right of way starting from the highest tide to the property line. (This distance may vary.) Permits to build over the water require a concession from the maritime authority and the Ministry of Finance. An exception to this is the island of Contadora, where certain properties have been specifically exempted from this restriction and are available for foreign ownership. See *www.InternationalLiving.com/Contadora.*

• **Malta:**

Real estate closing costs: Typically 6% of the purchase price.
Property taxes: None.
Foreign restrictions: Foreigners are subject to a minimum purchase price. You must spend at least US$81,300 for an apartment and US$135,500 for a house.

• **Australia:**

Real estate closing costs: Typically 4% to 6% of the purchase price.
Property taxes: The rate varies up to a maximum of 1.8% (applied to properties worth approximately US$977,500 or more).
Foreign restrictions: Non-resident investors may purchase only brand-new properties (fully finished or still under construction).

• **France:**

Real estate closing costs: Typically 8% to 10% of the purchase price, but may be as low as 3% for a new property.
Property taxes: The rate depends on the type of residence and its location. In rural Provence, one homeowner pays annual charges of $412, while a house in the Toulouse suburbs is taxed twice that amount.
Foreign restrictions: No restrictions on foreign ownership.

• **Canada:**

Real estate closing costs: Typically 2% to 4% of the purchase price.
Property taxes: The amount levied depends on location and can vary within the same city. In Kingston, Ontario, for example, the burden on a house valued at $150,000 varies from 1.6% to 1.8%.
Foreign restrictions: Some provinces impose restrictions on non-resident ownership. For details, contact the Canadian Embassy at *www.canadianembassy.org.*

Little black book for the world's top 10 retirement havens

1 PANAMA

International Living **Panama office:** Greg Geurin, director of operations, will be able to assist you from real estate to visas to accommodation, *17 Avenida Jose Gabriel Duque, La Cresta, Panama; tel. (507)264-2204; e-mail: Panama@ InternationalLiving.com website: www.InternationalLiving.com/panama*

Offshore banking: National Bank of Panama (Banco Nacional de Panama), *135 Panama, 9A Panama, P.O. Box 11181, Panama 6, Republic of Panama; tel. (507)263-9000; fax (507)263-9514.*

Attorney: Rainelda Mata-Kelly, *LL.M., Law Offices, Suite #305-307, Balboa Plaza, Balboa Avenue, P.O. Box 9012, Panama 6, Republic of Panama; tel. (507)263-4305; fax (507)264-2868; e-mail: rmk@mata-kelly.com*

Business: Panama's Chamber of Commerce, *Avenida Cuba No. 33a, Panama City; P.O. Box 74, Panama 1; tel. (507)25-0833; fax (507)64-8513.*

Government agencies: Embassy of Panama, *2862 McGill Terrace N.W., Washington, DC 20008; tel. (202)483-1407; fax (202)434-8413.*

2 MALTA

Real estate: Frank Salt (Head office), *2 Paceville Ave., Paceville, St. Julians, Malta; tel. (356)21337-373; fax (356)21318-037; e-mail: stjulians@franksalt.com.mt*

Attorney: Camilleri & Camilleri, *129 St. Dominic Street, Valletta, Malta; tel. (356)21242-540.*

Diplomatic representatives: United States consulate in Malta, *5800 Valletta, Malta; tel. (356)21235-960; fax (356)21243-339.*

Healthcare: St. Luke's General Hospital, *Malta; tel. (356)212241-251.*

Dental surgeons: Anthony P. Camilleri & George E. Camilleri, *Regent House, Floor 1, 315, Bisazza St., Sliema, Malta; tel. (356)21330-468.*

Bank: HSBC Malta, *32 Merchants Street, Valletta, Malta; tel. (356)21245-281; fax (356)21222-667; e-mail: infomalta@hsbc.com*

Accommodation: Hotel San Pawl, *Blacktail Street, St Paul's Bay, Malta; tel. (356)21571-369.*

Tourism representative: Malta Tourism Authority, *280 Republic Street, Valletta, Malta, tel. (356)21224-444/5; fax (356)21220-401; e-mail: info@visitmalta.com*

Website: *www.imalta.com* (Malta tourist guide. Includes attractions, flights, hotels, events, history and culture, sports, restaurants, and nightlife.)

(continued on page 215)

Residency Requirements

For most foreign nationals, North Americans included, a valid passport is sufficient for stays up to three months. Visas are not required. The Republic of Malta recognizes three levels of residency for non-Maltese nationals. Incidentally, unless you have been married to a Maltese national for five years, or are the child of Maltese parents, there is no provision to acquire Maltese citizenship, no matter how long you are a resident of the islands.

Foreigners can be classified as follows: non-resident, permanent resident, or temporary resident. For more information on the best option for you, contact the Embassy of Malta, 2017 Connecticut Ave. N.W., Washington, DC 20008; tel. (202)462-3611; fax (202)387-5470.

Outdoor Living—at a Price

Interested in a retirement haven that's even more remote?

Australia comes out in the top five for the second

year running, despite the fact that foreign residency is not an easy thing to obtain. This country is trying to control the number of foreign retirees and residents within its borders.

To be granted a retirement residency visa (extended temporary residence), you must be 55 or older (your spouse may be younger than 55). Plus, you must have at least $360,000 in capital that you are willing to transfer to Australia, or you must have at least $110,000 in capital plus a pension or investments that would provide you with an income of at least $25,000 a year.

The capital that must be transferred to the country can be used for personal investment in Australia, including the purchase of property.

You must also meet certain health and character requirements, and take out comprehensive health insurance with an Australian insurer. With this visa, working is not permitted.

The retirement visa is a temporary visa issued for

3 AUSTRALIA
Real estate: One of the most comprehensive sites, detailing properties throughout Australia is: *www.realestate.com.au*
International tourism and migration: a strong infrastructure for tourists and foreigners interested in taking up residence. For more information go to: *www.immi.gov.au*
Immigration: The Migration Institute of Australia, *tel. (61)292-793-140; fax (61)292-793-172; website: www.mia.org.au*

4 FRANCE
International Living's **Paris Office: Adrian Leeds,** director of operations, will be able to assist you from real estate to visas to accommodation; *43 Rue de Saintonge, BP 38, 75003 Paris, France; tel. (33)1-40-27-97-59; fax (1)801-640-2485; e-mail: Paris@InternationalLiving.com website: www.internationalliving.com/france*
Bank: Citibank, *125 Avenue des Champs-Elysees, 75008 Paris, France; tel. (33)1-44-79-79-79.*
Business and investments: Chamber of Commerce, *27 Avenue de Friedland 75008 Paris; tel. (33)1-55-65-55-65.*
Embassies and consulates: Embassy of France, *4101 Reservoir Road N.W., Washington, DC 20007; tel. (202)944-6000; fax (202)944-6166; e-mail: visas-washington@wash.fr website: www.ambafrance-us.org*
Healthcare: Harford British Hospital, *63 boulevard Victor Hugo, 92202 Neuilly, France; tel. (33)1-46-39-22-22.*
Tourism contact: French Government Tourist Office, *444 Madison Ave., New York, NY 10022-6903; tel. (212)838-7800; fax (212)838-7855; website: www.francetourism.com*

5 CANADA
Accommodation: Whistler Cascade Lodge, *4315 Northland Boulevard, Whistler, BC VON 1B8, Canada; tel. (866)5-806-643; e-mail: reservations@whistlerlodgingco.com website: www.whistler-cascadelodge.com* (Rates from $99 per night.)
Real estate: Coldwell Banker Rhodes & Company (Chris Rhodes), Ottawa, Ontario, Canada; *tel. (613)8-636-786; fax (613)2-362-692; e-mail: chris@rhodesrealestate.ca; website: www.rhodesrealestate.ca.*
Residency: Global Relocate (David Lesperance), *84 King Street West, Suite 202, Dundas, Ontario, Canada L9H 1T9; tel. (905)627-3037; e-mail: dsl@globalrelocate.com website: www.globalrelocate.com*
Tourism: Canadian Tourism Commission, *55 Metcalfe Street, Suite 600, Ottawa, Ontario, Canada K1P 6L5; website: www.travelcanada.ca*

(continued on page 216)

6 NEW ZEALAND

Immigration experts: Malcolm Pacific (Auckland) Limited, *Level 12, 49 Symonds Street, Auckland; P.O. Box 1219, Wellesley St. tel. (64)930-941-87; fax (64)936-647-30; e-mail: intl@malcompacific.com*

Real estate: Jim Mays Real Estate (Jim Mays), *P.O. Box 33-706, Takapuna, New Zealand; cell. (64)21-937-766; tel. (after hours) (64)9-489-8575; fax (64)9-489-8560; e-mail: jimmays@xtra.co.nz website: www.mays.co.nz*

Healthcare: Dr. Satish Chandra (Auckland-North Shore area), *tel. (64)9-486-3248.*

B&B: Peace and Plenty B&B (Machins), *e-mail: peaceandplenty@xtra.co.nz*

Useful website: *www.immigration.govt.nz* This immigration site provides information and has links to many other sites.

7 CYPRUS

Real Estate: Leptos Estates, *111 Ap. Pavlou Ave., P.O. Box 60146, CY-8129 Paphos, Cyprus; tel. (357)26-880-100; fax (357)26-934-719; e-mail: info@leptosestates.com website: www.leptosestates.com*

Visas/Passports: U.S. Embassy, *P.O. Box 24536, 1385 Nicosia, Cyprus; tel. (357)22-776-400; fax (357)22-776-841; e-mail: consularnicosia@state.gov website: www.americanembassy.org.cy*

Tourism: Cyprus Tourism Organization, *13 East 40th Street, New York, NY 10016, U.S.A; tel. (212)683-5280; fax (212)683-5282; e-mail: gocyprus@aol.com; website: www.cyprustourism.org*

Accommodation: Marathon Beach Hotel, *P.O. Box 54197, Limassol, Cyprus. For reservations, contact South Travels, tel. (971)65-591-426; fax (971)65-597-886; e-mail: info@southtravels.com; website: www.southtravels.com*

8 MEXICO

***International Living* local office: Dan Prescher and Suzan Haskins,** *e-mail: Mexico@InternationalLiving.com website: www.mexicoinsider.com*

Attorney: Peyton & Connell (Dennis Peyton), voicemail & fax in California *(619)374-1964; tel. in Mexico (52)664-634-2970; e-mail: inquire@lawmexico.com; website: www.lawmexico.com*

Banking and investing: Lloyds, *tel. (52)333-880-2020 or (52)333-880-2000; fax (52)333-647-2128; e-mail:lloyd@lloyd.com.mx; website: www.lloyd.com.mx/en*

Embassies and consulates: Embassy of Mexico in the United States, *1911 Pennsylvania Ave, Washington, DC 20006; tel. (202)728-1600; fax (202)728-1698;*

(continued on page 217)

an initial period of four years. However, extensions are possible— the immigration department has introduced provisions to enable self-supporting retirees to convert to permanent residence after 10 years in Australia. When you achieve this, you are eligible for many special senior discounts. For example, as a resident of Western Australia, age 60 or over, you're entitled to everything from a 50% discount on recreational fishing license fees to free public transport on Sundays and public holidays.

A Long Way from Home

Another drawback is the distance from the States—it's a 14-hour flight from L.A. to Sydney.

On the other hand, this country offers a relatively low cost of living, good weather, cheap real estate, and a great (outdoor) quality of life.

Part-Time Living

While we're in this part of the world, it's

worth noting another appealing retirement option: New Zealand. If you've seen *The Lord of the Rings*, you're familiar with this country's incredible landscapes. And if you like the great out-doors, you'll never be bored here. The cost of living is low, and real estate can be a bargain. But it's extremely difficult to obtain residency. Your chances are improved if you're young and highly qualified in a field that the government has targeted for growth.

Or, avoid the residency issue altogether by residing on this side of the world only part of the year (up to six months at a time).

Elsewhere in Europe

La belle France seems to have more than its fair share of good things—not least of which are food, wine, and haute couture. If you're looking to retire to Europe, France should also be on your list of possibilities (it takes fourth-place honors in our Index this year).

This country has all the ingredients we look for: a good climate, unspoiled countryside, top-notch culture, excellent healthcare, colorful traditions and history,

e-mail: info@embassyofmexico.org
website: www.embassyofmexico.org
Travel and tours: Agora Travel (International Living's travel agent), *tel. (888)671-8247 or (561)266-6276;*
fax (561)278-8765;
e-mail: Tours@Internationalliving.com
website: www.ildiscoverytours.com
Moving: MexiCo Forwarding, *tel. (888)306-980-76;*
website: www.mexico-forwarding.com

9 NICARAGUA
Attorney: Barrios and Associates (Dr. Emelio Barrios), *Calle Seductor, Los Robels 2da. Etapa, P.O. Box 4874, Managua, Nicaragua; tel. (505)278-0019 ext. 217, fax (505)278-6576, e-mail barrios@ibw.com.ni*
Architect and builder: Silvio Lacayo, *tel. (505)268-3568 ext.101; fax (505)266-2611.*
Business and investment: U.S. Embassy Managua, *Commercial Section, Unit 2703 Box 2, APO AA 34021; tel. (505)266-6010, ext. 4641, fax (505)266-9056; e-mail: usbusiness@amemb.org.ni*
Embassies and consulates: Embassy of Nicaragua, Consular Services, *1627 New Hampshire Ave., N.W., Washington, DC 20009; tel. (202)939-6570; fax (202)939-6542.*
Health insurance: Expacare International Health, *tel. (in England) (44)01344-381650.*
Accommodation: Camino Real (Managua), *tel. (505)263-1381; fax (505)263-1380.*
Real estate: *e-mail: Nicaragua@InternationalLiving.com*

10 GREECE
Real estate: Aegina Real Estate, *Aegina Town, Aegina Island, Greece; tel. (30)2-297-028-825; fax (30) 29-722-900; e-mail: info@aegina-realestate.com website: www.aegina-realestate.com*
Visas/passports: U.S. consulate, *Thessaloniki, Greece; tel. (30)2-310-242-906 (ext. 104); fax (30)2-310-242-927; e-mail: amcongen@compulink.gr website: thessaloniki.usconsulate.gov*
Tourism: Greek National Tourism Organization, *Tsoha 7 Street, 115 21 Athens, Greece; tel. (30)2-108-707-000; e-mail: info@gnto.gr; website: www.gnto.gr*
Accommodation: Hotel 7 Brothers, *Poros Island, Greece; tel. (30)2-298-023-412; fax (30)2-298-023-412; e-mail: 7brothrs@hol.gr; website: www.greekhotel.com (Rates from $45 per night.)*

and, of course, the glitter and sophistication of Paris—arguably the world's most bewitching capital. It's not surprising France is the world's favorite destination, receiving in excess of 70 million overseas visitors each year.

If you're contemplating a new life in Europe, you'll find that few European countries can match what France has to offer, especially when considering property prices—the choice of properties selling for less than $50,000 is incredible—and we're not just talking about ruins or renovation projects.

The downsides? Taxes are high, and the bureaucracy can be frustrating.

Originally published: September 2003 in International Living

International Living is the world's leading publication on living, retiring, and doing business overseas. For example, if you want to open a pub in Ireland… or spend a few months each year in Tuscany… or perhaps buy a vacation home in the Caribbean… International Living is the place to start. For the past 25 years, the publication has helped people realize their dreams to live better, cheaper, and more exciting lives by looking beyond U.S. borders. In addition to a monthly newsletter, International Living leads groups of subscribers on "Explorer Tours" of their favorite destinations. International Living's main offices are located in Waterford, Ireland, with satellite offices in Nicaragua, Mexico, France, Honduras, Argentina, Panama, and Italy. For more details on International Living's favorite places to live, invest, and retire right now, sign up for their free E-mail newsletter. Go to www.internationalliving.com.

How to Retire Overseas—A 12-Step Program

By Kathleen Peddicord

As those with us recently in New Orleans for our Live Overseas Conference discussed… it's not easy… but it can be much easier than you think to arrange a new life in paradise.

Easier yet, of course, if you have some help… and a game plan.

Here's our 12-step program:

1.) Make a list of your personal priorities and preferences.

2.) Narrow your list of potential paradises to three or four… and arrange to spend a little time in each one.

3.) After your visits, cut the list to one or two countries... and plan extended stays... preferably through the least agreeable time of year in each place (the offseason, the rainy season, the hurricane season, etc.).

4.) While you're in each country, trying it on for size, do three things:

Meet with as many expats already living in the country as possible.

Meet with as many real estate agents operating in the areas of the country you're interested in as possible. (Remember: Most real estate markets outside the U.S. do not come with multiple listing services.)

Look at as many properties for sale as you can.

5.) Meet with an international tax planner in the United States. You soon may have a new tax obligation... but don't forget that, as an American, you will never be free of your old one. Get advice from a U.S. tax expert who knows about things like the income exemption for non-resident Americans and the benefits of an offshore corporation.

6.) Meet with a tax expert in the country(ies) you're considering moving to... who, critically, is experienced in working with foreign residents. (It's important that you do this before taking up residence in the country. Otherwise, the most advantageous options for organizing your tax affairs may not be available to you.)

7.) Meet with a residency expert from the country(ies) you're considering... and determine which visa or residency permit would be most advantageous given your circumstances. (Again, we can make recommendations, depending on the country.)

8.) If you haven't already, narrow your list to one destination... and set a date for your move. Determine whether you want to ship your household belongings with you, or buy new when you arrive. Your decision may have something to do with the type of visa you're arranging (which may or may not allow for the tax-free importation of personal belongings, household goods, a car, appliances, etc.), but should have mostly to do with the hassle factor. Packing and shipping a household full of stuff across borders can be a pain in the neck... and expensive. We shipped a container load of furniture, etc., from the U.S. to Ireland... but wouldn't do it again.

9.) Set up a portable global office (to allow for reliable and efficient mail forwarding, e-mail, international telephone calls, bill paying, credit card usage, etc.).

10.) Do not buy... but rent a new home in your chosen haven... in the area where you think you want to relocate permanently. Rent for six months to a year before committing fully to buying. Had we not done this when moving to Ireland we probably would have bought wrong—that is, in town, rather than out in the country, which we've found suits us better.

11.) Open a local bank account. You probably won't be able to do this until you have a local address... and you may need a letter of reference from your bank in the States.

12.) Buy your tickets... you're ready to become an expat.

Good luck.

Originally published: December 2002 in International Living

Kathleen Peddicord is the publisher of International Living, a publication that identifies and reports on the world's best opportunities for living, retiring, investing, traveling, and buying real estate overseas. She has also edited several books on these and related subjects, including The World's Top Retirement Havens.

In the past ten years she has traveled extensively investigating real estate and retirement overseas, both for International Living and for personal interest.

In 1999, she finally took her own advice and moved her family to Ireland. She is currently restoring a charming Georgian Manor House and publishing International Living from its new offices in Waterford, on Ireland's south east coast.

For more info on International Living, visit: www.internationalliving.com.

How to Slash Your Taxes by 90%... and Live in a Tropical Paradise

The Best Places for Second Passports and Offshore Residency

By Robert Bauman

I often write about obtaining a second passport or dual citizenship as a means to hedge one's bets against future events. The last century (and already this one) has witnessed horrors when individuals or entire groups have been forced to flee their homelands. Millions of citizens each year choose to change their residence to another nation for a variety of reasons.

If you're a U.S. citizen, there's no need to surrender your U.S. passport if you do acquire a second nationality. U.S. law fully supports the right of Americans to enjoy dual citizenship.

What About "Economic Citizenship"?

If you don't qualify for alternative citizenship based on your ancestry, "economic citizenship" can be obtained from the two nations that still make it available; Dominica and St. Kitts & Nevis.

In 2002, Dominica sharply increased both the fees and administrative hurdles applicants for economic citizenship must overcome, making St. Kitts & Nevis the most viable program. While costs are still slightly lower in Dominica, the St. Kitts & Nevis passport is now a far more attractive travel document.

To qualify for citizenship in St. Kitts & Nevis, you must make a real estate investment of at least U.S.$250,000. There are also government fees of U.S.$35,000 for a single applicant, plus U.S.$15,000 for each dependent. Finally, there are application fees of U.S.$15,000 and due diligence fees, which vary depending on the number of persons included in an application. The Government recently increased these due diligence fees to U.S.$2,500 per adult applicant.

These requirements make the program relatively expensive but also more exclusive. However, St. Kitts & Nevis is an attractive place to own real estate, and there are some excellent real estate developments approved under the citizenship program. Further, relatively few passports have been issued under the program.

As a result, St. Kitts & Nevis passport holders enjoy visa-free travel to more than 90 countries, including the United Kingdom, Canada, Switzerland, Sweden, and many others. St. Kitts & Nevis passport holders, unlike Dominica passport holders, still have visa-free access to Canada. As a citizen of St. Kitts & Nevis you can live and work in St. Kitts & Nevis anytime, and as a Commonwealth citizen you enjoy special rights and privileges in the United Kingdom. You are not liable to taxation in St. Kitts & Nevis as there are no income taxes there at all.

Finally, owning real estate in St. Kitts & Nevis, two of the most attractive islands in the Caribbean, is a good investment that you can use for your vacation, as a *pied-a-terre*, for future retirement, or to generate rental income.

For more information, visit www.henleyglobal.com/stkittsnevis.

Eliminate State Tax, Pay Zero Estate Tax, and Slash Your Income Tax to 10%

Short of becoming a citizen of a foreign nation, you might consider the possibility of trying out a foreign homeland by first moving there and experiencing life as lived by the locals.

Several nations have residency programs especially designed to attract foreign citizens who may want to make their home abroad. These attractions include many special tax exemptions (some even total), reduced prices on many goods and services, plus home buying and building programs, also tax exempt.

Under a unique federal income tax arrangement applying only to the U.S. Territory of the Virgin Islands, it is possible for U.S. nationals and foreigners who make the islands their main residence to enjoy substantial personal and business tax benefits. These lower taxes make the islands an offshore tax haven option for wealthy U.S. citizens and for foreign nationals seeking U.S. citizenship. And for Americans, moving to the USVI is little more trouble than moving from one mainland state to another.

Like anyone else in the United States, USVI residents and corporations pay federal taxes on their worldwide income. However, they make their payments to the Virgin Islands Internal Revenue Bureau (IRB), not the U.S. Internal Revenue Service. This distinction has important legal consequences for those who are legal residents of the USVI or those who immigrate from outside the United States and become naturalized U.S. citizens while USVI-resident. For purposes of U.S. federal gift and estate taxes, such individuals are treated as non-U.S. residents.

Since the USVI has no estate or gift taxes, this means that upon death their estates owe zero federal or state estate or gift taxes.

That's just the beginning. To attract investment, the USVI government grants generous tax relief packages, including a 90% exemption on corporate federal income taxes. This package usually is offered for 10-15 years (with possible five-year extensions), and is available to USVI-chartered corporations, partnerships, and limited liability companies on their worldwide income. This allows investors to live in their second home anywhere in United States for the spring, summer, and fall, then come home to the USVI for the winter, to play golf, tennis, sail, and swim.

You too may be able to enjoy the unique legal privilege of paying 10% of your federal income taxes and no state or local taxes. To find out more, contact:

USVI Government Website URL: www.usvi.net/usvi/tax.html

Attorney: Marjorie Rawls Roberts, PC, LLB, JD, AB
P.O. Box 6347, St. Thomas, U.S. Virgin Islands 00804.
Tel.: +1 (340) 776-7235. Fax: +1 (340) 776-7951.
E-mail: jorie@marjorierobertspc.com
URL: www.lawyers.com/robertslaw

Panama: Leading Retirement Haven

Despite its relatively advanced industrial and financial infrastructure, Panama remains an affordable place in which to live. A live-in maid earns about US$120 a month; first-run movies cost US$1.50. Unlike much of Central America, Panama boasts a first class health care system with low costs compared to the United States—a doctor's office visit costs about $15.

The government makes retirement in Panama easy, and laws provide important tax advantages for foreigners who wish to become residents under its *pensionado* program. The only significant requirements are good health and a verifiable monthly income of at least US$500. There are no local taxes on foreign income and you can import your household goods tax-free.

Because of Panama's geographical diversity, there is considerable climatic variation. Panama City, the historical and financial center, has a year-round tropical climate. Yet only a few hundred miles away is a sub-tropical forest, with cascading waterfalls, mountainsides covered with flowers, and spring-like weather year-round. There are also many low-priced buys on condos and other real estate, particularly in Panama City and the surrounding areas. This is in part a byproduct of the U.S. government exodus after the Panamanian takeover of the Panama Canal in 1999.

For more information, contact: Greg Geurin, International Living (Panama), 17 Avenida Jose Gabriel Duque, La Cresta, Panama, Republic of Panama. Tel.: +(507) 264-2204.

Tax-Free Residency in Belize

Since 2000, this Central American nation has welcomed offshore persons with its Retired Persons Incentive Act. The program, which resembles the popular *pensionado* program in Panama, is designed to attract foreign retirees and foreign capital.

Known as the "qualified retired persons" (QRP) program, the law offers significant tax incentives to those willing to become permanent residents (but not full citizens). The program is aimed primarily at residents of the United States, Canada, and the United Kingdom, but is open to all.

As with Panama, a "qualified retired person" is exempted from all taxes on income from sources outside Belize. Import duties are waived for personal effects, household goods, and for a motor vehicle or other transport, such as an airplane or a boat.

There is no minimum time that must be spent in Belize and you can maintain your QRP status so long as you maintain a permanent local residence, such as a small apartment or condo.

QRPs can also own and operate an international business based in Belize exempt from all local taxes. Local income earned within Belize is taxed at a graduated rate of 15%-45%. However, you will need a work permit to engage in purely domestic business activities.

To qualify for the QRP program, you must be 45 years of age or older and prove personal financial ability to support yourself and any dependants. Initial fees for the program are US$700, plus US$100 for an ID card upon application approval. A spouse and dependents (18 and younger) qualify along with the head of household at no extra cost. Minimum financial requirements include an annual income of at least US$24,000 (or equivalent) from a pension, annuity or from other sources outside Belize.

For more information on the QRP Program, contact:

Belize Tourist Board, New Central Bank Building, Level 2,
Gabourel Lane, P.O. Box 325, Belize City, Belize.
Tel.: +(501) 231-913. Fax: +(501) 231-943.
E-mail: info@travelbelize.org

Ministry of Tourism,
Constitution Drive, Belmopan, Belize.
Tel.: +(501) 823-393. Fax: +(501) 823-815.
E-mail: tourismdpt@btl.net

For More Information

In an unsettled world, acquiring a second citizenship is a wise decision—an investment in your future. It can be a choice for life and a protective shield for your spouse and children as well. And offshore residency also opens doors, not only to new worlds, but to a new life as well.

Originally published: January 2004 by The Sovereign Society

Robert E. Bauman, JD is a former member of the U.S. House of Representatives from Maryland and the author of several books on offshore financial topics. Mr. Bauman serves as legal counsel to The Sovereign Society, an international group of citizens concerned with government encroachment on financial freedom. For more information, go to: www.sovereignsociety.com.

The Truth About Offshore Bank Accounts

6 Strategies to Achieve Maximum Banking Privacy

By Mark Nestmann

I n the minds of most Americans, there is nothing so mysterious, so enticing, as an "offshore bank account." The very phrase, particularly among the wine and Brie crowd, brings up images of exotic and possibly illegal financial dealings in a tropical setting, accompanied by absolute bank privacy. The movie *The Firm* greatly reinforced these stereotypes. It portrayed the Cayman Islands as a jurisdiction where you could simply land a plane stuffed with bags of cash and deposit that cash directly into a local bank account.

However, those days, if they ever existed at all, are long gone. The truth about offshore bank accounts is very different from what you hear at parties or see at the movies. In this column, I'm going to separate fact from fiction, and give you six recommendations that will allow you to legally protect the privacy of your offshore account.

The Truth About "Bank Secrecy"

For better or worse, the concept of "bank secrecy" has changed greatly in recent years. Thirty years ago, it was possible to hire an attorney in one of several offshore jurisdictions—including Switzerland, Liechtenstein, or the Bahamas—and have the attorney open up an offshore bank account, in his name, and operate it for you without the bank knowing your real identity.

In those days, secrecy was virtually absolute. No one—including agents of the U.S. government—could penetrate it, except in very unusual circumstances.

All this began to change in the 1970s, when the United States signed its first "Mutual Legal Assistance Treaty" (MLAT) with Switzerland. This agreement obligated Swiss authorities to waive bank secrecy when the U.S. government presented them with evidence that money tied to a serious crime in the United States was being held in Switzerland. Tax offenses, with the exception of tax fraud, were not covered.

Since then, the United States has ratified nearly 50 additional MLAT's, most with expanded provisions in comparison to the Swiss agreement. In addition, various international organizations, including the Organization for Economic Cooperation and Development (OECD) and its stepchild, the Financial Action Task Force (FATF), have prepared "blacklists" of countries in which "excessive financial secrecy" prevails, and tried to impose sanctions against those countries not agreeing to severely restrict it.

But bank secrecy has not been "eliminated," as some press reports would imply. The best way to view bank secrecy today is as a bulwark against prying eyes peering into your financial affairs, unless you are suspected of committing a serious crime.

No doubt, bank secrecy occasionally shields lawbreakers. But more often than not, it is used for legitimate purposes—to shield individuals and their families from retribution by corrupt or totalitarian governments; to give them access to investments forbidden or restricted in their own countries; or to hide wealth from kidnappers who typically target persons with visible wealth.

And today, even if some of the more powerful tools that individuals and companies could once use to keep their financial affairs secret have been severely restricted, opportunities remain for financial privacy "offshore" that simply don't exist domestically. You just have to be realistic in your expectations.

Offshore Bank Accounts and Privacy

While it's become more difficult to move money offshore, you can still take your domestic wealth off the radar screen to achieve practical, if not necessarily impenetrable, privacy.

The single best reason to move assets outside your own country is to protect yourself from the global litigation epidemic. The United States is unique in its approach to "tort liability," in which both sides in a lawsuit pay their own expenses, no matter who wins, and where lawyers are permitted to finance lawsuits, no matter how ridiculous the claim. In recent months, doctors have actually gone on strike in several states to protest skyrocketing malpractice premiums resulting from increased exposure to lawsuits.

However, truly frivolous litigation is no longer a U.S.-only phenomenon. The U.K. and Canadian legal systems are also undergoing quiet, yet revolutionary transformations that dramatically increase the odds of being sued and losing. (See www.overlawyered.com/places/canada.html for some mind-boggling Canadian lawsuits, including "Father files suit after son fails to make MVP award.")

An offshore bank account provides substantial protection from frivolous lawsuits. Since lawyers size up targets for lawsuits by looking for their money, someone considering suing you may decide to find a target with more visible wealth.

Unfortunately, the availability of offshore bank accounts with low minimums is rapidly diminishing. This is a direct consequence of the escalating cost of banks performing "due diligence" on their customers to comply with new initiatives from the OECD and FATF. However, minimum deposits for the Offshore Convenient Account still may start as low as U.S.$15,000.

Six Recommendations for Offshore Banking Secrecy

The advantages of dealing offshore—privacy, asset protection and investment diversification—remain in place, but only if you follow a few simple rules.

1. *Choose the right jurisdiction.* We believe the top offshore jurisdictions to be Switzerland, Panama, Liechtenstein, and Hong Kong. First-class offshore banking services are also available in Austria. Denmark offers low-cost offshore banking, but no privacy with regards to foreign tax authorities.

2. *Understand foreign "due diligence" requirements.* Along with the end of anonymous accounts in most offshore jurisdictions, most offshore banks now require prospective customers to prove their identity with a certified copy of their passport or other official document. You may also face questions regarding the origin of the funds you are placing into the account. Don't be afraid to answer these questions—the application for your account, along with all documentation you provide, is subject to whatever bank secrecy laws prevail in the jurisdiction you've chosen.

3. *Don't try to cheat the taxman.* Most high-tax countries impose taxes on the worldwide income of their residents. While domestic tax authorities don't generally have the authority to go on offshore "fishing expeditions" to uncover unreported offshore income, the momentum is clearly toward greater disclosure. There's also little doubt that the tools that governments are giving themselves to fight "terrorism" will ultimately be used to augment tax collection. Our recommendation is to report the existence of the account to your domestic tax authorities and pay whatever taxes are due. Doing so will not generally raise a red flag and will not negate the privacy advantages of the account with respect to prospective litigants. At least in the case of the IRS, there have been many more prosecutions for failing to report an offshore transaction than for engaging in an allegedly illegal transaction that was reported.

4. *Don't open an account at the foreign branch of a U.S. bank, or a foreign bank that has U.S. branches.* Either of these factors places the bank under the jurisdiction of U.S. courts, thus providing litigants with additional opportunities to penetrate offshore banking secrecy.

5. *Don't use offshore accounts to hold U.S. dollar denominated investments, including U.S. securities.* The U.S.A. Patriot Act gives U.S. authorities the right to demand to know the identity of individuals with interests in the U.S. "correspondent accounts" offshore banks maintain for their customers who maintain U.S. dollar investments.

In addition, the U.S. government is beginning to confiscate the proceeds of such accounts under the notorious "civil forfeiture" statutes. Finally, IRS "qualified intermediary" (QI) regulations enmesh correspondent accounts in a maze of red tape. U.S. depositors in foreign banks who purchase U.S. securities and refuse to identify themselves to the IRS under the QI regulations are subject to a 31% withholding tax—not just on income from the account, but on their entire investment. So make sure to set up your offshore account(s) so that you can use them to purchase U.S. securities or other dollar-denominated assets without actually holding them in U.S. dollars (sounds complicated, but it really is easy to do).

6. *Keep it simple.* It's a good idea never to get involved in an investment you don't understand, and this is doubly true for investments you make outside your own country. Ultimately, the value of offshore investing is to create a "nest egg" that can survive lawsuits, changes in public policy, or even a collapse in the value of your domestic currency. You don't need complex investments to achieve these goals.

Originally published: August 2003 in The Sovereign Individual

Mark Nestmann is the Editor of The Sovereign Individual, the monthly publication of The Sovereign Society, an organization dedicated to helping its members protect and grow their wealth. For more information, go to: www.sovereignsociety.com

The World's 4 Best Asset Havens 2003

By Robert E. Bauman

In preparing this survey of the world's top asset havens, we reviewed the laws, political stability, economic climate, tax situation, and the overall "clout" in dozens of different jurisdictions.

We narrowed our choices down to four top jurisdictions: Switzerland, Panama, Liechtenstein, and Hong Kong. Plus, we have listed several havens as "honorable mention."

To evaluate each jurisdiction, we reviewed five factors:

Government/political stability: How long has the current system of government been in place? Is the jurisdiction politically stable?

Favorable laws/judicial system: How long a tradition has the haven had? Does its legal and judicial system have a reputation for "fair play" with regard to foreign investors?

Available legal entities: Does the jurisdiction have a large enough variety of legal entities to satisfy the average person seeking an estate planning or business solution?

Financial privacy/banking secrecy: Does the jurisdiction have financial secrecy laws? How strictly are they applied? What exceptions to secrecy exist?

Taxes: Does the haven impose taxes on foreign investors? How easily can these taxes be avoided legally? Are there tax treaties or tax information exchange agreements in effect?

#1 Asset Haven: Switzerland

In spite of the many compromises the Swiss have been forced to make under world pressures, Switzerland today still stands as the world's best all-around offshore banking and asset protection haven.

U.S. depositors considering Swiss banks should avoid UBS AG and any other Swiss bank with U.S.-based branches, affiliates or banking operations, other than a mere "representative office."

Despite recent privacy setbacks, the Swiss financial system, warts and all, still has plenty going for it. Unless there is a strong suspicion of criminal wrongdoing, under Swiss law it is still a crime for bankers to violate the secrecy of their clients.

The Very Special Swiss Franc

Switzerland's currency, the Swiss franc, generally has reflected the state of Swiss banking: strong, valuable, and unaffected by inflation and stylish monetary fads.

Since 1971, the franc has appreciated nearly 300% against the U.S. dollar. U.S. owners of Swiss franc denominated assets have profited handsomely as a result. That profit came despite traditionally low Swiss interest rates and the bothersome 35% withholding tax on bank interest. In recent years, the value of the franc has fluctuated against the U.S. dollar, strengthening in the early 1990s, weakening from 1995-2001, and strengthening once again in the last two years.

World Class Banking System

Although Swiss banking privacy is legendary, secrecy is not the most important reason for Switzerland's success. Of far greater significance are the country's political, financial, and economic stability and strength. Most of the world's largest companies and hundreds of thousands of honest, law-abiding foreigners bank with the Swiss. Indeed, Swiss banks manage over two trillion Swiss francs, approximately US$1.6 trillion! Even the international intermediary banking institution, the Bank for International Settlements, is located in Switzerland.

Switzerland is home to several hundred banks ranging from small private and regional banks to the two giants, Union Bank of Switzerland (UBS AG) and Credit Suisse. These major Swiss banks have branch offices in most of the world's financial centers, from New York to Panama.

Swiss banks are unequaled as a base for global investing. Opening a Swiss bank account can be a first move in developing a strategy of safety and international diversification. An individual, corporation, trust, foundation, pension plan, or any other legal entity can open an account.

You can invest in certificates of deposit, U.S. and other national stocks, bonds, mutual funds, and commodities; buy, store, and sell gold, silver and other precious metals; and buy insurance and annuities. Swiss banks can act as your agent to buy and hold other types of assets. Of course, Swiss banks also issue international credit and ATM bank cards.

The biggest downside to banking in Switzerland is the high minimum deposits necessary at most banks. While only a few years ago, many banks were content with initial deposits of only a few thousand dollars, Switzerland's popularity among foreign investors, along with the cost of administering "know your customer" laws, has led to sharp increases in deposit minimums, which now average about US$100,000.

An option for smaller bank accounts can be found in banks run by the various Swiss "cantons," as the largely self-governing provinces are called. These banks offer full services, have relatively low minimum deposits and each cantonal government insures the deposits.

Contacts

Banks

- Bank Julius Baer, Tel.: +(41) 1 228-5111. Fax: +(41) 58-888-1122; Website: www.juliusbaer.com

- Banque Piguet & Cie SA, Tel.: +(41) 24-423-4300. Fax Human Resources: +(41) 24-423-4308. Banque *Financial Consultants.* Website: www.banque-piguet.ch

- SwissFirst Bank, c/o Ms. Julia Fernandez, Weber, Hartmann, Vrijhof & Partners; Zuerichstrasse 110B; CH-8134 Adliswil, Switzerland. Tel.: +41-1-709-1115. Fax: +41-1-709-1113. E-mail: whvp@active.ch. Website: www.swissbankaccount.com

- Marc Sola, NMG International Financial Services, Tel.: +(41) 1-266-2141. Fax: +(41) 1-266-2149. E-mail: marcsola@nmg-ifs.com

- Christian Kälin, Henley & Partners, Tel.: +(41) 1-267-6090.
  Fax: +(41) 1-267-6091 (send attn. to Mr. Kälin).
  Website: www.henleyglobal.com
  E-mail: zurich-office@henleyglobal.com

#2 Asset Haven: Panama

Alone among current offshore tax havens, Panama combines maximum financial privacy, a long history of judicial enforcement of asset protection-friendly laws, strong anti-money laundering laws, tax exemptions for foreigners, and—due to its unique historic relationship with the United States—a high degree of independence from outside pressures.

Panama is a very different place than I remember during my many visits in the 1970s when I served in the U.S. House of Representatives as the ranking Republican on the Panama Canal subcommittee. My visits then were made during U.S. legislative implementation of the Carter-Torjillos treaty negotiations.

Upon my return in 1999, I marveled at the modern skyscrapers, first class hotels and restaurants, excellent digital Internet and other international communications, as well as the reduced U.S. ambiance. Downtown Panama City, the balmy, tropical capital on the southern Pacific end of the Canal, suggests Los Angeles or Miami, except arguably more locals speak English here than in some parts of south Florida.

Privacy, Profits and No Taxes

According to Canada's Fraser Institute, Panama is near the top of the list of the world's most free economies, ranked eighth with Australia, Ireland, the Netherlands, and Luxembourg. Panama has adopted more than 40 laws protecting foreigners' financial and investment rights, including the Investments Stability Law (Law No. 54), which guarantees foreign and local investors equal rights.

Among the current 80 plus banks, the major players are the 58 multinational banks representing 30 countries that primarily conduct offshore business. They hold 72% of a reported total US$37 billion in total assets. Banking alone accounts for about 11% of Panama's GNP.

Nearly every one of the world's major banks has a full-service branch office in Panama, with representation from Japan, Germany, Brazil, and the United States.

IBCs and Foundations

Panama has liberal laws favoring trusts, international business companies, and holding companies. In 1995, it enacted Law No. 25, a new private foundation statute modeled after the popular Stiftung or family wealth protection and estate planning vehicle long used in Liechtenstein.

Panama's international business company (IBC) Law 32 of 1927, is modeled after the U.S. State of Delaware's corporation friendly statutes. There are about 350,000 IBCs registered in Panama, second only to Hong Kong's 400,000. A Panamanian IBC can maintain its own corporate bank account and credit cards for global management of investments, mutual funds, precious metals, real estate, and trade. Tax-free corporate income can be spent for business purposes worldwide and using the Panama IBC allows avoidance of home country zoning, labor, manufacturing, warranty, environmental, and other restrictions.

Leading Retirement Haven

Despite its relatively advanced industrial and financial infrastructure, Panama remains an affordable place in which to live. A live-in maid earns about US$120 a month; first-run movies cost US$1.50. Unlike much of Central America, Panama boasts a first class health care system with low costs compared to the United States. A doctor's office visit costs about US$15.

Because of Panama's geographical diversity, there is considerable climatic variation. Panama City, the historical and financial center, has a year-round tropical climate. Yet, only a few hundred miles away is a sub-tropical forest, with cascading waterfalls, mountainsides covered with flowers, and spring-like weather year-round.

The government makes retirement in Panama easy, and laws provide important tax advantages for foreigners who wish to become residents. The only significant requirements are good health and a verifiable monthly income of at least US$500. There are no local taxes on foreign income and you can import your household goods tax-free.

Contacts

Banks:

- Banco Continental, Tel.: +(507) 215-7000. Fax: +(507) 215-7192. Website: www.bcontinental.com

- National Bank of Panama (Banco Internacional de Panama), Tel.: +(507) 263-9000. Fax: +(507) 263-9514.

Trust companies:

- Trust Services SA., Tel.: +(507) 269-2438 or +(507) 263-5252. Fax: +(507) 269-4922. Website: www.trustserv.com E-mail: marketing@trustserv.com

Attorneys:

- Rainelda Mata-Kelly, Tel.: +(507) 263-4305. Fax: +(507) 264-2868.
  Website: www.mata-kelly.com E-mail: rmk@mata-kelly.com

Panamanian residency:

- Greg Geurin, c/o International Living (Panama), Tel.: +(507) 264-2204.
  Fax: (507) 264-2054.
  Mr. Geurin directs the operations of International Living in Panama and has
  excellent contacts in the Panamanian legal and real estate communities.

#3 Asset Haven: Liechtenstein

Liechtenstein's financial services provide some 40% of budget revenues, so anything that tarnishes its reputation is a major crisis. Its 16 locally owned banks, 60 law firms, and 250 trust companies employ 16% of the workforce, and its licensed fiduciary companies and lawyers serve as nominees for, or manage, more than 75,000 legal entities, most of them owned and controlled by non-residents of Liechtenstein.

Indeed, Liechtenstein was one of the first nations in the world to adopt specific offshore asset protection laws, as far back as the 1920s. Liechtenstein's unique role in international circles is not so much as a banking center, but as a tax haven. The nation acts as a base of operations for foreign holding companies, private foundations, family foundations, and a unique entity called an Anstalt (Establishment). The banks and a host of specialized trust companies provide management services for thousands of such entities.

Personal and company tax rates are low, generally under 12% for local residents. Any company domiciled in Liechtenstein is granted total exemption from income tax if it generates no income from local sources.

Liechtenstein is independent, but closely tied to Switzerland. The Swiss franc is the local currency and in many respects, except for political independence, Liechtenstein's status is that of a province integrated within Switzerland. Liechtenstein banks are integrated into Switzerland's banking system and capital markets. Many cross-border investments clear in or through Swiss banks. Foreign-owned holding companies are a major presence in Liechtenstein, with most maintaining their accounts in Swiss banks.

Secrecy Guaranteed By Law

Liechtenstein's secrecy statutes have historically been considered stronger even than those in Switzerland. The 2000 amendments to the money laundering laws weaken secrecy significantly, but Liechtenstein still boasts some of the strictest confidentiality statutes in the world. While banks must now keep records of clients' identities, such records may not be made public. Secrecy also extends to trustees, lawyers, accountants, and to anyone connected to the banking industry. All involved are subject to the disciplinary powers of Liechtenstein's Upper Court.

Contacts

Banks

- Centrum Bank, Tel.: +(423) 235-8585. Fax: +(423) 238-3839.
  Website: www.centrumbank.li

- LGT Bank in Liechtenstein, Tel.: +(423) 235-1122. Fax: +(423) 235-1522.
  Website: www.lgt.com

- Liechtensteinische Landesbank AG, Tel.: +(423) 236-8811.
  Fax: +(423) 236-8822.
  Website: www.llb.li

Trust Companies

- First Advisory Group, Tel.: +(423) 236-0404. Fax: +(423) 236-0405.

Financial Consultants: Use the Switzerland contacts above.

Asset Haven #4: Hong Kong

Even though it is controlled by the Communist government in Beijing, Hong Kong remains relatively free, a reflection of Beijing's need for Hong Kong as its financial powerhouse.

Hong Kong retains a strong set of common law based statutes governing banking and finance. If you're doing business in Asia, this is the place to be.

Hong Kong is proof that "money talks." China has too much invested in Hong Kong to destroy it all in a fit of rigid political ideology. Today, 30% of Hong Kong bank deposits are Chinese, and China accounts for 22% of all its foreign trade, including cross border trade, 20% of the insurance business and over 12% of all construction. More than 2,000 Chinese-controlled entities now do business in Hong Kong.

Doing Business in Hong Kong

As a matter of local custom, Hong Kong banks have always requested a judicial warrant before disclosing records to any foreign government. Access is much easier for the local government, but there are no double-taxation agreements with countries other than the People's Republic of China. A mutual legal assistance treaty (MLAT) with the United States was signed in 1998 and came into force in 2000.

Communist Connections

For non-Chinese wishing to conduct business in China, a secure option is to open a bank account at the Hong Kong branch of the Bank of Communications (BC).

Headquartered in Beijing, BC provides good openings to the mainland. Unlike the Bank of China, it has no U.S. branches subject to the kind of U.S. government investigative pressures that have been brought against other Hong Kong banks, such as Standard Chartered.

The Bank of Communications is likely to resist any U.S. pressure to lift bank secrecy practices. There are U.S. banks in Hong Kong, but when you open an account in one of those institutions, they demand a signed waiver allowing secrecy to be lifted at the request of U.S. authorities. That is a good argument for going Communist when banking in Hong Kong, or at least banking non-American.

Beware of Hong Kong's best-known bank, Hongkong & Shanghai Banking Corp. (HSBC). Thanks to its purchase of Marine Midland, the well-known New York bank, part of its diversification away from Hong Kong, it now is subject to pressure from American authorities.

Contacts

Banks

- Bank of Communications, Tel.: +(852) 2841-9611 / 2973. Fax: +(852) 2810-6993. Website: www.bankcomm.com.hk/e_index.htm

- Rabobank, Tel.: +(852) 2103 2000. Fax: +(852) 2530-1728.

Corporation & Trust Services

- Offshore Incorporations Ltd, Tel.: +(852) 2521 2515. Fax: +(852) 2810-4525. Website: www.offshore-inc.com E-mail: info@offshore-inc.com

- OCRA (Hong Kong), Tel.: +(852) 2522-0172. E-mail: ocra@ocra-asia.com

Honorable Mention: The following countries did not make our list of the top 4 asset havens, but still provide many benefits you might want to consider:

Andorra

Andorra, nestled in the Pyrenees between Spain and France, is both a residential haven and a banking haven, but only for the very wealthy. There are few taxes and only six banks, all of which adhere to the strictest financial secrecy laws applied anywhere on earth. Numbered accounts are still available to the mega-rich, but a 1995 anti-money laundering law is applied to any suspicious financial activities. A great place if you have lots of money and love winter sports.

Contact: Servissim, Tel.: +(376) 860-414. Fax: +(376) 863-797. Servissim is a relocation agent that provides, free of charge, a newsletter with information about Andorra's residency laws.

Austria

Austria is a banking haven in central Europe. Its major offshore attraction is its ironclad banking and financial privacy laws, uniquely guaranteed by its national constitution. Wherever your IBC, trust or other business may be located offshore, you can base your banking activities in Austria and take advantage of maximum privacy.

Contact: Anglo-Irish Bank, Tel.: +(43) 1-406-6161. Fax: +(43) 1-405 8142. The minimum deposit to open an account is US$100,000. Vice President Peter Zipper is a member of The Sovereign Society's Council of Experts.

Monaco

Monaco is an international home for people of wealth. Of the 35,000 residents, 80% are from other nations and virtually all of them rich enough to afford to live on some of the priciest real estate in the world. Tax-free for foreigners, its banks are supervised by the Bank of France. But bank secrecy is the rule, except where crime may be involved. Many wealthy people base their "family office" here, since wealth management is a major profession in this principality ruled by the princes of the Grimaldi family for over 700 years.

Contact: Christian Kälin, Henley & Partners, Tel.: +(41) 1-267-6090. Fax: +(41) 1-267-6091. E-mail: chris.kalin@henleyglobal.com Website: www.henleyglobal.com/monaco.htm

Nevis, Cook Islands, and Belize

Offshore Legal Entities

Several offshore centers combine high degrees of financial privacy with several decades of well-established statutory regimes offering asset protection trusts (APTs), limited liability companies (LLC), and international business companies (IBCs). In each, the local judicial system protects foreigners who have chosen to use their local legal entities.

These offshore centers include Nevis, one half of the Caribbean nation of St.

Christopher & Nevis; the Cook Islands in the far south Pacific and Belize in Central America.

Contacts

- Nevis: Nevis Services Ltd., Tel.: +1 (212) 575-0818. Fax: +1 (212) 575-0812. Contact: Mario M. Novello, President.

- Cook Islands: Asiaciti Trust Pacific Ltd., Tel.: +(682) 23 387 or 24 439. Fax: +682 23 385. Website: http://www.asiaciti.com E-mail: Cook_Islands@asiaciti.com

- Belize: Belize Offshore Center, Tel.: +(501) 223-3738. Website: www.offshoreservices.com E-mail: cititrust@offshore.bz

Originally published: June 2003 by The Sovereign Society

For more information on The Sovereign Society, go to: www.sovereignsociety.com.

Chapter 9

8 Ideas About Wealth and Money

How to Live like a Billionaire No Matter How Much You Make

By Michael Masterson

"Thou shalt not covet thy neighbor's house, thou shalt not covet they neighbor's wife, nor his manservant, nor his maidservant, nor his ox, nor his ass, nor anything that is thy neighbor's."
~Exodus 20:17

When you think about the rich—the really rich—you may find yourself marveling at their... well, their money. Take Bill Gates, the world's richest man. If you think $10 million is a fortune, then consider this: He has 8,000 of them. If he put his money in $1,000 bills, he'd have 80 million of them! His wealth is so great that the interest makes him $60 million richer every month. Bill Gates makes more money every time he takes a nap than most Americans make in 10 years.

But how much better does he live? Sure, he's got a huge house. And a yacht. He's probably got a jet, too. But who needs that crap? Really!

If you make at least $100,000 a year ($150,000 if you are attached to a family), you can live as well as Bill Gates does, and I'll prove it to you.

Let's start by identifying some of life's basic experiences:

* sleeping
* working
* dressing
* eating/drinking
* leisure

Now the purpose of becoming rich—you would think—would be to make each of these experiences as rewarding as possible. The more money you have, the more choices you have in terms of these experiences.

Take sleeping. What does a billionaire want out of his sleep time? I'd say the same thing you would: blissful, uninterrupted unconsciousness. And what will give you that? (Besides peace of mind which you can't buy?)

Answer: a great mattress.

And how much does the world's best mattress cost? Maybe $1,500. That means you can buy yourself a million-dollar sleep on a billion-dollar mattress for no more than $1,500. If you are making $100,000 a year, you can afford it.

So get rid of that lumpy thing you are sleeping on and find yourself the absolute best mattress you have ever sat on. Buy it and go to sleep content that Bill Gates can have it no better.

Buying Yourself the Best: How to Live Like a Billionaire When You're Not Even a Measly Millionaire

You can pay almost any price for anything, but after a certain price point you are no longer paying for quality, you are paying for prestige.

Take steak. Ask someone who knows about beef and you will be told that the quality of steak is entirely a matter of the meat you buy. (Let's face it—there's no great skill in cooking a flank of beef.)

If you buy a New York Sirloin at Ruth's Chris for around $30, you are eating the best steak money can buy. Eat the same piece of meat at Le Cirque and you'll pay $75. What's the difference?

Yes—just prestige.

The same thing is true when it comes to your clothing. Beautiful, comfortable clothes are not cheap, but they don't have to cost a fortune. You can buy the world's best pair of slacks for $150, or you can spend 10 times that amount. The difference will be the label on the waistband.

Champagne, anyone? *Consumer Reports* had some wine experts test a variety of champagnes and found that of the five best, four cost less than 40 dollars. Dom Perignon, listed fifth, will set you back $115. Better champagne can be had for only $28.

And so it goes on. The point is this: The best material things in life are affordable. They are not cheap—quality never is—but if you buy them selectively and use them with care, you can enjoy a life as materially rich as Bill Gates on an income that wouldn't get him through lunch.

Here's how you can live rich, starting today:

Your Dream House

I have lived in a three-room mud house in Africa and a 5,000-square-foot mansion, and I can tell you this: The quality of a home has very little or nothing to do with how much it costs or how big it is.

Think about the houses you most admire. They are probably *not* huge and flashy. One of my current favorites is a modest, three-bedroom house in Cleveland, which has been transformed by the lady who owns it into a luxurious museum of her love of travel, dance, and learning. Every room is a gem. I am completely comfortable and endlessly amused in this rich and interesting house.

It's value? As great as Bill Gates' 40,000-square-foot monstrosity in Seattle; yet this one has a market value of about $150,000.

Your Car

I have a friend—a wealthy friend—who loves cars, especially sports cars. He drives a Camaro. Why would he? Because he says it is as good as a Corvette, a Porsche, or even a Ferrari. Instead of forking out $150,000 plus... he gets his thrills in a car that costs one-sixth that price.

What about prestige? Well that's what you have to pay more for. But if you are willing to go the classic route, and buy a car whose design doesn't change every year or so, you can buy yourself prestige at affordable rates. For example, I drive a mint-condition NSX that you couldn't tell from a brand new one. My car is worth about $30,000. You'd have to pay almost three times that amount for a new one. The same holds true for older Mercedes and BMWs.

In fact, in terms of "living rich," you should never buy a new car. You'll save a bundle by purchasing a late model vehicle with low mileage. If you shop around, you can find a five- or 10-year-old car that will cost 25% or 30% of the new car price, but will be just as good.

Your Wardrobe

What does it cost to dress like the world's richest? Much less than you think.

If you can forget about brand names and learn about quality, you will save thousands and look better. As with cars, you'll do better by going after a classic look in clothing. That's because you won't have to discard perfectly good items simply because the lapel has changed.

The other big secret of dressing rich is this: Less is more.

Ralph Lauren—a guy who has the money and the access to dress as rich as can be—wears the same thing almost every day—classic cut jeans and a tee shirt. Pat Riley, one of the best-dressed men in America, wears nothing but Armani suits. He has a number of them, but nothing near the number you'd think to look at him.

You can dress beautifully in second-hand clothes. What could be more impressive than a vintage suit, properly tailored, impeccably clean?

There are books on this subject. They all say pretty much the same thing. A few, really nice items are much better—more enjoyable for you, more impressive to others—than a huge wardrobe of trendy, ordinary stuff.

Want specifics? Get yourself two or three pairs of slacks (or skirts). One or two suits (or dresses). Two or three pairs of shoes. Buy only what you love.

Make sure your socks are cashmere ($19.50 at Banana Republic) and that your tee shirts and underwear are the finest cotton (or silk). Use only one cologne or perfume, but love it. Do the same with hair products and cosmetics. The rule is to have much less, but love everything you have.

Buy classic. Insist on quality. Few are better than many. Simple is better than complex. Understated is better than flashy. Do this, and you will have what Bill Gates can afford to have: A very pleasant feeling each time you pull on your shirt or buckle your belt.

Food and Drink

Want to have a billion-dollar meal? Take a good bottle of wine, a baguette of freshly baked bread, some cheese, ham, and butter, and go to the nearest park with a friend or loved one. You need only a knife and a corkscrew (what you have in your kitchen is fine) to prepare and serve a truly memorable meal.

Le Cirque? Well, I told you my opinion about that. But if there's an expensive restaurant you are dying to try, go ahead and treat yourself. But not too often. As someone who has eaten countless expensive meals, I know how tiring rich food can be. More important, I can remember few expensive meals that surpassed the simple wine and cheese lunches my wife and I have enjoyed when we were lucky enough to have them.

Music, Books, Movies, Etc.

With today's audio technology, even a $300 boom box sounds great. Spend a grand. Don't even try to tell me you need to spend more than that. The secret is in the music you select. There is music that can make you feel like a billionaire.

And it's the same with books—the best ones cost no more than the worst ones. Treat yourself richly—read only that which makes you feel richer afterward. The same is true for movies, theater, and just about any form of entertainment.

There is only one extravagance for me that I can't buy reasonably: Front-row tickets to professional basketball games. I have made the mistake of becoming a Miami Heat fan. If you are smart, you will learn to love college ball.

Your Office

Warren Buffett, one of the world's richest (and smartest) men, keeps his office in a simple building. His walls are paneled plywood. His desk is a tabletop. He doesn't need the prestige of a cathedral-sized room and an altar-sized desk. He is not God. And he knows it.

But what he does have is a room that is uniquely his, with a comfortable chair and a place for everything he needs. On the surfaces and hanging from the walls are souvenirs to inspire him. Warren Buffett's office is his own. It looks like no one else's office, and it works for him.

That's what you want in an office. The right amount of space. Good lighting. A very good chair. And toys that stimulate and inspire you.

Everything else is a distraction. And anything that is there simply to make you seem "important" will only turn off your guests and visitors.

I'm not saying your office should not be luxurious. I am saying it should be luxurious in a personal way. You will be spending most of your waking life in your office, so put as much thought and care into it as you do your home.

Silverware

Shopping for a Christmas present for my wife, I wandered into an antique shop in town that specialized in silver. The proprietor, a genteel, 86-year-old lady from Georgia, showed me this and that—and then, when she sensed I was looking for something very special, took me to the back room and showed me an absolutely beautiful collection of silverware by the Baltimore-based silversmith Reed & Barton. It was the Francis I design—the finest they ever made. "If you were a millionaire," she said in her seductive Southern drawl, "You could not buy a finer set of silverware than this."

It cost me $4,500. Nothing to be sneezed at, but that was for a set of 14 place settings and a lot of serving utensils. A regular full service set might cost $2,500. Now think of that. You can own the finest silverware that money can buy—and an antique at that—for $4,500. Such a set of silverware could last you all your life, give you pleasure and prestige, and make even your ordinary meals elegant. The Queen Mother herself couldn't do better.

I'm thinking about throwing away the rest of my silverware—and using only this. That's how much I like it.

If You Fill Your Life With All The Best Luxuries... A Great Home, Great Clothes, Delicious Food... But You Are Too Busy Running Around To Enjoy

Them, You've Missed The Boat.

Of all the things money can buy (it can't buy happiness… I've admitted that), time and freedom are the most important.

Here's my prescription for buying time. Think about your schedule and pick a half-hour a day to do nothing but luxuriate. (For some people, this is easy. For others, it's tough.) Tell yourself you'll work smarter this way. Take this half-hour and do something that a billionaire might do. Sip a cup of espresso. Smoke a cigar. Have a cognac. Contemplate how good life is. Thank the gods for your good fortune. Breathe deeply. Smile.

Now get back to work.

It's All Entirely Within Your Reach.

The way you dress, the way you eat and drink… even the home you live in… can be as good as any billionaire's. Spend time shopping. Buy very selectively. Limit your possessions. And take a half-hour a day to really appreciate the good things you have. That's all there is to it. (Oh, yes. And don't scrimp on the mattress.)

Originally published: June 9, 2000 in Early to Rise.

A successful entrepreneur who has owned and run many businesses, including two that grew beyond $100 million, Michael Masterson, offers practical advice for growing wealth through his popular daily e-column, Early to Rise. He continues to act as advisor and consultant to dozens of start-up and established businesses, helping them grow from struggling enterprises into multi-million dollar successes. To sign up for Michael Masterson's wealth-building advice, visit: www.earlytorise.com.

The #1 Secret of Every Successful Businessman I Know

By Michael Masterson

"We must use time as a tool, not as a couch."
– John Fitzgerald Kennedy (1917-1963)

Every successful businessman I know (or have read about) gets to work early. It's such a universal trait of accomplished individuals, I'm tempted to say it is a secret for success. "Early to bed and early to rise," Ben Franklin said, "makes a man healthy, wealthy and wise." I used to think that was propaganda from a Puritan. Now I think it's an observation from a very wise man.

Healthy, wealthy and wise. Let's start with wealthy—since that's what we're here for.

How Does Starting Early Make You Rich?

There is no better time to collect your thoughts and plan your day than early in the morning when the office is quiet. Not only are you undisturbed by phone calls and interruptions, but also ahead of you is the potential of an unopened day. The solitude promotes a kind of relaxed, contemplative mood. You feel free to think in an expansive way. Later on, when the place is noisy and the pressure is on, it's difficult to pay attention to what's important. You feel your attention drawn in several directions at once. You feel the pressure of deadlines. And you may be hit with bad news, which could put you in a bad, unproductive mood.

A Near Perfect Morning Routine

Over the years I've studied hundreds and experimented with dozens of timesaving techniques and organizational systems. The simple three-step program that follows is the best of the best.

Step One: Getting Your Inputs (Time: about 15 – 30 minutes)

Start with your weekly to-do list. On a sheet of paper, jot down anything you need to get done. Make sure you give primary attention to your top goal.

Now scan your e-mail. Don't read the messages. You will get bogged down if you do. Just give them a quick once-over to see if there is anything waiting for you that may need to be taken care of right away and/or will take some extra time.

Next check phone messages, faxes and your in-box. Don't respond to anything. Your job is simply to organize it all, to figure out what you will do today and what you can delegate or do later.

When you have done all of this you will have completed the first step of your morning routine. You will have gathered up all the work you might want to do that day. You will already be thinking about much of it. You will not have to worry about forgetting something important. And you will have a realistic idea about how much needs to be done.

Step Two: Sorting and Ordering (Time: 15 – 30 minutes)

Now comes the fun part. Get out a clean sheet of paper, or even an index card, and write the date on top. Referencing all the inputs you have just gathered, select 15 to 20 that you intend to accomplish before the end of the day.

Don't be unrealistic: There is no way you can do more than 15 or 20 significant things in a 10-hour day. And you don't need to work more than 10 hours a day to accomplish everything you need.

Of the 15 or 20 items, highlight 4 or 5 of them. These should all be important-but-not-urgent tasks.

To the right of each item, you might want to indicate how much time you think it will take. (I run a subtotal of the cumulating times so there is some relationship between what I want to do and how much time I have to do it.)

As a general rule, it's a good idea to structure all of your tasks so that none lasts more than an hour. 15-minute and 30-minute tasks are best. If you have something that takes several hours to do, break it up in pieces and do it over a few days. It will be better for the extra time you give it and you won't get crushed on any one day.

You will have now finished step two. Your day is organized not according to what others want from you, but according to what you want from yourself. If you have never done this before, it will be a major change.

Step Three: Give Your Day a Boost.
(Time: 15 – 60 minutes)

Here's the best step. Do one of the highlighted tasks. If you can, select a task that will make you feel good. That might be something you enjoy doing or something you really don't want to do (because it will make you feel so good when

---

How to Make Friends in High Places
By Michael Masterson

I'm going to open a little door into your future.

First, answer this question: Who in your industry would you like to know? Whose trust or confidence would you like to gain? Who could help you succeed? (I'm talking about someone you know of, not someone you know personally.)

Next, think about something this person has done that you admire. It may be a product he has recently developed. It may be the standard of service he sets. It may be an award he has won. Anything you genuinely admire.

Now—on some very nice, dignified stationery—write him a note expressing your feelings.

Don't fawn. Be direct and complimentary.

End by saying something like, "I know you are a very busy man, but if you ever have a spare half-hour, I'd love the chance to get some advice from you on my own career."

Insert your business card and post it.

Repeat once a week until you run out of names.

it's done).

Do these three things right away—first thing when you get in (which should be about 90 minutes before everyone else)—and you will have accomplished more by starting time than most people do by lunchtime. (Or all day for that matter since most people see most of their day consumed by unimportant emergencies.)

Success is What Happens When You Do A Little More Each Day Over and Over

Success can come in a single windfall but most often it arrives bit by bit. This is a way for you to give yourself a significant advantage over the people you compete with in life.

It actually gives you three advantages. You get much more done. You have to deal with many fewer unnecessary crises. And, most important, you spend a much greater percentage of your time doing things that move you along toward the goals you desire.

A Clever Way To Keep Track...

This system can be complemented by a file-indexing system that a famously organized newspaper publisher showed me several years ago. It requires two accordion folders. One with a pocket for each month and another with pockets for 31 days.

As you go through your e-mail or read correspondence and memos, put aside anything you want to follow up on. Place it in the pocket of the month in which you intend to address it. When that month arrives, there will probably be thirty or forty sheets of paper stuffed inside, which you can sort through and place in some kind of manageable order in each of the days of the month.

Then, as each day arrives, you simply extract from that day's pocket the files you've placed there. This is a very easy way to keep hold of all your vital data and correspondence without resorting to large, messy stacks of paper.

Originally published: June 7, 2000 in Early to Rise.

To sign up for Michael Masterson's wealth-building daily e-mail sevice, visit: www.earlytorise.com.

The World's Most Valuable Skill

By Michael Masterson

If you want to be wealthy, there are four things you absolutely must do…

1. Master a financially valuable skill.
2. Develop a high income.
3. Invest conservatively in other businesses.
4. Invest aggressively in a business you know.

Today, I'd like to talk about *the* most valuable skill you can have, and share with you some of the secrets I've learned over the years that can help you become very good at it, very quickly.

On the road to wealth, developing a financially valuable skill is the most important step. It's the foundation upon which every other step is based.

What is the world's most valuable skill? Simple: the ability to sell. Not just products and services, but ideas, concepts, and beliefs.

You know it as well as I do, in any organization, power moves inexorably to those who are persuasive. This is true for every business in every country in the world.

What matters is that you have a way to convince people (your boss, colleagues, customers, investors, etc.) that your ideas (and your work) are worthwhile.

I've identified a few fundamental secrets of selling over the years—a few tricks of the trade. And that's exactly what I'm going to share with you right now.

I can't give you all my secrets in this one message, but I can give you the basics behind every great piece of salesmanship.

I call them **The Three Fundamental Rules of Selling**, and they are…

#1. People don't like the idea of being sold.
#2. People buy things for emotional, not rational, reasons.
#3. Once sold, people need to satisfy their emotional decisions with logic.

Let's look at **Rule #1**: People don't like to be sold. On the face of it, this doesn't make sense. Every year, trillions of dollars worth of goods and services are bought and sold, billions through the mail alone. Think about your friends. Many of them, no doubt, love to shop.

People like to buy things. But they don't like to be sold. Remember this. Whether you're writing a sales letter or trying to convince your friend to go to a concert, don't apply pressure. Offer to give something. Don't force. Tempt.

Let's say you want to get your friend to buy a piece of chocolate cake. You wouldn't start off by listing 10 reasons why cake is good for him, would you? Of course not.

In real life, if you really wanted to get a friend to buy a piece of cake, you'd probably start by describing how great the cake smells, how gooey it is, how thick the icing is, and how it will just melt in his mouth…

In other words, you'd create a verbal picture that teases his desires—his hunger, his craving for chocolate. You'd tempt him by appealing to his emotions. You would not bore him with reasons or bully him with force.

Understand this first principle and you'll have people eating out of your hands.

Rule #2 Hit 'Em Where It Hurts: People buy things for emotional, not rational, reasons.

If people acted rationally, you couldn't sell chocolate cake. There's no logical reason to eat it. It's not nutritious. It makes you fat. It screws up your metabolism. And it's expensive.

So why is chocolate cake a multi-million-dollar industry? Because it makes you feel good!

To be persuasive, you have to appeal to your prospect's feelings and desires.

Here are seven very important ones: *Fear, Greed, Vanity, Lust, Pride, Envy, and Laziness.*

Rule #3: Once the prospect is emotionally sold, he needs to justify his irrational decision with rational reasons.

Think about TV commercials for cars. How do they work? First, you see a stirring image of the car itself—beautiful, stylish, new. The background says something too: There's a mountainous landscape for the prospect that wants to see himself as rugged; a five-star hotel for the prospect that wants the car to enhance his status; a beautiful woman for—well, you get the idea.

Next, you see an interior shot to show how luxurious your life will be with this car. You get to listen to the state-of-the-art sound system. (The type of music depends on the feeling required.) Then, there's a shot of the car driving by the ocean. Put it all together and you have an effective 20-second movie that's designed entirely to appeal to emotion.

But car commercials don't stop there. They usually give you numerous bits and pieces of information—the size of the engine, statistics on fuel economy, speed, weight, interior space, rankings in national surveys and customer satisfaction reports, and so on.

All this data isn't meant to sell the car. It's to make the prospect feel good about the decision he's already made. And in the final analysis, this is almost as important as the emotional appeal. Though the information doesn't sell the car, it does justify the sale.

These secrets are, of course, only the beginning.

But the great thing about the secrets of selling is that once you understand how they work, you can use them in every aspect of your life: to land a better job; to get a promotion; to sell more of your company's products; even to convince your friends to follow your advice for your next vacation.

Over the years, I've taught many of my students the little-known psychology of selling. Two of my top protégés took these secrets and, with my help, developed an organization called the American Writers and Artists Institute (AWAI). It's a group that helps regular folks become top-notch, high-paid sales writers (or "copywriters," as they're called in the advertising industry).

One graduate of this program is a student of mine who turned the sales knowledge he learned from AWAI into a life of high-paying freedom as a copywriter. Believe me, he's not the only one. I could show you literally dozens of people who have used these very same techniques to make a heck of a lot of money—and to enjoy a freedom few people will ever know.

Make no mistake about it; sales writing is one of the highest paid professional skills in the world. (I've personally seen ads that make writers tens of thousands of dollars each year—year after year.) But because so few people understand what copywriting is—much less how to do it effectively—there's a great shortage of good copywriters.

Whether you want to become a professional writer, or simply want to learn how to communicate much more persuasively, mastering the basics of selling can really give you an edge. And there's no better program to help you do this than AWAI's. Period.

If this is the type of financially valuable skill that interests you, learn more about how it works today. Go to: www.thewriterslife.com

Originally published: September 3, 2001 in Early to Rise.

To sign up for Michael Masterson's wealth-building advice, visit: www.earlytorise.com.

Secure Your Future: Educate Your Kids and Grandkids

By Justin Ford

I'd like to show you how, starting today, you can get your children to apply a little effort over time in a crucial area of life that is usually neglected when it comes to kids. I'm talking about money.

By beginning a hands-on program today, not only can your kids or grandkids grow wealthier year after year, they can do it without giving up the dreams they most want to pursue. They'll have the luxury to choose careers that match their interests, values, energy, and talents like kids at play, rather than simply working for a paycheck.

What's more, they'll have done it themselves—but with your guidance. That's because I'm not talking about a trust-fund program or raising your children with silver spoons. I'm talking about a natural way to *train* your children in matters of money and actually get them to begin *practicing* good money habits from a very early age.

They'll begin to understand exactly how you're going to help them create this wealth, once you introduce a very simple, yet very effective savings technique I call…

The Two-Box System©

The moment you first introduce the idea of saving and investing to your children, you're going to help make that idea a reality by doing two things: First, you'll give them two dollars so they can make their first allocation among spending money and savings. Second, you'll make sure they have two distinct boxes (or other receptacles) to put their money in.

These can be cardboard boxes, colored and designed by your child. They can be desk safes or piggy banks. One will be for their spending money (which is the same as "temporary savings"). The other will be for their permanent savings.

And that's really all they need to *begin* to build wealth and develop good money habits right away.

You'll explain how these two types of savings are to be used with an example—to make sure they understand the importance of always saving and investing before spending. To do that, you might say something along the following lines:

> "One of these boxes is labeled 'permanent savings' and the other is labeled 'temporary savings.' They're both going to go on your dressers. Every time you get a buck, two bucks, twenty bucks, or a hundred bucks, half goes into the permanent and half goes into the temporary.

> "I've just given you two dollars, so what's going to happen with those two?

> "Right, one will go into the temporary savings and one will go into the permanent. From that permanent savings box you're going to grow a few dollars into a small fortune—or maybe even a big fortune—by the time you're around my age or a little older.

> "The temporary savings you can spend whenever you want on whatever you want.

> "Let's say you get $20 from grandma, what do you do with it? Right, you put $10 in the permanent savings and $10 in the temporary savings.

> "Now, what happens if you want to buy a new skateboard? Can you ever use money from your permanent savings to buy it?

> "The answer is 'no.' You can buy the skateboard, but to do that, you'll have to get the money together from the temporary savings. The easiest way to do that is to set up a separate box for the skateboard. We'll call it the "Skateboard Fund"—and it's only to be funded from your temporary savings—*never* from the permanent.

> "The permanent savings are never to be <u>spent</u> for any reason—at least until you're about my age. They're only to be invested so they can grow into a lot more money as you grow up."

Why Half Is Good

Now, in case you think you're asking a lot of your children by having them save half of every dollar they receive, let me ask you this: When was the last time you could spend 50% of every dollar *you* made on whatever *you* want?

For most people, the answer is "never."

By the time you're done paying the mortgage, food, clothing, income and property taxes, utilities, car payments, medical and dental bills, current education expenses for the kids, health insurance, homeowner's insurance, gas, auto repairs, and home maintenance—and fund your retirement plan and the kids' college funds—you're lucky if you have more than 10% of your income left to spend as you please.

And yet, children don't have any of these bills. In effect, they have 100% disposable income. They don't have to pay rent or alimony, the government doesn't tax their allowance or household chore money (up to the $11,000 gift tax exclusion), and they can even earn up to $4,700 a year from a "real job" tax-free (since the effective tax rate on the first $4,700 of earned income is zero).

And keep in mind that if you don't train your children to build wealth now, while they have 100% disposable income, they may learn the opposite lesson: to automatically spend all they earn or even more than they earn as adults.

Six Super Savings Ratios

The 50% savings rate applies, of course, only to children five and older while they live at home and have no real living expenses. For other stages in their life, I recommend other savings rates.

Here are my six recommended savings rates for various stages of life. I call them the Seeds of Wealth saving ratios, and I believe they form a combination that can assure your children enjoy lifelong financial success:

Tycoon Tots: 100%. Until the time your kids are ready for kindergarten, you're likely to automatically save 100% of every dollar they receive, simply because they're too young to want or need to spend money.

Wonder Years: 50%. From the ages of 5 through 17, while they're living at home, I suggest you have them save half of every dollar they receive, for reasons already explained.

College Days: 10%. In college, I suggest you counsel your kids to save 10%. Money is extremely tight at this time, but by at least saving 10% of whatever they scrape together, they learn that there is never a reason to make an excuse not to save.

Single Working Adult: 15%. Once a child has graduated and is on his or her own in the working world, I advise they save 15% of current income. While this may seem high compared to most young adults who tend to consume all of what they earn, it shouldn't be a burden for your kids.

After saving 50% at home during childhood and seeing how saving and investing can create significant wealth over time, this 15% mark should be a piece of cake. Also, in my opinion, when you're in your twenties you don't need to spend a lot of money to have a very rewarding life. It's when young adults begin to have children and mortgages and broader health and education expenses, that money becomes a more pressing concern.

Just Married: 15%. When your children first marry, it still shouldn't be a burden to save 15%. In fact, it may be even easier since they may find themselves with two incomes in the house—helping them create more investment capital more quickly.

Married, with Children: 10%. When your kids begin to raise their own families, at that point they will be able to easily shift to what was for a long time the traditional savings rate of 10%. But also by that time your kids will have built up a significant amount of wealth that will compound for them along with their 10% savings year after year.

Making the Seeds Grow

Let's see what happens when you combine the Seeds of Wealth saving ratios with investment returns ranging from 10% to 20% over the long run… starting with $730 at the age of 1.

By the age of 30—when most young adults are only just beginning to build wealth—your children could own investments worth somewhere in the range of a quarter million dollars

Another way to look at it is to see that if your child averages just 10% returns (about the total returns of the broad market during the entire 20th century, including all bull and bear markets), he would accumulate approximately $500,000 by the age of 36.

At that point, 10% returns would generate $50,000 in gains a year… or about $4,167 a month.

At 15% returns, you child could amass roughly $350,000 by the age of 28. From that point, the same 15% returns that would generate over $52,500 a year, or over $4,300 a month.

Finally, if you achieve high-watermark returns of 20% over the long term, your child accumulates assets worth over $274,000 by the age of 23. From that point, 20% returns then generate approximately $54,800 a year or more than $4,500 a month.

Quite a monthly allowance he'll be paying himself!

If your children decide to take on a new life challenge in their twenties or thirties… perhaps start a family of their own… begin to build their own business… go back to school for their master's degree or doctorate… or dedicate some time to writing the Great American Novel… they would be in a very good position to do so.

Originally published in Seeds of Wealth

Justin Ford is the author of Seeds of Wealth, a step-by-step program filled with wealth building strategies designed to show you and your child how and where to invest. For more information, go to: www.seedsofwealth.com.

How Much Money Do You Really Need?

By Bill Bonner

"Women," said my old friend, Mark Ford. That's the reason we earn money. I misunderstood at first. Yes, a woman can cost a lot to maintain. She will need food, clothing, transportation, and shelter. Her children will need braces and tuition. But it is not need that underlies man's drive for wealth... it is desire.

People do not buy chateaux because they need a place to live. Nor do they invest in stocks because they need pocket money. They seek wealth and its trappings for other purposes.

Dorothy Parker said, "You can't be too rich or too thin." But when Howard Hughes died, it looked like he was both. Hughes had the kind of wealth that meant he could do what he wanted. He didn't have to listen to anyone. He was so rich he could eat Campbell's chicken noodle soup every day if he wanted and wander around with Kleenex boxes on his feet.

In the end, Howard's wealth may not have helped him much. It cushioned him from reality, protecting him from the things that might have brought sanity to his life.

He might as well have been on welfare. Those people, too, are cushioned from the reality of everyday life, so they never have to learn how to earn a living and get along in the real world. That is also often true of the children of rich people. They don't have to learn how to hustle, and many never do. In this sense, wealth is not merely a burden like the Chateau de Bourg Archambault, but a threat.

At the chateau I bought about 7 years ago called Ouzilly, deep in the French countryside, you can live well on very little money. On a beautiful day, you can sit out on the terrace of a stone farmhouse... you can drink local wine... you can eat local food... you can putter in your garden and take day trips to visit medieval towns. Life can be quite good—even with very little money.

But when you don't have money, you don't have the option of changing your lifestyle. As long as I am content to live in rural France, or rural Arkansas, for that matter, I can do so on little money. But what if I want to live in New York? Or Paris?

I'm going to find out how much it costs to live in Paris in a couple of weeks. We're moving to an apartment near the Trocadero. The modest, 4-bedroom apartment rents for 17,000 francs per month—about $3,000. Not bad. Cheap by New York standards. Paris is actually one of the cheapest major cities in the world. Still, with school fees, meals, transportation, maintenance, furniture, utilities, and professional fees... we estimate it will cost us about $100,000 a year to live there. But the tax rate in France is 60%, so I will have to earn $250,000 just to keep my head above water.

Hmmm... this won't be cheap. How much capital would I need to earn $250,000 per year? Well, if I could get a reasonably safe return of 6%, it would mean that I would need $4.3 million. This does not provide a luxurious lifestyle by any means. In fact, it barely pays the bills of a bourgeois American family... with six children in school.

Most people think you need at least $10 million before you can be considered rich. That amount would provide you with about $600,000 in income. Most people could live comfortably on that much.

But wealth is not always forthcoming when, and in the amounts, we want it. So, in practice, people don't really calculate how much they "need" to live the way they want. Instead, they try to earn as much as they can and adjust their sights accordingly. They do not need to live in Manhattan—life in Omaha is good enough for Warren Buffett, after all. They do not need to go to the Tour d'Argent for dinner. The food at Madame Grammond's is just as nourishing. So why the pressure to earn ever more money?

Bunker Hunt said that money was "just a way of keeping score in life." But to what end? What's the prize, in other words? Once you have a comfortable place to live, and decent food to eat, does additional wealth really add to your quality of life? Does it help your children... or does it hurt them? Does it make you happier? More secure?

The major thing it does is expand your field of choice. You can decide for yourself whether you want to live in Omaha or New York, for example. More choice leads to more thought, about what living well really means. This, in turn, may have the effect of enriching your life in unforeseen ways. Or it may simply make life more complex and difficult, like having to choose a long distance phone service or an insurance program.

"Women," repeated Mark, "without women, money would mean nothing." At last I grasped his meaning. He was reaching for the deeper truth. For all the practical advantages of having wealth, men strive for it for impractical reasons. Money is status. There is some reproductive imperative that causes men to seek status and women to prefer men who attain it. To express it crudely, money is a way of scoring (metaphorically, of course)... not just keeping score.

Originally published: August 20, 1999 in The Daily Reckoning

Bill Bonner is the founder and president of Agora Publishing, and the author of the free daily e-mail service called The Daily Reckoning. Mr. Bonner is the author, with Addison Wiggin, of the New York Times Business bestseller Financial Reckoning Day: Surviving The Soft Depression of The 21st Century (John Wiley & Sons New York, London). To sign up for The Daily Reckoning, go to www.dailyreckoning.com.

The Burden of Capital

By Bill Bonner

Having money is such a burden, say rich people. *Because you have to figure out how to preserve it... and what to do with it after you die.*

I was lucky... Thanks to the collective wisdom of the credit industry of the '60s and '70s, I passed through young adulthood with neither credits nor debits.

Neither a borrower nor a lender was I. I had neither money, nor debt. I could not be accused of wasting the family fortune, for there was nothing to waste. I was free from the burden of wealth.

But my children may not be so lucky. Their father tries to make life easy for them... and may end up making it much harder.

And if he does not ruin himself by following his own investment advice, or impetuously running off, penniless, for the purpose of mixing his genes with those of a French cocktail waitress, he may even leave a farthing or a sou after he is gone. The bequest will be announced in his Last Daily Reckoning, to be read solemnly in the presence of an estate lawyer and an IRS agent.

I may even suggest that my executor hire a few women to come and weep openly and dramatically, as if they missed me.

It was Doug Casey who first described rich investors such as Warren Buffett and George Soros as "idiots savants." The term applied, said he, because these men were geniuses at making investment profits but almost complete imbeciles otherwise.

International Herald Tribune recently brought further evidence that these titans of investment are midgets at other matters.

"Some 120 wealthy Americans, including Warren Buffett, George Soros and the father of Bill Gates," says the IHT news article, "are urging Congress not to repeal taxes on estates and gifts."

The father of Bill Gates was so agitated by the prospect of letting his fellow Americans decide for themselves who gets their money that he organized a petition effort against it. Signers include Soros, a few Rockefellers, and Ben Cohen, founder of Ben and Jerry's ice cream company.

Mr. Buffett said he did not actually sign the petition because he thought it did not go far enough. He said he believes it would be a "terrible mistake" to stop taking away accumulated savings after death. It would be, he said, like "choosing the 2020 Olympic team by picking the eldest sons of the gold medal winners in the 2000 Olympics."

I will try to help you make sense of that remarkable statement, dear reader, by pointing out that making money is a game to Buffett. He has far more money than he can ever spend. Or that his children can ever spend.

Economists point out that the more you have of something, the less each additional unit is worth to you. A hungry man really appreciates his first hamburger. A 10th hamburger is welcomed only by a person with an eating disorder. This is called the principle of declining marginal utility.

Every additional dollar made by Warren Buffett has a marginal utility near zero. It is just the sport that interests him, not the money. As Bunker Hunt once put it, "money is just a way of keeping score in life."

Well, according to the most recent *Forbes* ranking, Warren Buffett is the 2nd highest scoring person in the nation.

In Buffett's view, making money is just a game. The government is like a referee, who makes sure that all the contestants start the race at the same time and from the same position.

Government employees, of course, are not impartial referees at all. They're in the race too. Their goal is make sure that they emerge the big winners.

One way or another all savings end up in someone's hands. Either they go to the children of the people who did the earning and saving, or they go to someone else's children.

Buffett imagines a pure meritocracy, where all players begin with the same grub-stake and where all wealth is distributed to the people who earn it. "You have mobility," he says, "so people with talents can be put to the best use. Without the estate tax you in effect will have an aristocracy of wealth, which means you pass down the ability to command the resources of the nation based on heredity rather than merit."

Existing capital can either be destroyed, or passed along to the next generation. It cannot be earned—because it was already earned, by the previous generation. The only question is whether the people who built the fortunes should have the right to decide who gets them, or whether someone else decides.

Buffett's world exists only in his imagination. People start out in life with different talents, different handicaps, different burdens... and very different attitudes. Their challenge, though, is always the same—to make the best of things.

My poor children. I can already see the corrosive influence of unearned wealth. Rather than set his hand immediately to a career, my oldest son intends to backpack around Europe this summer... following his graduation from college. I paid his tuition and supported him during his college years, so unlike so many young Americans, he has no college loans weighing upon him.

Sophia, too, is searching her soul and the Internet to try to find something to do with her life. The poor thing. Should she work with the destitute in India? Or spend a year on a dude ranch, earning a pittance but getting an entirely different experience?

I had no such cares or concerns when I was her age, I merely had to find the best paying job I could, which turned out to be painting radio towers. It paid more than $5 an hour as I recall—because it was almost unbelievably tedious, dumb and dangerous. All day long I would climb around on steel girders, hundreds of feet off the ground, dipping my mitted hand into a bucket of paint that was hooked to my belt. Then, I smeared the paint on the rusty metal with one hand while I held on to the swaying tower with the other.

Many college boys were attracted to the work by the pay, but few actually stuck with it. One, a large blond football player, climbed up the WBAL TV tower in Baltimore with me one morning, his first day on the job. After a while, he looked down, and froze with fright. He held onto a girder with both arms and refused to move. We thought about leaving him up there like a cat up a tree; we figured he'd eventually come to his senses and come down.

On the other hand, if he didn't come down, we'd have to deal with him, probably in even worse condition, the next morning. Finally, a supervisor and I managed to pry his hands loose and escort him down.

The work was miserable, but the money was good for a summer job in 1968.

Yet, without the hot breath of financial necessity on the back of my neck, combined with youthful recklessness, I probably would have preferred to do something different.

I would have backpacked around Europe, for example.

And maybe that would have been for the better.

Originally published: February 16, 2001 in The Daily Reckoning

To sign up for Bill Bonner's free Daily Reckoning e-mail service, go to www.dailyreckoning.com.

The Handicap Principle
By Bill Bonner

"Why do humans and animals alike do such dumb stuff? Stuff that is unnecessary, flamboyant, and often downright deadly?"
-Richard Conniff, Discover Magazine

"I don't want to buy 'Diversity'," said Elizabeth. "I'll buy 'Ingenuity' instead."

"Oh no... I'm stuck in a traffic jam," said Edward. "But I like jam."

"It's not that kind of jam, you moron," said his older brother Jules, who turned 14 on Christmas Day.

The game was "America!" It entertained the family while I read the latest financial news. It was just a game, of course... a silly one. Still, each of the players wanted to win. And the way to win was simple—to get the most money. So eager was Edward to come out on top that his little hand slipped down towards the "bank" when his mother wasn't looking.

Why do people spend so much effort on something that doesn't really matter, I wondered? They play games as if their lives depended on them. If the theory of evolution is correct, it doesn't make sense that people should devote precious energy to things that give them no survival edge. At the margin, the animal that wastes its time playing games should die, while the one that stays busy storing nuts and grains should survive and reproduce.

And yet, most of what people do seems to have little or no evolutionary benefit. After basic needs are met, men spend almost all their time, effort, and money trying to impress other men... or trying to feel superior to them. That is what is so nice about a place like Baltimore, after all; there are so many men there to whom it is easy to feel superior.

But why would a man spend millions on an apartment on Avenue Foch when he could spend just a couple hundred thousand for one, just as big, just as comfortable, just as convenient, on the rue Mouffetard? It probably makes no difference, since in today's world, a man with an apartment on rue Mouffetard is probably just as likely to survive and reproduce as one with digs on the Avenue Foch. But how did the instinct to this kind of conspicuous consumption ever get started?

Surely, at some dark and distant point in humanity's past, there were men who spent all their time hunting and gathering, and others who spent some time making ornate headbands or other prehistoric equivalents of a Louis Vuitton handbag. Why didn't the genes of the headband maker die out, since they were less likely to survive a famine?

No sooner had I posed the question than an answer presented itself. There, in my pile of reading material, beneath *Grant's Interest Rate Observer* and on top of Doug Casey's *International Speculator*, was an article from *Discover* magazine entitled "Why We Take Risks."

Buying a Louis Vuitton bag, I remind readers, is risky. In nature, everything happens at the margin. At least in theory, the money lavished on extravagance might someday be needed for food. So, too, might the calories used up in a tribal dance someday be needed for survival. Yet, everywhere you look, some common instinct tells people to boogie and buy, even when, at that very moment, they may be in danger of losing their jobs.

"Grandstanding is common in the natural world too," writes Richard Conniff, "For instance, antelopes pursued by hungry cheetahs often leap acrobatically straight into the air, a practice called stotting. Common sense says they should be springing straight for the far horizon."

Common sense tells men to avoid buying stocks at 30 times earnings... and eschew unnecessary consumer spending. (Who knows, some day you may need the money for something important.) But nearly everywhere and all the time, men seem to prefer to buy both their investments and their consumer items when they can get less of them for their money. When investments are cheap, hardly anyone wants to hear of them. But when they are expensive, such as at the crest of a bubble market, they become the dearest subject of conversation among the most beautiful people in the chicest quarters of the city. Likewise, women will want to show off the new hat they bought from Franck et Fils for $200... but rush upstairs to change when company comes rather than show themselves in the serviceable threads they bought from Sears.

Everybody stots.

"Down in the Riviera," Bernard Vuitton explained, "people try to see who can come into port with the biggest yacht. You know, they change hands all the time. Paul Allen has one of them one year... then he sells it to Kashoggi... who then sells it to someone else."

Owning a big yacht is, of course, ridiculously expensive. So the idea is to own it for just long enough to show it off to your friends... then get rid of it as soon as you can. "A friend of mine has a yacht so big that he couldn't get into port at all. He had to buy a smaller boat to come into the harbor. His yacht was so big people thought it was a cruise ship. He's still trying to sell it, I think."

But why do we stot?

"These behaviors are how we advertise how prosperous, how fit, how fearless we are," explains Conniff. "And because the world is a jaded, cynical place, we have to incorporate a significant cost, or handicap, in our advertising to make it persuasive. Thus, antelopes really are indulging in a dangerous waste of energy when they stot in front of a cheetah. But their willingness to risk it is how they tell the cheetah: 'Don't even bother trying.'" Recent research suggests that stotting actually does seem to give the antelopes an evolutionary advantage: Antelope that stot get eaten less often than the non-stotting ones.

The "Handicap Principle" is the invention of Israeli biologist Amotz Zahavi. Why do male birds of many different species have such bright, heavy plumage, he wondered. The extra feathers make the birds more vulnerable to predators. Why do men prefer women with large breasts—when smaller ones are more efficient? Why do many animals show themselves to predators... and even taunt them? Why do Irish elk have antlers with a 12-foot span?

The simple answer to all these questions: They give themselves a handicap to prove that they are superior.

But why prove they are superior?

To encourage the opposite sex to accept them as mating partners.

The "Handicap Principle" also explains why people make ostentatious gifts, such as Ted Turner's $1 billion pledge to the U.N. or Bill Gates' $23 billion to his foundation. In theory, the donations demonstrate how rich and superior the donors are.

But theory often diverges from practice, as we often observe in these letters. The trouble with doing something stupid to impress other people is that that they might be impressed by how stupid you really are. The handicap you give yourself may backfire; you may be regarded as severely handicapped. Thus, buying stocks at 30

.mes earnings may not be a sign of fitness... but mental infirmity. And Ted Turner's gift, in our view, hardly designates him as a good breeding partner. Instead, it suggests such a severe handicap that he should be a prime candidate for forced sterilization.

Likewise, we caution readers in search of mates: The richly plumed pheasant makes as good a meal as the drab one. And he's easier to shoot.

Originally published: December 28, 2001 in The Daily Reckoning

To sign up for Bill Bonner's free Daily Reckoning e-mail service, go to www.dailyreckoning.com.

Virtues of the Very Rich

By Bill Bonner

"I don't care about money," said "Smokin' Joe" Frazier.
"It just steadies my nerves."

The former champ, after having been hammered by Ali and numerous others in his career, seems to have suffered less brain damage than the president of Indonesia.

I was thinking about that last night on a long walk home from the office. It came to me just as a beautiful woman entering the church at St. Sulpice diverted my attention. She was tall with swept-back blond hair. And there was something about her expression. She was at ease in some personal way... not vacant like a Hare Krishna at an airport terminal... her nerves were steady, not deadened.

Here's a provocative idea: Virtue can improve your financial performance.

I mulled that idea over, realizing how absurd it is.

Think about the very rich people you know. The boneheads, the morally challenged, the perverts and the profane. Ted Turner, Donald Trump... the corporate raiders... the stock market mavens...

If the battle for wealth is won with weapons of virtue... a lot of these guys are, well, unarmed.

The subject of morality has certain parallels... and intersections... with investing. Both can be dull. And both can be perplexing and paradoxical.

I am coming more and more to the belief—first announced by Jim Grant—that markets work on the principle of irony. More and more, I find irony to be the driving force... as well as the secret key to understanding market movements. The very moment when the public comes to believe that stocks will go up forever... stocks begin to decline. When a technology is certain to be a big success, you can almost be sure that an investment in the company's stock will be a big loser. When gold is pronounced dead... that is the moment to hold a mirror to the nostrils and recheck the pulse.

The same may be true for the way morality affects your investments.

We are dealing here with cause and effect relationships. Primitive peoples, lacking a sophisticated view of cause and effect, partake of a primitive one. They see spirits hiding behind every bush. And the spirits are dangerous. The spirit of a tree may get mad because you chop off a branch. The sun spirit may decide to hide himself if he doesn't like the way you dress. A volcano may hunger for a maiden or two.

In the Old Testament days, it was still thought that God would punish sin in this life rather than the next. Sodom and Gomorrah did not prosper... they were obliterated. If a person fell ill... or a drought ruined crops... the elders would ask, "Who sinned?"

This sentiment is still a strong part of our emotional programming. We feel we will be punished, in some way, for sin. What better way, in this materialistic age, than in the stock market? And from yesterday's example, it is obvious how certain sins (avarice) at certain times (a bull market top) may produce negative returns. Wouldn't it be ironic, and perhaps poetic, for a jealous God to punish the mammon worshippers in such a way? By putting their mammons through the wringer of a bear market?

Wouldn't it be fun to watch the yuppies and masters of the universe get what they deserve? Uh-oh... taking pleasure in their loss... that delightful sensation of "schadenfreude," as the Germans say, that is probably a sin too! Maybe not a capital sin... maybe a sin of the lower case... or sub-prefecture variety. But still a sin. And if God is going to punish the big ones... he's bound to punish the little ones, too. Those who delight in irony will have irony done unto them, too.

But, if God is to punish sin... will he really reward virtue? Think about the virtuous people you know. Are they rich? All major religions have a similar vision of a virtuous person. The virtuous soul cares not for material things. I learned yesterday that the philosopher Wittgenstein, born into one of Europe's wealthiest families, gave away all his money. One of Julius Nyerere's virtues was that he didn't seem interested in money. Virtuous people are beyond caring... and not just about money. They are satisfied if not happy... people who can walk by a Paris pastry shop in their bare feet, with no desire to stop in and have an éclair. They can get a tip on an IPO and have no urge to call their broker. They can watch a beautiful blonde pass on the street and not lust after her... neither in their hearts nor other anatomical parts.

Shakespeare was not describing a virtuous man... translated into Swahili by Nyerere... when he spoke of Cassius as having "a lean and hungry look." Virtuous people do not have a hungry look. They lust not. Neither do they sin. And neither do they make a lot of money. They don't care about money.

I don't care about money either. But as "Smokin' Joe" put it, it steadies my nerves. I am not a virtuous man. I lust after profit, pulchritudinous company and profiteroles just like everyone else. Besides, I need to lust after money. I have six children to put through college. Six times $20,000 per year... times four years... after tax... well, you can do the math.

I don't know if God will punish me by sending me to the poorhouse. But, like Blaise Pascal, I'd rather not find out. And I'm not desperate for money, anyway. Or pastries. Or blondes, for that matter. And maybe that's the real key. Desperate gamblers are bad gamblers. Starving people will eat anything... even Dinty Moore stew. A man who hasn't had sex in 12 years... well... you fill in the rest.

I am not desperate. So, I can tolerate a little virtue in my life, from time to time... within reason. And a little virtue is probably not a bad thing in investing, just as it is not necessarily a bad thing in the rest of life. It helps prevent you from doing something really dumb.

Originally published: October 21, 1999 in *The Daily Reckoning*

To sign up for Bill Bonner's free Daily Reckoning e-mail service, go to www.dailyreckoning.com.

Oh Where Oh Where Will My Baby Boomers Go? Too Old to Rock & Roll, But Too Young to Die.

By Bill Bonner

Gary Scott moved to Ecuador. Doug Casey just bought a ranch in New Zealand. Jim Davidson got an apartment in Buenos Aires. What's going on with these guys?

Baby boomers have set the tone for our culture and our economy. There are just so many of them. They flooded the job market in the '70s, drove up home prices in the '80s, and drove up stock prices in the '90s. What's ahead?

I try to figure out what they will do by looking at my friends and myself. We are all baby boomers. Maybe not representative, but in many ways indicative.

What are my friends doing? Well, they are not preparing for retirement. But they are changing the way they live. They are entering a new period in their lives.

Psychologists say there are three main phases to a person's life, to which I will add a fourth. From the time you are born until you are out on your own, you are being cared for by your parents and schools. You are being prepared for life. You have little control over the process. You take what comes your way. This phase lasts longer and longer, as more and more people stay in school for longer, but it typically ends after 20 or so years.

In the next phase, you take over, and make what you can of your life. You get a job. You get a spouse. You get children. You raise them. You buy a house. You progress in your career. You build your life.

But after 30 years or so, the house is paid for. You have gone about as far as you are going to go in your career. The children are raised. Maybe you are still paying college expenses, but the hard work is done. By this time, you have finally come to terms with your spouse, or split up. In short, you are ready for a new phase in your life.

This is where many of my friends find themselves. It is a new phase—a new exit on the highway of life. It used to be that you would continue in your home, your office and your family until you reached 65. Then, the third and final phase would take its course. But now there is something new and different... it's a new stage of life for boomers who are "too old to rock and roll, but too young to die."

This period is not well defined. Many people in their 50s still have small children—myself included. Others are still developing careers and businesses. Still others are remarrying and starting the process all over again.

The common denominator is that they are not willing to stick with their Phase II lives until they reach 65. They do not imagine themselves working until traditional retirement kicks in at age 65. They are ready to do something different. They do not share the retirement dream of their parents—to retire and move to Florida where they will walk on the beach and try to amuse themselves until they finally cast off their mortal shells.

Retirement, to the boomers, is a bore. It is the end of the line. It is something that old people do, people who don't have enough life left in them to do anything else. Boomers may be ready for it someday, but they're not ready yet.

Instead, they are searching for a new kind of fulfillment—a "payoff" phase in their lives, when they are no longer under the pressure or tedium of normal work in normal places and normal routines. I call it the Bed & Breakfast stage, because they either want to stay in Bed & Breakfasts... or they want to start one of their own. Maybe in a tropical paradise. Maybe in a quaint New England town. Something, somewhere, with some charm and romance to it. One of the hallmarks of the Bed & Breakfast stage is the mid-life crisis. More and more, the Internet plays a role. If you notice your husband or wife spending a lot of time on the Internet, you may want to worry. Just in my own small circle of friends and relatives I know two people who met their spouses over the Internet.

Another source of worry is financial. It costs money to finance the Bed & Breakfast stage. And if you compound savings at 5%, you'll have to wait a long time. Boomers don't want to wait. That is, I believe, a big reason for the popularity of day trading—and stock market investing in general. The boomers do not have the patience to wait until they are 65 to reap life's rewards. They want them while they are still young enough to enjoy them. They want them now. And they need money to get them.

The most recent issue of *Forbes* includes a confession by a former day trader. He expressed the sentiment that led him to begin trading: "I'm sick of sitting on the sidelines while all these idiots are getting rich." Boomers are too young to remember the last bear market. And life has generally been very kind to them. Is there any reason to think that they won't get what they want now?

Well, one reason is just arithmetic. We have looked at many of the arithmetic problems that lie like landmines between where the average stock investor is today and where he hopes to be in five years. The same *Forbes* writer, for example, highlighted the forbidding arithmetic of day trading:

"Suppose you open a day-trading account with $25,000... margin yourself to the hilt... turn it around twice a week. Even with commissions as low as $9.95 per thousand shares, your transactions costs will run to nearly $2,000 per year. Throw in spreads, and you have to earn 20% annualized just to break even."

It is possible to earn 20%. But only if the market is booming. Which can happen for a while, but not forever. The boomers can drive up prices for Internet stocks, just as they have for suburban real estate and the Dow, but sooner or later they must sell if they are to realize this new Bed & Breakfast dream. But to whom? And at what price? And what will they buy in their place?

The answers to these questions will help us identify the best places for your money over the next 10 years, including one that almost has to be a winner. A hint: it's slimy.

Originally published: September 8, 1999 in The Daily Reckoning

The Great Depreciation

By Bill Bonner

I had intended to talk about oil in this article, which I regard as one of the best long-term investments you can make. Not the oil itself... but the infrastructure for getting it to you... shipping, for example. But I'm going to put that on hold and stick with a theme I took up recently: what the baby boomers are doing.

The title I have given this comes from a book by Craig Karpel. The book has a simple premise: that, as it says in Ecclesiastes, there's "a time to get, and a time to lose... a time to keep and a time to cast-away." The boomers are soon reaching the castaway stage of their lives. Traditionally, people build assets during their working careers and dispose of them when they retire. They sell the house in Hackensack and buy a condo in Del Ray Beach, for example. They downsize their own lives.

This downsizing was no problem for the last generation. They made good money on the houses they bought after WWII. And they found plenty of ready buyers among the boomers who succeeded them.

But now three new developments totally change the picture.

The first is the relative size of the boomer generation.

When the boomers cast away their stocks and houses... there will be relatively few buyers standing in line for them. It will take lower prices to clear the market— hence, Craig's Great Depreciation.

But in addition to that that, the boomers are different.

They have a new and different vision of how to lead their lives. They have been spoiled by good times. They expect a lot. And they're not willing to wait to get it. Thus, they're introducing a whole new stage into the human life cycle. I named this ambiguous new stage previously—the Bed & Breakfast Stage. It is when boomers begin living in a different way... and often, a different place. Ask almost any boomer about his vision for the future. Will he say he intends to stick with his job and retire at 65... and then move to Florida? No... he will almost invariably offer some ambiguous idea of working as a consultant... or on a freelance basis... part-time... while pursuing personal interests more seriously—elsewhere.

Technology has favored the boomers too. This is the third, and critical, new piece of the puzzle.

For the first time in human evolution, people have been liberated from the constraints of geography. During the hunter-gatherer period, humans survived on a slim margin... following the plants and animals on which they lived. When farming developed, the margins fattened ever so slightly allowing for huge increases in human population. But humans were then tied to their fields, herds, and orchards. And in the industrial age, commerce consolidated around the mills and factories. There was no question about living where one wanted to live... you had to live within commuting distance of the job in the factory or in those "machines of commerce" (skyscrapers) in the cities. Suburbs were the logical expression of the machine age... they allowed the proletariat to rest on shelves in suburban split-level warehouses until they were needed on the job.

But the Internet changes everything. The leading industry is no longer manufacturing... and certainly not farming. It is the work done by what Charles Murray calls "the cognitive elite," people who work with ideas, words, and information. These people make up a larger and larger part of the workforce. And as I am living proof... they can work from almost anywhere. I live in Paris. But I work with people all over the world, via the Internet. As recently as 10 years ago, this would not have been possible. It is certainly hard to run a business... or to hold an ordinary job... remotely. But, for the baby boomers in their Bed & Breakfast Stage, it is ideal.

And what it means is that the boomers will not wait until they are 65 before they cast away their suburban homes. The suburban home was the dream of the '40s and '50s... and maybe '60s. It is no longer part of the dream. Not for the boomers. Nor for the next generation. Just ask them. It may be convenient. It may be practical. But it is no longer something people aspire to.

It is difficult to generalize about real estate. But, on the average, you may expect that suburban residential real estate will be a losing proposition over the next 20 years. Instead, you would do better to put your money where the boomers want to put their own money: Sand, Small Towns, and Old Towns.

Seashore property, for example, has been rising rapidly. Makes sense. People always want to live where they have had fun. I have a lot of friends who have always wanted to live near the beach. Now they do.

Oceanfront property in America is expensive. But the baby boomers are not afraid to leave the country. *The Wall Street Street Journal* noticed the trend in a piece about Nova Scotia, which featured a photo of the oceanfront property bought by my friend Bob Fordi. Nova Scotia has both the cheap oceanfront property... and the small-town quality that boomers like.

But Nova Scotia can be cold. Beachfront property in Belize, Honduras and Costa Rica, meanwhile, has already taken off. Nicaragua looks as though it will be next. I was so sure of this I bought an interest in a development on Nicaragua's Pacific Coast. The place is like Big Sur, but warm. And it has probably the cheapest oceanfront left in the hemisphere. I'll tell you more about it some other time.

Property in pretty small towns is increasing in value too.

I wrote about this as I drove through Massachusetts and New York this summer. It's a step up from the suburbs. And usually cheaper.

And guess what other areas are rising in value? Old, inner city areas. People over 50 get tired of cutting the grass. They want to walk to theaters and coffee bars. They don't want to drive around in station wagons anymore. Already, even in Baltimore, this trend is picking up. You have to be careful about choosing a neighborhood. But the Italian and Ukrainian neighborhoods have always been pretty safe. Not surprisingly, property prices are rising rapidly. Small houses that could have been bought for $60,000 five years ago are now selling for $150,000.

Look for safe neighborhoods with history... places that could be tarted up... where you can imagine people drinking designer coffee and reading the *New York Times* on Sunday morning.

Personally... I'll stick to Paris, for now.

Originally published: September 9, 1999 in The Daily Reckoning

To sign up for Bill Bonner's free Daily Reckoning e-mail service, go to www.dailyreckoning.com.